Transformative Time Travel

Transformative Time Travel

*Deepening Discipleship through Meditation
on the Future, Past, and Present*

JAY S. LOWDER

WIPF & STOCK · Eugene, Oregon

TRANSFORMATIVE TIME TRAVEL
Deepening Discipleship through Meditation on the Future, Past, and Present

Copyright © 2024 Jay S. Lowder. All rights reserved. Except for brief quotations in critical publications or reviews, no part of this book may be reproduced in any manner without prior written permission from the publisher. Write: Permissions, Wipf and Stock Publishers, 199 W. 8th Ave., Suite 3, Eugene, OR 97401.

Wipf & Stock
An Imprint of Wipf and Stock Publishers
199 W. 8th Ave., Suite 3
Eugene, OR 97401

www.wipfandstock.com

PAPERBACK ISBN: 979-8-3852-2774-7
HARDCOVER ISBN: 979-8-3852-2775-4
EBOOK ISBN: 979-8-3852-2776-1

10/11/24

Unless otherwise indicated, Scripture quotations are from the ESV® Bible (The Holy Bible, English Standard Version®), © 2001 by Crossway, a publishing ministry of Good News Publishers. Used by permission. All rights reserved. The ESV text may not be quoted in any publication made available to the public by a Creative Commons license. The ESV may not be translated in whole or in part into any other language.

Scripture quotations marked NASB are taken from the (NASB®) New American Standard Bible®, Copyright © 2020 by The Lockman Foundation. Used by permission. All rights reserved. lockman.org.

To Christy Lowder, beloved wife, avid church history and theology student, artist, fellow meditative memorizer, and co-time traveler. Your zeal for memorization, meditation, and music has encouraged me every day of our marriage!

Contents

Acknowledgments	ix
Introduction: Humans Are Time Travelers	1
Chapter One: Meditation as Time Travel	10
Chapter Two: For the *Future*—Be Alert!	16
Chapter Three: Toward the *Future*—Do Not Be Anxious!	30
Chapter Four: Toward the *Past* and the *Future*—Be Appreciative!	53
Chapter Five: Toward the *Past* and the *Future*—Don't Be Amnesic!	74
Chapter Six: In the *Present* for the *Future*—Be Disciplined!	93
Chapter Seven: In the *Present* for the *Future*—Time Travel Together!	114
Chapter Eight: Time Travel Tested by Decline and Death	140
Conclusion	169
Bibliography	171
Author Index	183

Acknowledgments

To God be the glory! His glory is often seen in the lives of others and in the grace they extend to us. There is no one for whom I am more thankful than my wife, whose zeal for Jesus and daily encouragement has served to "stir up" (2 Pet 1:13) my faith. She has been my first-line editor-in-chief.

In a book that includes a chapter on appreciation and another chapter on time-traveling together in communities, let me thank some special people by type of community.

- Community of Family: I am thankful for my parents, stepparents, and in-laws, all of whom have supported my years in seminary both spiritually and financially.

- Community of Educators: Some pastors never receive the blessings of seminary education. I have been blessed twice! The faculty of Southwestern Baptist Theological Seminary and the Southern Baptist Theological Seminary devoted time to me inside and outside of the classroom. Though both schools are known for their academics, my passion for the spiritual disciplines was kindled at both. In particular, I was blessed during my PhD years by Dr. Ronald Nash, Dr. Ted Cabal, Dr. Thomas Schreiner, Dr. Bruce Ware, Dr. Steven Wellum, Dr. Tom Nettles, and Dr. Jonathan Pennington.

- Church Community: On this side of heaven, we cannot know fully how much church members and leaders have shaped us. I have been blessed to be an active member at several churches and on staff at others. Thank you to the families of First Baptist Church of Springdale, Arkansas (now Cross Church), Crestmont Baptist Church, Sagamore Hill Baptist Church, Clifton Baptist Church, First Baptist Church

Acknowledgments

of Duxbury, First Baptist Church of Pinckneyville, and First Baptist Church of Beebe. In Louisville as a science teacher and in Massachusetts as the principal, the Portland Christian School and Good Shepherd Christian Academy families blessed me.

- Editorial Community: I am thankful for the staff at Wipf and Stock Publishers. They were professional and personal, graciously providing extra assistance for a first-time author. I also appreciate that in this new era of publishing, when companies have to be creative and careful to remain profitable, Wipf and Stock's publishing model permits them to "accept book projects based on merit rather than a book's projected sales."

Introduction
Humans Are Time Travelers

> You should look *backward*, to Jesus on the cross. You should look upward to Jesus at the right hand of God. You should look *forward* to Jesus coming again on the last day. Happy is he who takes these three looks every day that he lives!
>
> J. C. Ryle (1816–1900)[1]

The adage says that "time waits for no man." That is true, for time passes us by relentlessly. Yet, in another sense, time does wait for us, right at the foot of the bed! From your first conscious thought in the morning to your last one as you collapse in bed at night, you think, act, and react to your *past* and *future*. Whether you travel time consciously or unconsciously, you are a time traveler! You do not travel in some science fiction time machine but by something much more powerful: your mind!

Your *past* awaits your rising. How do you know who you are? Your memories will tell you. What will you eat for breakfast? Don't worry! Your *past* memories contain all the information you need about what you want to eat or, if you are dieting, what you should eat! How will you decide what to do *today*? Will you go to work, school, church, or stay home? Don't sweat it! Your *past* will tell you what you should do in your immediate *future*. Your memory saves you from considering the almost limitless number of other things you could do!

The *future* awaits you, too. You cannot get very far from the bed *before* feelings of hope or dread overtake you. Will you have a good day full of

---

1. Emphasis added.

opportunities to advance your goals for the *future*?[2] Will you have a bad day, frustrating at best or disastrous at worst? Compared to yesterday, do you anticipate a better day *ahead* or a worse one? Will this day have significance, or will it be just another monotonous rat race to complete everything? Regardless of the day's outcome, your mind is the professional *predictor* of what it thinks *will happen*. Based on what *has happened before* and your *future hopes* for something better, you *already* anticipate the day *before* you live it out.

AT OUR BEST, WE ARE TERRIFIC TIME TRAVELERS!

Humans have the remarkable ability to use the *future* to improve the *present*. Created in the image of God, whose wisdom "always chooses the best goals and the best means to those goals," we can plan how to move toward success.[3] In families, parents envision a better *future* for their children, being willing to sacrifice *present* time working for their children to thrive. Likewise, remembering the joys of *yesterday* can brighten dark days *today*. The hope of *future* days in which long-term goals will be reached can propel us *forward*.[4] People often work their whole careers for their *future* selves. They regularly set aside some money they could have spent for *present* enjoyment toward a better *future* retirement.

In the workplace, the employees who anticipate *future* promotions naturally work harder in the *present*. They invest in their *future*, a *foreseen* better one. If they cannot see opportunities for *future* advancement, they will seek better work environments and better compensation elsewhere. Recognizing this, savvy companies invest money in training and retaining *present* employees.

The *future* also drives economics and consumer choices. Buyers make thousands of decisions each year about spending money. Some are weighty and have significant impacts on the *future*. But even smaller ones involve trade-offs between anticipated *future* product performances and parting with funds in the *present*. Competing visions of the *past* and the *future* drive politics, too. Informed citizens work to improve their government. They listen to elected politicians and political candidates as they identify pressing *current* issues, and propose *future* solutions. Who should get their

2. Lewis, *Mere Christianity*, 134.
3. Grudem, *Systematic Theology*, 231.
4. Amen, *Stones of Remembrance*, xiii.

Introduction

vote? The candidate with the best plans for the best *future*! Election season is a referendum on voters' perceptions of the *past* and their hopes for the *future*. Moreover, if an elected official seems inefficient, it is only a short time *before* voters want a *present* recall election or a *future* electoral defeat of the *once*-promising, *now*-disappointing official.

Not only does time influence us, but we are captivated by thoughts of it. Time management books claim to tell you how to save time and achieve *future* goals. Historical books transport many readers through literary time travel *back* to *past* times for academic study or for musing about life in radically different eras. Fiction pushes the idea of time travel even further. Ever since H. G. Wells's (1866–1946) 1895 novel *The Time Machine*, generations have been fascinated with the thought that people could at least try to change their *future*. Time travel has been the subject of thousands of fiction books and hundreds of movies and TV shows. Currently, Amazon lists several thousand fiction books under the category of time-travel fiction, showing just how much time travel intrigues us.

AT OUR WORST, WE ARE TERRIBLE TIME TRAVELERS!

By failing to consider the *future* and the *past*, having an unhealthy obsession with them, or missing the capacity to let the *past* and the *future* change us, temporal problems plague many. Ever since our parents in the garden unwisely chose temporary, fleeting pleasure (Gen 3:6) over heeding God's warning about *future* death (Gen 2:17), people have been making mistakes in the *present* that mess up their *futures*. In families, parents can be shortsighted, selfishly living in the *moment*, and failing to save for their children's *futures*. On the other hand, some become *workaholics*, toiling away for their children's *futures* that may never arrive as anticipated. Some pursue *careerism*, seeking significance and value more at work than at home. They forget that family relationships will last, for good or bad, long *after* work ends.

Citizens can fail to care about politics and allow the *future* to unfold without their input. Or worse, politicians lure them into poor decisions using selfish promises at the expense of the moral good. Governments and their citizens pay high *future* prices when they forsake wisdom, focusing only on short-term gains *today* instead of wisely planning for *tomorrow*. For example, in the United States, *present* and *future* generations will inherit the ever-increasing national debt, a failure of *previous* generations to insist on temperate government spending.

Marketing works, sometimes too well! Consumers may live paycheck to paycheck, failing to plan and indulging in advertisement-driven reckless spending that jeopardizes their lives and families. We all know too many who short-circuit their lives on the altar of materialism and instant gratification. They should heed Benjamin Franklin's (1706–90) advice against accumulating debt *tomorrow* for good things *today*: "Rather to bed supperless than rise in debt."[5] Finally, apart from such decision-making, anyone can experience moments of worry, which is a wasteful process of *predicting* a terrible possible *future* and inflicting actual harm on themselves in the *present*.[6]

BECOME A BETTER TIME TRAVELER!

This book will guide your journey toward becoming a savvier time traveler. If you improve your time-traveling skills, you will be blessed! J. C. Ryle (1816–1900) recommended three daily directions of mental travel: "You should look *backward*, to Jesus on the cross. You should look upward to Jesus at the right hand of God. You should look *forward* to Jesus coming again on the last day. Happy is he who takes these three looks every day that he lives!"[7]

You meet different types of time travelers with various skill levels. But everyone travels time—some for the better, others for the worse. Many are sloppy time travelers whose bodies move throughout their days, unaware of how their minds travel destructively to the *past* and *future*. They lessen their enjoyment of the *present* and imperil their *future*.[8] Think of the worrier who consumes his time by being *preoccupied* with what might happen and misses what is happening around him. Or imagine the woman deeply hurt by the pains of her *past*, maybe even trauma, who cannot live in the *present* without the *past* tainting it. As the Stoic philosopher Seneca (4 BC–AD 65) observed, the *past* and the *future* often make humans miserable: "We, however, are tormented alike by what is *past* and what is to come. A number of our blessings do us harm, for memory brings *back* the agony of fear while *foresight* brings it on *prematurely*. No one confines his

---

5. Franklin, *Autobiography and Other Writings*, 174.
6. Welch, *Running Scared*, 50.
7. Ryle, "Are You Looking?," 514 (emphasis added).
8. Calamy, *Art of Divine Meditation*, 68–69.

Introduction

unhappiness to the *present*."⁹ There can be terrible pain and suffering in life, but, like card players holding a lousy hand, we often double down on our pains and fears, mishandling them and increasing our torment.

A person's advancement in life can be harmed by sloppy time-travel issues: anxiety about the *future*, forgetting the *past*, or living undisciplined in the *present*. Children and teenagers can struggle to stay focused on the *present*, especially if they have gifted, creative imaginations. Those active imaginations that may serve them well as *future* adults *now* hamper their *present-day* learning in school. On the other end of life, everyone knows a senior adult so addled with the seemingly innocent lure of nostalgia, so in love with the *past*, that they find little passion for the *future* and less ability to rejoice in the *today* the Lord has made (Ps 118:24).

Others are intentionally sinful time travelers. They use their "image of God" ability to *premeditate* sins and how to commit them in the *future*, rather than thinking about God and His will in the *present*. They may get ahead in life or enjoy the passing pleasures in the *present* time, but they are progressing toward a terrible *future* destiny. Commenting on Rom 8:5, Wihlelmus à Brakel (1635–1711) wrote about the time travel of unbelievers:

> Such a person thought and mused upon sin, reflecting on *previously* committed sins in order to yet find delight in them. He would think upon *future* sins (or sins never to be committed in the *future*) in such a fashion as if he were *presently* committing them, or in order to provide his imagination with sufficient matter to reflect upon. He would devise and formulate means to actually commit such a sin—be it to commit it in very deed or to merely muse about the manner in which this sin could possibly be committed. For sin, rather than God and His will, was the object of his contemplations.[10]

People often eventually commit the sins they contemplate, but even if they do not, they have sinned in their evil, imaginative *future* gazes. Coveting that leads to wanting to obtain something unreachable or unlawful is a perfect example of this dangerous path. That is why coveting, something entirely internal, was highlighted in the Ten Commandments (Exod 20:17; Deut 5:21). Jesus himself warned that covetous lusting for another person is *already*, in the *present*, committing adultery! Therefore, such impure impulses

---

9. Seneca, *Letters from a Stoic*, 38 (emphasis added).
10. Brakel, *Christian's Reasonable Service*, 2:252–53 (emphasis added).

Transformative Time Travel

must be fought against *now* at any price, lest they cost an eternal *future* (Matt 5:27–30).

Not all ponder inherently evil things all the time. Some skilled time travelers harness the *past* and the *future* to achieve great things. People do not need to be Christians to benefit from God's design of humans as time travelers. Many women and men of history have shaped the world by being sensible and skilled regarding their *past* and *future*. Whether they use their skill for selfish reasons or God's glory, they achieve extraordinary earthly results. Napoleon Bonaparte (1769–1821) attributed his skill in handling the unexpected to his meditation: "If I always seem to be ready for everything, to face up to anything . . . it is because I never undertake anything at all without first having meditated for a long time and *fore*seen what might happen."[11]

There are also spiritual time travelers, maturing Christians who have come into an intimate relationship with the Eternal Father through Jesus the Son, who is himself the "same *yesterday* and *today* and *forever*" (Heb 13:8; emphasis added). They were saved when they anchored their faith to the life, death, and resurrection of Jesus, accepted his *past* payment for their sin, and committed their *future* well-being to him. They have *already* entered a higher quality of unending "eternal life," just as Jesus promised: "Truly, truly, I say to you, whoever hears my word and believes him who sent me has eternal life. He does not come into judgment but has passed from death to life" (John 5:24). As they mature, they are learning to live in light of their *past* and *future*. From within, the Holy Spirit nurtures a growing appreciation for God's goodness in their *past* since they have "*already*" received many of God's promises and are eagerly awaiting the ones "not *yet*" fulfilled.[12] By the eyes of faith, they can see more than human sight can perceive. Richard Sibbes (1577–1635) observed that faith "sees things far off in place. Faith sees things in heaven; it sees Christ there; it sees our place provided for us there . . . and for distance of time, the eye of faith it sees things *past* and things to come."[13]

Not all Christians can travel time well, and too many struggle with worry about the *future* and weariness from the *past*. But God has given teachings and examples from Scripture and church history to help. Not surprisingly, Jesus himself is the best model. Randy Alcorn's insight is worth

---

11. Castelot, *Napoleon*, 231 (emphasis added).
12. Schreiner, *Magnifying God in Christ*, 19.
13. Sibbes, *Works*, 7:423 (emphasis added).

Introduction

reflecting upon: "When Jesus walked the Earth, he lived with divine happiness in his *past*, the happiness of an eternal perspective in his *present*, and the anticipation of unending happiness in the *future*."[14]

The journey *forward* includes your *future*, your *past*, and your *present*. Chapter 2 is a call to biblical "alertness," that is, time travel toward the *future*, obeying the admonishments of Jesus to be "alert" about the *future* (Matt 24:42; 25:13). Chapter 3 is a caution against the destructive time travel of anxiety, also emphatically forbidden by Jesus (Matt 6:25, 27, 31, 34). Chapters 4 and 5 *present* opposite approaches to the *past*—a person either appreciates it or develops spiritual amnesia.

Chapter 6 shows how your views of the *past* and the *future* directly influence your *present* choices about being disciplined. Chapter 7 happily reminds you that you do not time-travel alone. You have fellow time travelers alongside you and *ahead* of you. In your *present*, they are with you to inspire and encourage you with their models and their words. Looking into the *past*, you have countless biblical and church-history heroines and heroes to inspire you! What a blessing also to have spiritual shepherds who show the way *forward*. Learning to think about members and ministers in terms of time travel will reignite your passion for God's people, with whom you can regularly gather for time-traveling tips and encouragement.

Chapter 8 puts your transformative time-travel skills to the test. By *preparing now*, you can overcome the ultimate tests of faith—your inevitable decline and approaching death. Many people are paralyzed by the challenges near the end of their lives, but you do not have to be. Seasoned, spiritual time travelers have *already* mentally and emotionally journeyed *forward* in time to their deaths and *back* to their *present* many times. They face both decline and death with remarkable grace and insuppressible joy, inspiring hope and resilience in those who follow their path. This book assists you, the reader, on the road of time travel. So here are four tools that will help you remember what you read, decide if you agree with it, and respond to it wisely by the power of the Holy Spirit. Take advantage of them!

---

14. Alcorn, *God's Promise of Happiness*, 40–41 (emphasis added).

FOUR TOOLS FOR YOUR JOURNEY

1. "There Is No Escaping Them!"—*Italicized* Temporal Words

Temporal words like *past, present, future, now, earlier, later, before, after, beforehand, once, already, prior, back, ahead, behind,* and prefixes like *pre-, post-, fore-,* etc., are *italicized* throughout the book to show that even how we talk about *time travel* and spiritual disciplines is unavoidably *time sensitive*! Even if someone does not like the idea of time travel, they cannot speak long about their faith without invoking temporal terms. As you step *forward* toward better time travel, notice how you think, speak, and write almost constantly in terms of time. It will be a paradigm shift in your perception. There is no going *back*!

2. "The *Past* Is Still *Present*!"—Intentionally Leaning on *Past* Christian Teaching

Christians have been thinking, speaking, and writing about the *past, present,* and *future* for centuries, so a growing knowledge of Christian history will change you. To assist you in thinking historically, the frequent references to great Christians will include their life dates to show that Christians *today* exist in a community with the saints *before* them. Like Abel, their lives of faith "*still* speak" (Heb 11:4). They have won the race, and their testimonies yield glorious riches to those who look to and learn from them. Reading their testimonies will spur you to run the race for your *future* so that God will find you faithful, too.[15] As they *now* see Jesus face-to-face (Matt 5:8), so may we run our race!

3. "Read More about It!"—Suggested Further Readings

By the grace of God, many great Christian authors from the *past* and the *present* have written on these chapter topics. At the end of each chapter, there are recommended reading lists. I am deeply indebted to *past* and *present* generations of saints whose writings have benefited my Christian life and made this book possible. You, too, should enrich yourself with the wealth of your church history family.

---

15. Piper, *Desiring God*, 363.

4. "Take Them with You!"—Suggested Memorization Verses

You carry *today*'s experiences and lessons into *tomorrow*, whether you discover a new food to keep eating or a new insight into how you live your faith. But time fades memories. For a short while, you will remember what you read in this book and then lapse into vague recollections. Since each chapter is drawn from the Bible, why not memorize a verse to remind you of what God wants you to remember and act upon? For example, if you are reading about facing your fears, memorize a verse that tells you what you should do in the *future* about what you fear in the *present*, such as, "When I am afraid, I put my trust in you. In God, whose word I praise, in God I trust; I shall not be afraid. What can flesh do to me?" (Ps 56:3–4).

Nothing new is written in this book, that is, nothing not taught *before* (Eccl 1:9). But this book will give you refreshing and helpful tools for meditating on your life in light of the Bible. That will fulfill my intent, an echo of George Müller's (1805–98) goal for his writing: "The hope of being instrumental in this way to lead some of my brethren to value the Holy Scriptures more."[16]

---

16. Müller, *Narrative of the Lord's Dealings*, iii.

CHAPTER ONE

Meditation as Time Travel

> In our Christian pilgrimage, it is well, for the most part, to be looking *forward*.
>
> CHARLES SPURGEON (1834–92)[1]

This talk about spiritual time travel might be unsettling to you, just a bit too novel! But did you know that mental journeys to the *past* and *future* are simply forms of biblical meditation? The Bible teaches that you can find comfort in *present* distress by remembering God's grace in the *past*: "I will *remember* the deeds of the Lord; yes, I will *remember* your wonders of old. I will *ponder* all your work and *meditate* on your mighty deeds" (Ps 77:11). Remembering is a meditation on the *past*, a form of time travel that brings comfort in the *present*.

Moreover, the Bible has many examples and exhortations to look to the *future*. Despite decades of discouraging circumstances, Abraham never wavered in his faith (Rom 4:19–20). He was "looking *forward* to the city that has foundations, whose designer and builder is God" (Heb 11:10; emphasis added). Healthy time travel begins with your scheduled morning devotional time. You *first* apply the daily Scriptures you read to the day *ahead*, praying for God's guidance and grace. *Then*, throughout your

---

1. Emphasis added.

day, you move from *temporary* experiences and emotions (such as anger, anxiety, and apathy) *back* to the *eternal* realities of God's word. It does not matter whether you begin with Scripture or end with Scripture, as long as one end of the meditative time-travel journey anchors to God's word. The connection to the word of God is what makes meditation genuinely godly and profitable!

STAY TETHERED TO THE TRUTH!

Humans meditate, but tragically, often they meditate on evil. Secular, Eastern, and religious speculative forms of meditation fail to profit spiritually because they do not connect to God's revelation of himself, either at the beginning of the reflective journey or at the end of it. Imagine exploring the gondola of a hot air balloon. While you explore it, it remains safely tethered to the ground. As long as the ropes stay secure, keeping you safe, you can play out the rope and ascend as high as you want, gaining beautiful views of the surrounding scenery. But cut those ropes and you lose the safety you *once* enjoyed. Where will you go? Where will you land? You do not know, especially if you have never flown before, much less piloted, a hot air balloon *before*. Meditation is delightful for the Christian life while connected to God's word. But detaching it from the security of divine revelation is a perennial danger. This insidious mistake results in evil meditation methods, sometimes even tragically promoted as "Christian" meditation. It is subpar at best and sinful at worst, erring both in using strange techniques and drifting into dangerous subject matters.

Genuine, godly, Christian meditation inseparably connects to God's revelation. This makes sense when you recognize that only the redeemed can meditate properly.[2] Time travel from God's word to your *future* or *past*, or from your *future* or *past* to God's word, "transforms." You are filled with God's word, and, over time, your life becomes godlier. This is the opposite of vain, Eastern, and eminently dangerous methods like "transcendental" meditation.[3] Observe William Bridge's (1600–1670) warning to keep a connection to the Bible: "Let nothing fall within the compass of your meditation that does not fall within the compass of the Scripture."[4] Either beginning with Scripture or moving toward the safety of Scripture is so essential that if you

---

2. Allcock, *Deeper Still*, 40.
3. Morgan, *Worry Less*, 93.
4. Bridge, *Sweetness of Divine Meditation*, 33.

do not commit to staying within these bounds, do not meditate! It would be better to be ignorant and impoverished than arrogant and deluded!

MOVING FROM EXPERIENCES TO SCRIPTURE

Broadly, Christian meditation is "a serious, practical, and devout contemplation of divine things."[5] It often begins with reflecting on an observation or experience and then connecting it to Scripture. For example, John Stott (1921–2011) reported that in his solitary walks, he focused on "remembering that every fresh breath, every heartbeat, was a gift from God which could be taken away at any time."[6] He was connecting his experiences *back* to the truths of the Bible. Time travel throughout the busyness of life begins with personal experiences and then relates them to God's truths. This is "spontaneous meditation," occurring at unplanned moments. Instead of drifting through your day without reflecting, this is seizing your rush of thoughts and looking heavenward.

If you are a believer, you may *already* practice Christian meditation as you daily consider the advice you receive, the books you read, the personal circumstances you encounter, the songs you hear, and how all of them connect to Scripture. If so, you are well on your way to mature Christian thinking and the development of a consistent Christian worldview. If not, then start that process of reflective thinking *today*. The idea of transformative time travel is a helpful walking stick for that journey.

When we consider time travel to the *future* (chapters 2 and 3) and the *past* (chapters 4 and 5), we begin with our experiences and move toward Scripture. Experiences and emotions can be fastened to the rock of God's holy word, which will correct perceptions and change passions. Understanding the difference between passively "listening to yourself instead of talking to yourself" is a fundamental deciding factor in your spiritual happiness and holiness.[7] Instead of getting swept away in the stream-of-consciousness emotions, you can choose to meditate and anchor yourself to Jesus, the "sure and steadfast anchor of the soul" (Heb 6:19).

---

5. Newcomb, *Young Lady's Guide*, 167.
6. Stott, *Stott on the Christian Life*, 133.
7. Lloyd-Jones, *Spiritual Depression*, 20–21.

MOVING FROM SCRIPTURE TO YOUR EXPERIENCES

If Christians mention meditation, they usually think of filling "your mind with God's word, chewing it until you have digested spiritual morsels."[8] This form of meditation on Scripture connects you each day to your *past* and *future*. It is "scheduled" meditation, done as the outflow of personal Bible intake.[9] For example, Christian missionary and martyr Betty Stam (1906–34) wrote about the sacrificial nature of the Christian life as she reflected on the week-long consecration of Aaron and his sons in Lev 8:33: "When we consecrate ourselves to God, we think we are making a great sacrifice, and doing lots for Him, when really, we are only letting go some little, bitsie trinket. We have been grabbing, and when our hands are empty, He fills them full of His treasures."[10] Through such devotional reflections, she matured as a believer, traveling *backward* in time to the dedication of the priests and *forward* in time to contemplate her unknown *future*. She became unconditionally committed to whatever God willed for her and ready for whatever hardships and victories lay *ahead*. When it was time for her to actually make a "great sacrifice, doing lots for Him," she was *already pre*pared for it!

In your devotional reading of Scripture, you should be moving from what you read to what you are praying. You can reflect on how to apply the truths just read to your life that day (scheduled meditation). As the day progresses, you can connect your experiences and emotions *back* to biblical truths (spontaneous meditation). With practice, both forms of meditation work hand in hand. Whether starting from God's word in meditation (Ps 1:2) or meditating on the glory of God displayed in the heavens (Ps 8:1–3), you can meditate day and night, which sparks praying without ceasing (1 Thess 5:17). It is a more joyful path to Christian growth, empowering you to do good works for the glory of God (Matt 5:16) and strengthening you to battle against sinful meditations such as brooding anger and coveting lust (Matt 5:21–30).

Both ways of meditating nourish your soul on God's word. If you struggle with a quick temper, perhaps your daily Bible reading plan will bring you to the words of Jas 1:19–20: "Know this, my beloved brothers: let every person be quick to hear, slow to speak, slow to anger; for the anger of man does

---

8. Tripp, *Journey to the Cross*, 140.
9. Richard Baxter called this "set and solemn." Baxter, *Saints' Everlasting Rest*, 192.
10. Taylor, *To Die Is Gain*, 35.

not produce the righteousness of God." Healthy meditation would be pausing to ponder this truth, acknowledging that you fail this standard, confessing these sins to God, and asking for strength to be patient in the *future*.

Later in the day, when someone frustrates you, remember this truth, and your morning commitment to it will help you slow down to consider a better response. Instead of your typical knee-jerk angry response, you can exhibit the patience God expects. What you had in the morning promised God in secret (Matt 6:6), you will *now* actually perform publicly! People around you may wonder what has gotten hold of you when you do not lash out at them anymore, but the truth is God's power has gotten ahold of you. Maybe in the *future*, this will open the door for you to share the gospel with them, telling them about God's grace offered to sinners like you and them.

This process is simply healthy Bible study and personal application, but it involves meditation, an intermediate step that occurs in your mind, even if you are not conscious of it. Not only does it help to call it what it is biblically—that is, meditation—but it also helps to see that when you study and apply the Bible, you are engaging in mental time travel. The daily spiritual habits of Robert M'Cheyne (1813–43) were described as a healthy blend of both of these forms of meditation: "His morning hours were set apart for the nourishment of his own soul; not, however, with the view of laying up a stock of grace for the rest of the day,—for manna will corrupt if laid by,—but rather with the view of 'giving the eye the habit of looking upward all the day, and drawing down gleams from the reconciled countenance.'"[11] He specifically meditated on God's written word in the morning and then strengthened himself with broader meditation on the things of God throughout each day.

Beginning with *future* time travel, jumping *back* to *past* time travel, and ending up in the *present*, you can be better equipped for a Christian life of "making the best use of the time" (Eph 5:16). We begin with the journeys to the *future* that we all take, whether they produce holy and happy alertness or unholy and unhappy anxiety. May the Eternal God who was, is, and will be ever-*present* bless the time-traveling *ahead*!

RECOMMENDED READING ABOUT MEDITATION

Linda Allcock, *Deeper Still: Finding Clear Minds and Full Hearts through Biblical Meditation* (Charlotte, NC: Good Book Company, 2020).

11. Bonar, *Memoir and Remains*, 64.

Joel Beeke, *How Can I Practice Christian Meditation?* (Grand Rapids: Reformation Heritage, 2022).
Edmund Calamy, *The Art of Divine Meditation* (Monee, IL: Lulu Publishers, 2022).
Joseph Hall, *The Art of Divine Meditation* (Lafayette, IN: Sovereign Grace, 1964).

MEMORIZATION PASSAGES ABOUT MEDITATION

Psalm 1:1–2
Blessed is the man who walks not in the counsel of the wicked,
nor stands in the way of sinners, nor sits in the seat of scoffers;
but his delight is in the law of the Lord,
and on his law, he meditates day and night.

Psalm 77:11–12
I will remember the deeds of the Lord; yes,
I will remember your wonders of old;
I will ponder all your work,
and meditate on your mighty deeds.

CHAPTER TWO

For the *Future*
Be Alert!

Alert people achieve the best *future*; those who think seriously about the *future* prepare for it. That is just natural common sense, and the Bible goes a supernatural step further: God blesses the spiritually alert, who stay in tune with him and are *pre*pared to act. That alertness is not a fearful mindset, for anxiety is as wrong as not being *pre*pared. Like all Christian traits, Jesus lived out alertness without anxiety perfectly, utterly aware of what was to come and yet filled with the joy of the Holy Spirit. John Piper remarks, "It is not glorious to be gloomy. Therefore, Christ has never been gloomy."[1]

ALERTNESS IS LOOKING *FORWARD* TO THE *FUTURE*

Alertness is "looking *forward*" to the fulfillment of God's great promises with a sober-minded awareness that there are many hardships, trials, and temptations *before* we cross the finish line.[2] Throughout the Bible, there

---

1. Piper, *Seeing and Savoring*, 36.
2. Biblical calls to be on guard or watchful: Exod 23:13, 21; Prov 13:3; 22:5; Eccl 5:1; Jer 9:4; Mic 7:5; Mark 13:9; Luke 12:15; 17:3; 21:34; Acts 20:28; 2 Pet 3:17. Calls to be alert and sober-minded: Matt 24:42–3; 25:13; Mark 13:3–7; Luke 12:37; 21:36; Acts 20:31; 1 Cor 15:34; 16:13; Eph 6:18; Col 4:2; 1 Thess 5:6, 8; 2 Tim 4:5; 1 Pet 1:13; 4:7; 5:8.

are warnings of potential dangers and promises of possible *future* blessings from God. At least twenty-seven passages command us to be on guard, alert, and sober-minded. In addition, there are prayers for God to guard believers, examples of being on guard, and the recognition that, ultimately, unless God himself guards us, we cannot protect ourselves.[3] On the positive side, Jesus's famous eightfold Beatitudes promise a positive *future* for those alert enough to hear and respond. Be alert for good opportunities to be blessed by God in the *future* by choices *today*.

Society recognizes the need for physical alertness while ignoring the greater need for spiritual vigilance. The disastrous consequences of physical and emotional dullness are frighteningly evident. For example, there is the decades-old problem of traffic accidents caused by driver "pedal confusion," the switching up of the accelerator and the brake, which can happen to anyone but especially seniors. The National Highway Traffic Safety Administration estimates that in 2015, approximately sixteen thousand car crashes were caused by not paying enough attention to which pedal to push.[4] More recently, the technology that enables memorable selfies also permits "killfiles," where people taking risky photos die from dangers that more sober-minded realists would have avoided. Hundreds of tragic deaths each year occur from avoidable risks.[5]

Being alert is vitally important, but it can also be difficult.[6] While some lament new eras of technology and blame modern devices for distractibility, human nature has never changed. Even in the seventeenth century, Thomas Manton (1620–77) complained that unless we retire into solitude for prayer, "sinful distractions will crowd in upon us when in company, and we are thinking of this and that."[7] So be encouraged that, just as billions of believers *before* you have successfully battled spiritual distraction by the Scripture and the Spirit, you can, too.

---

3. Personal commitments either to stay on guard or acknowledging the importance of having been on guard in the *past*: Ps 39:1; Prov 21:23; John 17:12; 1 Tim 6:20. Deferring to God as the One who must keep us safe as we travel *forward* in time: Pss 91:11; 121:18; 127:1; Prov 2:8, 11; 4:6, 13; 13:6; Isa 27:3; 52:12; 58:8; Phil 4:7; 2 Tim 1:12; 1 Pet 2:25.

4. "NHTSA Safety Advisory."

5. "Data Scientists Chart."

6. Bavinck, *Reformed Ethics*, 406.

7. Manton, *Complete Works*, 1:17.

GOD'S *FUTURE* GRACE GIVES *PRESENT* JOY AND HOPE

Forward-looking Christians are full of joy and hope, assured that God has the *future* planned; therefore, you can fill up each day with good works (Eph 2:10) until your *last* day on earth (Ps 139:16). God wrote the pages of your life in *advance*. Therefore, you can *now* live with alert anticipation of what is on the *next* page! Commenting on Romans 8:28, John Piper notes that "the freest life of love is the life saturated with the confidence that nothing comes to me but what is good for me."[8] So, although you must be alert for hard days that may come, be assured that where danger might abound, God's grace superabounds.

ALERT FOR GOOD: DUTY AND FAITHFUL RELATIONSHIPS

Wise followers of Jesus who are alert see the opportunities for good works that God places before them in their workplaces, homes, and communities. But those who are distracted by the cares of this world (Matt 13:22) miss the joy of that better way of life. Such people view their careers as a mere means for achieving good things for themselves. They endure *present-day* work to get to the *future* rewards. They want "ample goods laid up for many years" (Luke 12:19). They work *this* week to reach the *next* weekend, work all year for their *next* vacation, and work their whole careers for that anticipated retirement.

Tragically, even relationships can become an occasion for goodness for themselves rather than others being valued. They often live in relationships simply because they enjoy them in the *present*, not out of faithfulness to *past* commitments or *future* hope. As a result, their relationships rise and fall depending on whether it is stormy or fair weather. Even if they are *temporarily* satisfied, there are temptations to wonder if the grass is greener elsewhere, imagining a better possible *future*.

In contrast, alert Christians, enlightened by God's word, see each day's work in the workforce and home as an opportunity to do good works for God's glory and their joy. They honor their *past* commitments to others, willing to endure any hard season for God's glory and their ultimate good. Everyone knows them as all-weather friends instead of fair-weather friends, steady spouses instead of shifty ones, and exemplary overseers instead of

---

8. Piper, *Future Grace*, 129.

abusive overlords (1 Pet 5:3). Their relationships are covenantal instead of "contractual." Jesus's parables about his imminent return emphasized that believers should be found completing their duties. For example, Jesus will find the "faithful and wise servant" doing his duty (Matt 24:45–47). But he will catch the "wicked servant" idle and abusive, living it up *today* like there is no *tomorrow*. That wicked servant deserves the punishment coming for him in the *future* (vv. 48–51).

Savvy, time-traveling Christians anchor to their *past* commitments to God and others and walk faithfully through the dark valleys. They maintain their integrity by reaching for the *future* and anticipating God's abundant grace. They keep their ultimate goal in sight: to glorify God in everything they do *now* (1 Cor 10:31) and ultimately to see God in the face of Christ (Matt 5:8; 2 Cor 4:6). Likewise, when daily duties turn more demanding, the healthy fear of God's *future* evaluation motivates alert believers to keep working. Martyn Lloyd-Jones (1899–1981) wrote about this believer-only motivation: "The Christian is the only man in the world who does life always with and under this sense of judgment. He must do so because our Lord tells him to do so. He tells him his building is going to be judged, the test of life is going to come."[9]

Sober-minded saints do not forget Jesus's warnings that no one would expect his return (Matt 24:42–43; 25:13; Mark 13:35–37; Luke 21:36). Whether their faithful service ends in death (chapter 8 "Time Travel Tested by Decline and Death") or the descent of Christ (Matt 24:30), they work in the *present* to be ready for the *future*. The *future* holds no fear! They stand firm, looking for eternal reward rather than punishment, with a joyful, *forward*-looking gaze.

ALERT FOR GOOD: SPIRITUAL DISCIPLINES

There are many wonderful reasons to spend time with God through spiritual disciplines such as Bible reading, meditation, and prayer. However, the two most important are communion with God and conformity to his image (Rom 8:29; 2 Cor 3:18). You move toward them through your devotional practices. Those who are alert practice them, and those who practice them are alert. Alert believers protect "scheduled" times to read their Bibles and pray meditatively, often beginning in the morning. Think of Daniel, whose zeal for his daily three times of planned prayer landed him in the lion's den

---

9. Lloyd-Jones, *Studies*, 27.

(Dan 6:10–24). Wise believers also redeem spare moments in their days to pray "spontaneously" as they meditate on God and the good things around them (Phil 4:8). If you begin the day with spiritual devotional time, you have *pre*pared your heart for fellowship and transformation for the rest of the day. This pattern of Bible reflection and prayer, both scheduled and spontaneous, is itself a reward for the spiritually alert and leads to greater rewards.

We are never spiritually neutral. Although created to stay alert for good, we are capable of yielding to sin and replacing alertness for good with seeking opportunities for evil. It is wrongly assumed that the opposite of being alert is "distracted." But distraction is simply being alert for less important or evil things. Opportunities to "alertness" for good things get twisted into seeking wasteful or wicked things. Think of the man who whips out his phone while standing in line and catches up on his social media stream. He could be praying or meditating, but instead, he wastes those moments pursuing lesser things. Envision the woman who snatches spare moments to think about her friends and social connections instead of focusing on God-given tasks before her. Even without their cell phones, students are experts at getting distracted in school, escape artists daydreaming about everything except the subject at hand, much to the age-old chagrin of teachers everywhere.

ALERT FOR GOOD: GOD'S GOODNESS AND THE BELIEVERS' DELIGHT

Uncertainty can either paralyze you or propel you through life. By faith, Christian time travelers live with alertness, aware that they will not know the hour of Jesus's return or their death. Yet they anticipate an "abundant" life of good gifts (Ps 119:17; John 10:10), not a life barely scraping by. Even when faced with dire circumstances, they can praise God like Jeremiah, the weeping prophet: "The steadfast love of the Lord never ceases; his mercies never come to an end; they are new every morning; great is your faithfulness" (Lam 3:22–23).

Based upon God's promises and his unbroken pattern of *past* faithfulness, alert believers can look *ahead* for God's goodness as they serve and work each day. Since they do not fear death or the end of this *present* age, they anticipate the *future* and, with the Prov 31 woman, "laugh" (v. 25). Unlike *pre*occupied souls, they look *forward* to God being *present* in their daily lives. They are mastering contentment in the "*now*" of their lives, having "no higher ambition than to belong to the Lord and to be totally at His disposal in the place He appoints, at the time He chooses, with the provision He is pleased to make."[10]

ALERT FOR *FUTURE* DANGER: KEEPING YOURSELF SAFE

What would you do if you caught on fire? You would probably subconsciously do what has been drilled into you since childhood: "Stop, drop, and roll."[11] Should you put oxygen masks on your children first if your plane suddenly depressurizes? No, you will follow the ingrained, oft-repeated airline safety protocol subconsciously embedded in your mind: "If you are traveling with a child or someone who requires assistance, secure your mask on first, and then assist the other person."[12] When it comes to issues like this about physical safety, there is almost no end to the training you receive. Parents, public service announcements, and primary school teachers have *pre*pared you to respond to dangers. Living in a society that trains you to respond to dangers is valuable. Still, if you stop there, merely concerned only about physical dangers, then you miss the true identity of the greatest threat to your life: yourself!

ALERT FOR *FUTURE* EVIL: KEEPING WATCH OVER YOUR HEART

Jesus warned against the foolishness of seeking to gain the whole world *now*, yet *later* losing your priceless soul (Matt 16:26). You could seek prosperity for yourself and your family, yet all of you perish in unbelief! Or, as a believer, you could fail in shocking ways in the middle of your life like David (2 Sam 11–12) or at the end of your life like his son Solomon (1 Kgs 11). Spiritual watchfulness means "the unending effort of guarding ourselves against idols while resting in the promises of the gospel. To keep your heart is your primary business as a Christian, and it cannot be done with just passing interest or any small amount of energy."[13]

---

10. Ferguson, *In Christ Alone*, 190.
11. "Stop, Drop, and Roll."
12. Halsey, "Flying and That Oxygen Mask," para. 3.
13. Thorn, *Note to Self*, 97–98.

Through frightening warning passages, the author of Hebrews seeks to keep us spiritually alert for the protection of our souls. Notice the severity of this warning and the danger of acting carelessly: "Therefore, we must pay much closer attention to what we have heard, lest we drift away from the faith. For since the message declared by angels proved to be reliable, and every transgression or disobedience received a just retribution, how shall we escape if we neglect such a great salvation?" (Heb 2:1–3). Believers must live with alertness against drifting away from Christ and suffering judgment. Recognizing that theologians across the centuries have interpreted the warning passages of the Bible differently, this chapter adopts the view articulated by Thomas R. Schreiner, New Testament professor:

> The warnings are addressed to believers and threaten them with eternal destruction if they fall away. I would contend that all true believers (all the elect, all those who have the Holy Spirit and enjoy the forgiveness of sins and are members of the new covenant) heed the warnings and are thereby saved. In other words, the warnings are one of the means God uses to keep his own trusting him and persevering in faith until the end.[14]

THE TIME-TRAVEL MISTAKE OF WORLDLINESS

Worldliness is sinister because it is sneaky! It is simply focusing on what you can see around you, focusing on this physical world at this *present* time instead of the spiritual world *now* and in the *future*. It is to live as if the *future* will never be different from the *present*. Instead of rejoicing and being rescued out of the "*present* evil age" (Gal 1:4; emphasis added), this is the opposite: reveling in this world. It is all too easy to get caught up in this world of pleasure and pain, distracting yourself from the importance of what is spiritual and in the *future*.

For example, many forms of anxiety (the next chapter's subject) are signs of worldliness. Jesus reminded his disciples that life is more than having physical needs met (Matt 6:25). R. T. France (1938–2012) wrote that "a life which is dominated by worry about food is missing out on that 'more,' . . . the pursuit of God's kingship and righteousness. A life that does not prioritize these deeper concerns has fallen prey to materialism."[15]

---

14. Schreiner, *Run to Win the Prize*, 92.
15. France, *Gospel of Matthew*, 267–68.

Beware of the ever-*present* danger of becoming worldly in thinking and desiring (Matt 6:24; 13:22; Luke 21:34; Titus 2:12; Jas 4:4; Jude 1:19). Though it is necessary to be in the world to be on a mission for the kingdom, your *forward-looking* faith must latch on to your *future* with Jesus in heaven. If you maintain your *forward* focus, you can resist many worldly desires and deeds, such as those Paul lists in Gal 5:19–21. Those dominated by the world in the *present* will not "inherit the kingdom of God" in the *future*.

Anything good in your life *now* or that you hope for in your *future* can distract you. It was not the rich man's wealth that was keeping him from eternal life but his idolatrous love of money (Matt 19:16–22; 1 Tim 6:10). That is why Jesus demanded something exceptional of him not demanded of anyone else. He was to sell everything and give to the poor to combat the worldliness of this *present* age that was blocking *future* grace.

Further, anyone could distract you. How many Christians "skip church" on Sunday because their family will not attend with them? How many families abandon church for their children's Sunday sports events? You cannot be alert for all the good God might do through you or be protected against evil unless you are regularly gathered in your local church. Jesus demonstrated himself (Matt 12:46–50; Mark 3:20–21; John 2:4) and demanded of his followers (Matt 4:21–22; 8:21–22; 10:37) an alert allegiance of "follow me" that could override even the value of family.

ALERT AGAINST EVIL: WINNING AGAINST TEMPTATIONS

Be alert to fight immediately against temptation using the power of God's word. Temptations cannot be allowed to linger, waiting for moments of weakness. Yet be careful to fight only in the strength God supplies through his Scriptures. You would be safer to wrestle a python than to attempt to resist sin apart from the power of Scripture! You will be tempted, just as every human is tempted. Even Jesus experienced temptation. But looking at his model, you can see the path toward victory. The same Holy Spirit who led Jesus into the wilderness to be tempted also *pre*pared him for those temptations. Jesus fasted forty days in *pre*paration, meditating on God and his word during that isolation (Matt 4:1–2). When the devil spoke to him, he spoke back with only the memorized scriptures that flowed from his heart (vv. 3–11). An alert lifetime "of fervent and regular prayer" and "a life devoted to the word of God" had *prepared* him to defeat the devil.[16] He set for you the perfect pattern for victory. Learn from Jesus's example that *past preparation* is essential for your *present* struggles to gain a victorious *future*. William Bridge (1600–1670) observed that "if the heart is filled with holy and heavenly thoughts by meditation, there is no room for evil and sinful thoughts."[17]

Like Jesus, you can store up God's words, and you have even more Scripture available, more readily accessible than he did! God has given you a complete Bible full of encouraging promises and frightening warnings, both of which make excellent ammunition against temptations. Many of them show the value of transformative time travel, using the *past* and *future* to win in the *present* heat of the battle. Think of Joseph facing the pressure of the temptation to yield to Potiphar's wife. He glanced at his master's *past* trust in him and gazed at the *present* goodness of his father's God, who was still "with him" (Acts 7:9). Then, he defeated both sexual temptation and any fear of rejected retaliation through a *future* focus on his accountability to God. Regarding his *future*, he not only knew he would have to give an account to God for so blatant a sin, but he also knew from childhood that God had an extraordinary *future* planned for him: "His refusal was strengthened because he was convinced that God had called him to a special task—he had seen evidence of that in his rise from slavery. If one is to fulfill God's plan, he cannot sin against the God who will bring it about."[18]

David also relied on *past* experiences, like God delivering him from dangerous animals (1 Sam 17:34–36), to *predict future* victory through God: "The Lord who delivered me from the paw of the lion and the paw of the bear, He will deliver me from the hand of this Philistine" (v. 37). Recognizing God's *past* faithfulness made him alert for good opportunities to rely on him again. With that confidence, he resisted the temptation to take matters into his own hands by killing Saul. Instead, he waited on the Lord. He could *foresee* God's *future* vengeance without advancing it by his hand: "May the Lord judge between you and me, and may the Lord avenge me on you; but my hand shall not be against you" (1 Sam 24:12).

David faced the temptation to take Saul's life not once but twice. Though David was unfairly hunted by Saul and lived a life of hardship, he refused to kill God's "anointed" (1 Sam 24:6–10; 26:9–11), anticipating that God's *past* promise of becoming king (1 Sam 16:12–13) would become a

---

16. Ware, *Man Christ Jesus*, 87.
17. Bridge, *Sweetness of Divine Meditation*, 33.
18. Ross, "Genesis," 90.

future reality. Surely, David grew weary of being mistreated and wanted vengeance, but he resisted his desires and his companions' suggestions. Instead of helping him consider the godly response, they urged the wrong course of action. But David would not be swayed either by personal passion or external persuasion. In resisting the temptation to end Saul's life, David drew strength from God's *past* judgment on Nabal. Against his inflamed passions, David had spared the fool, but God did not, showing David in whose hand vengeance should lie.[19] David expected that God would bring about his promised *future* despite any *present* problems.

INCREASING ALERTNESS: TIPS FOR *FUTURE* TIME TRAVEL

When you grasp the nature of alertness as transformative time travel to the *future*, then life applications for the *present* come naturally. Stay alert in your personal, family, and church life! Alertness forms the middle, and often overlooked, step in many areas of obedience to God. For example, parents want to be excellent parents, and they will be when they live alert to the spiritual forces arrayed against their children. Pastors want God to find them faithful, and they will be successful when they guard the flock of God with alertness (Acts 20:28–31). Couples stand at the altar and envision many years of marital bliss *ahead*. That will likely happen if they remain alert and ready for that *future* instead of coasting along and assuming everything will be fine. Think, for example, of the wisdom of the couple that invests time in *pre*marital counseling to guide their journey *ahead* versus the foolishness of the couple that cannot conceive of why any advice would be needed! So, prayerfully consider this council regarding three areas of *pre*paring to be alert: conditions, conditioning, and community.

Conditions for Increased Alertness

Stay alert to the conditions around you! Not every day is a challenge, and not every season of life is as hard as others. It is wise to reflect upon where you are in your faith journey and what dangers might come. Just as you should check the road conditions *before* you travel and then maintain extra

---

19. Baldwin, *1 and 2 Samuel*, 154–55.

vigilance while driving in treacherous weather, you should anticipate more significant dangers at certain times.

In his marvelous book *On Keeping the Heart*, Joseph Flavel (1627–91) listed seasons in life that require maximum watchfulness: prosperity, adversity, troubling times in the church, danger, need, duty, abuse, trials, temptations, doubt, suffering, and sickness and death.[20] Notice that Flavel called for maximum alertness in challenging circumstances. Besides the possibility of being lulled to sleep at the wheel in beautiful, bright sunshine, most driving dangers come from treacherous weather conditions that can lead to accidents. In the same way, seasons of pain prove particularly dangerous for many people. In these times, be careful not to sink spiritually like Job's wife, who, in a season of deep sorrow, turned from God in pain and told Job to "curse God and die" (Job 2:9).

Just as the conditions around you affect your alertness, so do the conditions within you! Your health impacts your soul, likely more than you know. Spiritual conditioning is more important than physical conditioning, but you need both. Do not separate what God has joined together, your body and soul. Your physical health, primarily determined by your commitment to temperate eating, regular physical exercise, and *proactive health*, will influence your spiritual life. So many Christians struggle through their morning prayers, half asleep, and gain little watchfulness for the day because of too little sleep overnight or too much physical indulgence the day *before*. Others do not have the physical stamina to make it through a long workday and remain alert enough to watch their tempers and tongues around family members.

In contrast, John Stott (1921–2011) testified about how his soul benefited from attention to his body: "I have never really been tempted to this because I have taken *pre*cautions. I have recognized that human beings are psychosomatic creatures, so that our bodily condition has a powerful influence on our spiritual life. I have tried to maintain a disciplined life, ensuring adequate sleep, food, and exercise."[21] What can you change in your life physically to become even more alert spiritually for running the race of faith? Commit *now* to keeping a close eye on the conditions around and within you!

---

20. Flavel, *On Keeping the Heart*, 22–90.
21. Chester, *Stott on the Christian Life*, 133 (emphasis added).

Conditioning for Increased Alertness

Bible reading, meditation, and prayer are spiritual exercises that improve your spiritual stamina, which is why they have been called spiritual disciplines. Their importance is seen by the identity of the one who most vigorously opposes them: Satan! Martyn Lloyd-Jones (1899–1981) noted that if the devil can hinder such watchfulness, you have *already* lost ground against him:

> Neglecting self-examination is one of the most significant causes of defeat in the Christian life. If the devil can discourage our watching, all is going to be well from his standpoint. If he causes us to neglect the reading and studying of the word and the understanding of the word, it will suit him admirably. If he causes us to neglect praying, we shall faint, and in that condition become an easy and obvious prey. . . . There is nothing more terrible than to neglect self-examination. So the devil in his wiles comes to us and does his utmost to discourage us at every one of these special points.[22]

Your *present* and *future* spiritual health depends on these spiritual disciplines (1 Tim 4:7–8). Your *future* readiness for what God has *pre*planned for you can never exceed your passion for spending time with him *preparing*. That closeness to him experientially will produce exponential conformity to his likeness.

What would it look like to read your Bible with the goal of increased alertness? Perhaps as you *prepare* in the morning to serve the Lord, your day's Bible reading brings you to David, who was *already pre*pared to face Goliath because of his *past* trust in God (1 Sam 17:34–37). Reflecting on his life, you could pray that lesson *forward*: "Lord, *prepare* me *now* that I may be ready *later* to trust you in moments that test faith so that I can succeed, too!"

Days *later*, when you read about David's *later* life (2 Sam 11:1–5), you observe that David was not guarding his heart on the rooftop that infamous night when he fell into terrible and life-altering sin. That could prompt you to pray that lesson *forward*, too: "Lord, I trust that you will meet all my needs according to your wisdom, so guard my heart against temptations that suggest otherwise. Keep me from sins like those that consumed David in his moment of weakness!" Whether you encounter happy stories of faith to imitate or sad stories of sin to avoid repeating, you benefit by moving

---

22. Lloyd-Jones, *Christian Warfare*, 153.

from meditative Bible study to prayers for alertness. Your meditation on them naturally leads to praying biblically from them!

Community for Increased Alertness

God has made your church invaluable for your journey toward the *future*. You cannot live fully alert without sisters and brothers in the Lord to help you. Let members and ministers teach you and encourage you to have persevering faith. They guard you, too! If you begin to go astray from walking with the Lord, they may need to rebuke you to save you! Remember that in nature, predators use the tactic of separating weaker animals from the larger herd to make them more vulnerable. So much the more does the wilier stalker of your soul, the devil, want you isolated from the protection of the flock of God.

Because these fellow time travelers are at different stages of life than you, they can spot dangers to your life that you have missed. Their advice should provoke prayerful reflection. You also have a responsibility to look out for others. For this reason, the author of Hebrews commands the church community to look after each other's destiny: "Take care, brothers, lest there be in any of you an evil, unbelieving heart, leading you to fall away from the living God. But exhort one another every day, as long as it is called 'today,' that none of you may be hardened by the deceitfulness of sin" (Heb 3:12–13; emphasis added).

Just as living believers help increase your alertness, so can Christians from the *past*! Those who have *already* run their races have set outstanding examples for you. Let the Holy Spirit encourage and caution you from their lives. In addition to encouragement, they often provide a fresh perspective on our *contemporary* issues. C. S. Lewis (1898–1963) noted that since each generation has blind spots in their faith, reading from *past* Christian writings helps correct each generation's shortsightedness. Even their failures can be instructive. All heroines and heroes of church history were imperfect sinners saved by grace, just like you. Learn from their models what is worthy of imitation and what to avoid.[23]

---

23. Lewis, Preface to *On the Incarnation*, 10.

For the Future

ALERTNESS AND OTHER FORMS OF TIME TRAVEL

The investigation of mental, meditative time travel turns *now* to a toxic form of *future* travel: anxiety! But you are *pre*pared for that tough topic because alertness is an excellent antidote to the sin and suffering of anxiety. Alertness and anxiety are combatants. Alertness transforms, while anxiety poisons. Embrace one and the other yields!

Staying alert for both delight and danger will keep you from anxiety as surely as anxiety will keep you from remaining alert. Not surprisingly, anxiety often masquerades as alertness. "I am not worried, just cautious," many anxious people say. But God always judges it as a sin even though it "seems" helpful. In the next chapter, you will discover that thinking about meditation as time travel is a necessary step in combating anxiety.

RECOMMENDED READING ABOUT ALERTNESS

John Flavel, *On Keeping the Heart* (Monee, IL: Lulu Publishers, 2022).
John Piper, *Future Grace* (Sisters, OR: Multnomah, 1995).
Thomas R. Schreiner, *Run to Win the Prize: Perseverance in the New Testament* (Wheaton, IL: Crossway, 2010).
Joe Thorn: *Note to Self: The Discipline of Preaching to Yourself* (Wheaton, IL: Crossway, 2011).

MEMORIZATION PASSAGES ABOUT ALERTNESS

Matthew 7:15 (NASB)
Beware of false prophets, who come to you in sheep's clothing but inwardly are ravenous wolves.

Matthew 24:42 (NASB)
Therefore, be alert, for you do not know which day your Lord is coming.

1 Peter 5:8 (NASB)
Be of sober spirit, be on the alert. Your adversary, the devil, prowls around like a roaring lion, seeking someone to devour.

CHAPTER THREE

Toward the *Future*
Do Not Be Anxious!

> An experienced worrier can go for days leapfrogging from *past* to *future* and *back* again, never landing in the *present*. When they travel into the *future*, they see it in Technicolor and vivid detail.
>
> EDWARD WELCH[1]

Everyone knows that anxiety is problematic and pointless. It has been said that "worry is like a rocking chair. It gives you something to do, but you never get anywhere."[2] Yet many people dismiss worry as merely a mistake, even though it is a far more severe issue. It is actually a sin and terribly destructive to one's soul. Tragically, it is both prevalent among Christians and persistent, being hard to defeat.[3] Martyn Lloyd-Jones (1899–1981) cautioned against underestimating its power:

> Worry, after all, is a definite entity; it is a force, a power, and we have not begun to understand it until we realize what a tremendous power it is. We so often tend to think of the condition of worry as one which is negative, a failure on our part to do certain things.

1. Emphasis added.
2. Attributed to Vance Havner (1901–86).
3. Lloyd-Jones, *Studies*, 147.

It is that; it is a failure to apply our faith. But the thing we must emphasize is that worry is something positive that comes and grips us and takes control of us. It is a mighty power, an active force, and if we do not realize that, we are certain to be defeated by it.[4]

Jesus frequently addressed this problem of anxiety. He commanded his followers to "not be anxious" three times in the Sermon on the Mount, expecting that with divine help, Christians could defeat this oppressive enemy (Matt 6:25, 31, 34). Anxiety is foolishly attempting to face *tomorrow's* problems *today*. But you do not have to live this way! As you move toward the *future*, being alert about the *future* without living there, you can trust that God's grace will supply your needs *then* as he does *now*.

Worry is an acid eating away at health, relationships, and faith. Even worse, anxiety is a root sin, bearing much poisonous fruit. John Piper observes that though silent, anxiety inevitably leads to other more destructive sins: coveting, greed, hoarding, stealing, irritability, lying, and apathy toward others.[5] How anxiety harms you and others (functional problems) will be investigated *later*, *after* answering the question of how anxiety dishonors God (faith problems). Then we can see God's prescribed medicine for it. The elixir for anxiety is biblical meditation as transformative time travel.

PHONY APPEALS OF ANXIETY

The hard truth is that often, people do what they want to do, even as they complain that they do not want to do what they are doing! Anxiety is a perfect example. It is appealing, full of false promises. Recognizing why people would want to worry marks the first step toward resisting its seductive power. The devil craftily tempts you only with what can distract you from duty and devotion. For many, anxiety is more attractive than adultery![6] What could be attractive about it?

First, anxiety is actually a better choice than apathy and its fruit of idleness. Anxiety, apathy, and idleness are all sins and have costs, but the anxious person is better *prepared* to handle the unexpected *future* than the apathetic. Worrying is an overreaction to the *future*, but at least it is a

---

4. Lloyd-Jones, *Studies*, 463.
5. Piper, *Future Grace*, 53.
6. Lewis, *Screwtape Letters*, 25.

reaction! There is a spiritual and emotional pulse to the anxious soul not found in those who do not care. To those who do not look to the *future* at all, bad things will happen sooner or *later*: "Love not sleep, lest you come to poverty" (Prov 20:13).

To their credit, the anxious are open-eyed toward the *future*, anticipating all sorts of trouble. Of course, their worry brings them extra pain as they over-anticipate and overreact to what has not happened and may never happen. Still, they generally fare better in life, work, and relationships than the idle. Many successful professionals are chronic worriers, but there are few successful lazy people. Some charge *forward* on emotional stress instead of peace because they think that is the only way to approach the *future*. Think of the unhealthy emotional states of many well-known actors and actresses whose professional achievements are impressive but whose personal lives exhibit frequent crises, failed marriages, bitter rivalries, and sometimes even the tragedies of suicide.

Second, anxiety seems to be a reasonable reaction to *past* pain. It comes from vowing never to be ill-*pre*pared or naive again. Ask yourself if this is what is happening the next time you see yourself becoming anxious. Is your anxiety an overreaction to *past* hurts that could have been avoided but were not? For example, a parent whose child was injured in the *past* may become hypervigilant in the *present*. But that hyped-up emotional state may cause both the parent and the child additional *future* pain. A woman hurt in *past* relationships might stay obsessively worried about being hurt again. A betrayed man may be too anxious to trust again. Such emotional overreactions cause more harm in the *future* than they *prevent*. For example, if you drive too close to the shoulder of the road, the worst (but too common) reaction is to jerk the wheel hard, sending your car out of control across the street and into the other lane. But the wiser driver calms down and eases the vehicle back into the right lane unharmed. Overreactions are always bad reactions!

God has given you a better way to *pre*pare for the *future*: proactive alertness. When you see problems in your *past*, even if you could have avoided them, you can pray that God will make you more attentive for the *future*. In addition, learn to trust that God has control of even your *past* mistakes and their lingering consequences. For believers, there is always hope in *future* grace. No child of God will fully experience the bleak *future* they *once* deserved while still a sinner (Rom 5:8). *Now*, even more, your Father will intervene to provide a better *future* than you anticipate.

If you do not redeem the emotional energy that leads to anxiety, a terrible irony will overtake you. Anxiety makes you less fit, rather than more fit, to fulfill your *present* duties. Then, when it makes you fail to do the wise things you should have done, your anxiety will increase even more! This is a dark cycle to get stuck in. Worry, like other sins, never achieves what it promises up front.

Third, anxiety seems to show concern and love. What do you do with the emotional pressure of not knowing if the *future* will work out? Since you cannot guarantee the *future*, surely you must do something! And if you are not "uptight" about anything, anxious people will interpret that as uncaring. Surely, some "white-knuckle fliers" likely look around the plane aghast and irritated that others are relaxed and enjoying the flight. Tim Challies dispels the notion that worry indicates authentic caring: "Our willingness to fret about something is not a necessary indication that we care deeply about it. Our unwillingness to fret about something is not a necessary indication that we are ambivalent about it. In those times we are fearful or uncertain, we can make ourselves believe that our worrying displays just how much we care, just how much our hearts are engaged. But it's a false connection."[7] These are time-travel mistakes, thoughts like "my worry *today* will bring about better *future* results" or "my deep *past* love for my family members justifies my *present* anxiety about their well-being." What should spur prayer stirs up stress instead!

Fourth, "pessimistic peddlers" are all around you. Whether they are misguided fellow worriers or conniving manipulators, they make your anxiety worse. Stay alert to recognize and avoid professional alarmists. Multitudes of secular alarmists dole out dire *predictions* about the bad times to come. The *future* will likely prove they were mistaken, but instead of apologizing, they will sound the alarm about other things. Going beyond informing the public or raising genuine concerns, such people benefit from inflaming panic by enhancing their popularity and lining their pocketbooks. Do not allow naysayers to discourage you. Turn off the television and set down the phone more often so that you can spend less time consuming news and more time communicating with the God of perfect peace. Writing to John Adams (1735–1826), Thomas Jefferson (1743–1826) insisted that people should be sanguine instead of gloomy, for "how much pain have cost us the evils which have never happened!"[8]

---

7. Challies, "Not Worrying ≠ Not Caring," para. 3.
8. Jefferson, "To John Adams," para. 2.

Churchy anxiety about worldly things is as deadly as personal anxiety and just as distracting from the glory of God. Do you still remember the Y2K scare? "Experts" dominated newscasts and filled church pulpits, *predicting* the end and giving panicky advice! I remember sitting in a Sunday service of a large evangelical church in December *before* the infamous Y2K date arrived. Instead of hearing from the church's pastor about the hope or joy of Jesus and the gospel during Advent, a "Y2K expert" spent the whole service telling wealthy church members how to stock up on groceries and where to hide their money *before* the banks folded. When such crisis-of-the-moment experts are wrong, do they apologize to the many worriers they pushed into heart palpitations and drastic *preparations*? They do not! Instead, they find other looming *future* crises around which to build their speaking and writing careers. Perhaps such pessimistic peddlers have always been around, but the growth of social media has increased their influence.

Thankfully, you can look to Jesus as a model of living under tremendous pressure yet never being worried. He faced unimaginable suffering for our sake and knew his *future* perfectly in advance, but he was never gloomy. If anyone had the right to panic, he did! He knew all that was coming upon him (John 18:4)! But Jesus was not worried and calmly spread a message of hope instead of hopelessness. The same Holy Spirit on whom he relied can also grant you peace. You, too, can be alert and ready for God's plans without staying alarmed.

The appeal of anxiety is why conventional advice dispensed to worriers, although true, usually does not help them. When they hear "just don't worry about it," they either discount their advice-giver as naive or agree temporarily, only to fall *back* into it again. Just like the sobered-up drunk will often vow not to do "that" again, so the worrier, in moments of clarity, will nod along with a preacher's appeal not to be anxious, but stumble right *back* into worrying *before* leaving the church parking lot. Something more substantial than human exhortations must be applied to remedy this problem. Heart surgery is needed instead of the Band-Aids. You must ask the Holy Spirit to operate on your heart, giving you peace about the *future* rooted in your *past*. Your part as a spiritual cardiac patient is to meditate on why anxiety is so wrong and then direct your heart to meditate on the goodness and greatness of God.

FAITH PROBLEMS OF ANXIETY

Anxiety weakens your faith and can even shipwreck it. The most severe consequence of anxiety is failing to trust your Heavenly Father, believing, often without admitting it, that either he cannot or will not bring about good in your *future*. George Müller (1805–98) cautioned that it "is impossible to be anxious without dishonoring God."[9] For this reason, others have identified anxiety as "sub-Christian," "an ungodly practice," "injustice done to God," and "practical atheism."[10] These strong labels are appropriate because childlike trust honors your Heavenly Father. But anxiety attacks God's character and dishonors him. In your moments of angst, Satan whispers, "Did God really promise to provide for you? Can he? Will he?" Take courage! Your God is generous and always provides! He paid the costliest payment for your salvation, the "precious blood of Christ" (1 Pet 1:18). *Now*, as his child, you can confidently expect that he will "give us all things" for life and godliness (Rom 8:32; 2 Pet 1:3). But doubting that God will meet your needs is character defamation.

It is only natural for unbelievers to worry.[11] But it is spiritually unnatural for believers to worry. So, learning to trust God is a sign of spiritual growth, and as your trust grows, your worry will wilt. Many great stories of the Bible involve women and men exercising childlike faith in crushing circumstances. They glorified God, and he filled them with joy. The widow believed that God would provide for her and her child, so she obediently made bread for Elijah from the last of her supplies (1 Kgs 17:8–16). Likewise, Jesus commended the great faith of the centurion, who believed that Jesus could and would heal from a distance through spoken words (Matt 8:5–13). On the other hand, you read the disappointment of Jesus with his disciples every time their fears smothered their faith: "O you of little faith" (Matt 8:26; 14:31; 16:8; 17:20).

Doubting God almost inevitably leads to a second related problem: idolatry. You must trust something or someone for your good, or else you will never get out of bed and face the day. The firmly grounded believer trusts that God holds the future. But a believer unsettled by anxiety turns away from trusting God and relies on himself, a close family member, a

---

9. Müller, *Counsel to Christians*, 79.

10. Thomas, "Authority of Scripture," 27; Schwertley, *Sermon on the Mount*, 455; Calvin, *Commentary on Matthew, Mark, and Luke*, 464; Mounce, *Matthew*, 61.

11. MacArthur, *Matthew*, 425.

friend, a professional, or an institution. He decides he can face tomorrow because of somebody or something other than God! That lie leads to idolatry, trusting in something other than God.

You worship whatever you depend on for a promising *future*, whatever will "give you what only God can give."[12] Some people rely on themselves and are encouraged by cultural can-do messaging; ultimately, their trust is in themselves. Thomas Schreiner notes, "Worry is a form of pride because when believers are filled with anxiety, they are convinced that they must solve all the problems in their lives in their strength."[13] Sometimes, people lean too heavily on others, slighting God, who alone deserves your dependence. Only God can claim to "declare the end from the beginning," having complete and perfect knowledge of the *future* and fulfilling his plans (Isa 46:10).

WORRY IS HIJACKED MEDITATION

Worry is a failure to trust God, leading to trusting others in his place. It is a replacement sin, displacing God from his role as your caring Heavenly Father. What lures a person down the path to fear? It is thoughts running unexamined and unhindered. You need to take your "inconsistent thoughts" that are "very fleeting and feathery" and think about God and His goodness in your *past*, *present*, and *future*.[14] God desires that you should meditate "day and night" on his law (Ps 1:2). That means "to see all things in God, and God in all things."[15] But that often does not happen in the Christian life and rarely happens for those afflicted with anxiety. Why? Because anxiety hijacks meditation! It overpowers the cure!

Anxiety exploits the God-given ability to contemplate, gaze at, muse over, and regard persons and things "worthy of praise" (Phil 4:8). Instead of healthy meditation that produces peace within and praise to God above, worry leads to constant turmoil within and dishonor to God above. Biblical meditation is the cure-all for worry and all other forms of toxic mental time travel. Holy and helpful meditation flows from what you know about God's faithfulness and leads to prayer. Think of Peter sinking into the water, weighed down by worry. He knew Jesus could save him (knowledge of

---

12. Keller, *Counterfeit Gods*, xviii.
13. Schreiner, *1, 2 Peter, Jude*, 241.
14. Bates, *Whole Works*, 115.
15. Bates, *Whole Works*, 117.

God), that he needed saving (meditation), and cried out urgently in prayer, "Lord, save me" (Matt 14:30).

Worry is hazardous because it is messed up meditation. Meditation is a powerful tool, but in this situation it harms you instead of helping you: "Anxiety is nothing more than meditating on problems rather than the One who holds the solution. God commands us to meditate on His word instead."[16] The power of meditation is hijacked: "Anxiety is a form of negative meditation, which can only be countered by chewing the cud of the gospel."[17] Richard Baxter (1615–91) wrote about worriers that "their fantasy most erreth in aggravating their sin, or dangers, or unhappiness: every ordinary infirmity they are ready to speak of with amazement, as a heinous sin: and every possible danger they take for probable, and every probable one for certain."[18]

Believers may panic when contemplating possible *future* events, like challenging relationships, academic struggles, employment issues, hostile workplaces, sicknesses, and losses in life. They forget to cling to God's promises and presence, which can carry them through the valley (Ps 23:4). These excessive thoughts in *advance* of what may or may not happen do no good and reap much harm. There is asphyxiating, anxious panic when a person realizes that they cannot make it in life ("It will be a disaster!"). It is wrong to be *prematurely* anxious about the *future*, and the focus is off, too. Even if a person spends all their time thinking about the *future* without getting carried away in anxiety, that is still worldliness. Attempting to live for God while filling your mind with worldly thoughts is a clear case of being "double-minded" (Jas 1:8; 4:8).[19]

Further, behind all fearful thinking about the *future* lurks a dangerous assumption: if only you knew what would happen, then surely everything would turn out better for you. But what every worrier seeks in vain to know—the *future*—is better not known. Charles Spurgeon (1834–92) cautioned that even "if there were ways of reading the *future*, it would be wise to decline to use them. The knowledge would create responsibility, arouse fear, and diminish *present* enjoyment."[20]

---

16. Barnett, *David's Spiritual Secret*, 127.
17. Bush and Due, *Live in Liberty*, 162.
18. Baxter, *Practical Works*, 218–19.
19. Calamy, *Art of Divine Meditation*, 85.
20. Spurgeon, "My Times," 285–86.

ANXIETY IS DEFEATED ONLY THROUGH MEDITATION

The bold but biblical claim here is that worry is best battled through Christian meditation. This battle demands serious and sustained reflection on God's grace in your *past*, *present*, and *future* through mental time travel. Maturing believers may not know how they have tamed anxiety. However, whether they recognize it or not, the victorious believer has discovered the power of meditation, just as David did: "When I am afraid, I put my trust in you. In God, whose word I praise, in God I trust; I shall not be afraid. What can flesh do to me?" (Ps 56:3–4). Meditation on Scriptures like this, especially if you sing them, shifts the gaze from worry to God's worth. You stop staring at the source of the anxiety and start acclaiming God's character. This always terminates trembling!

As a citizen of heaven, you should set your mind on the things above (Phil 3:20; Col 3:1–2). The key to becoming more heavenly minded is to meditate on the glimmers of God's glory in inherently good things on earth: "whatever is true, whatever is honorable, whatever is just, whatever is pure, whatever is lovely, whatever is commendable" (Phil 4:8), or by direct, formal meditation on God's person and works through meditation. Your imagination, which *once* made your worry worse, can *now* help you out of that mess with thoughts of what you can see *now* by faith and *later* by sight. What believer has not thought of heaven and then had a spring in her step as she moved through her day? Or what Christian has not imagined hearing, "well done," and has worked even harder at faithfulness (Matt 25:21, 23)?[21]

Singing is a particularly powerful form of meditation and a potent weapon against worry. By worldly standards, Paul and Silas had many reasons to be worried. But they worshiped with meditative hymn singing late into the night (Acts 16:25). They had the comfort of heaven on earth in their souls long *before* God unleashed his power through the earthquake. The meditating Christian experiences the joys of heaven as often as she fixes the eyes of her heart on it: "Heaven came down, and glory filled my soul."[22]

If you struggle against anxiety or try to comfort someone with anxiety issues, relief may seem elusive, if not unobtainable! But God has provided meditation, by which, through mental time travel, you can unlock your

---

21. "One of the great duties of the Christian mind is imagination." Piper, *Life as a Vapor*, 69.

22. Paterson, "Heaven Came Down," 573.

memory of his remarkable *past* performances for his people and his *future* promises for you! Charles Orr (1844–1913), confident in the power of meditation, declared that from its practice, "there will be a holy flame enkindled in your soul and such heavenly sweetness and peace that the cares of this life, and fret and worry will no more light on you than flies on a heated furnace."[23]

MEDITATE ON GOD'S CHARACTER

What should Christians be thinking about throughout each day to alleviate anxiety? Focusing on God's characteristics is the best battle plan against anxiety. All of God's characteristics are beneficial for relieving frightened hearts, but we will focus on the three that are particularly powerful for worriers: omniscience, omnipotence, and loving faithfulness. This progression moves from attributes of God's greatness to his attributes of goodness. Pensive people need first to know that God can help (great enough to intervene) and then that he will help (good enough to intervene).[24]

Meditate on God as Omniscient (All-Knowing)

For a man facing a life-threatening illness, his mind can run wild with regrets about the *past* and uncertainties about the *present*: fears about losing loved ones, financial pressures from loss of income, mounting medical bills, and uncertainty regarding which recommended treatments to take. The *future* looks bleak, too! Who will provide for his family in the short term or long term? The threat of death can provoke troubling questions such as the one that bothered Leo Tolstoy (1828–1910): "Is there any meaning in my life which can overcome the inevitable death awaiting me?"[25]

Peace will not come from thinking about life only *now*. As the Holy Spirit elevates the sick man's gaze to see his Lord's omniscience (Job 28:24; Ps 139:1–4, 17; Isa 46:9–10; Matt 10:29–30; Heb 4:13), anxiety will be banished as often as he thinks of the Lord. His God knows everything and will bring about the ultimate best for each of his children (Matt 6:30–32). God never

---

23. Orr, *Helps to Holy Living*, 5.

24. Millard Erickson uses these categories for God's attributes: goodness and greatness. Erickson, *Christian Theology*, 289.

25. Tolstoy, *My Confession*, 23.

has to revise his opinions or reassess the best course. He *foresees* what is best and will bring it about.[26] Like trees placed by God in just the perfect suitable locations and conditions for flourishing, God "places us amid the circumstances and experiences in which our life will grow and ripen the best."[27]

Meditate on God as Omnipotent (All-Powerful)

In addition to knowing God has all knowledge, the shaken sufferer can rest in God's omnipotence, his all-powerful nature (Gen 18:14; Jer 32:27; Ps 115:3; Prov 21:1). In the Bible, even tyrants had to confess, "He does according to his will among the host of heaven and the inhabitants of the earth; and none can stay his hand" (Dan 4:35). No one, not even demons, can ward off the long arm of the Lord from doing his holy will, which includes providing the best *future* blessings for his servants, even if those blessings lie on the other side of the grave. Nothing can ultimately thwart his will or overturn his plans.

This does not justify rash decision making but assures you that you can be at peace when faced with difficulties, even as great as persecution for your faith! Like Shadrach, Meshach, and Abednego, faith that God controls life and death will empower you to face the *future* with confidence. Standing in their confidence that God could deliver them from the furnace of fire, they proclaimed precisely that to the king instead of trembling before his threats: "If this be so, our God whom we serve is able to deliver us from the burning fiery furnace, and he will deliver us out of your hand, O king" (Dan 3:17). Yet, submitting to the sovereign freedom of God to plan the best *future* for them, they did not *pre*sume to know his omniscient plans. They did not worry but worshiped with their willingness to leave their lives in his wise and wonderful hands: "But if not, be it known to you, O king, that we will not serve your gods or worship the golden image that you have set up" (v. 18). God not only delivered them, but he also prompted praise for himself from that pagan king: "There is no other god who can rescue in this way" (v. 29). They even received promotions (v. 30)!

---

26. Erickson, *Christian Theology*, 302.
27. Miller, *Workday Religion*, 12.

Meditate on God as Loving and Faithful

Meditating on God's loving faithfulness will also calm you. You know, and the Holy Spirit will remind you, that God loves you and that you can trust his promised faithfulness (Exod 34:6–7; Deut 32:4; Lam 11:22–23; Pss 36:5; 89:8; 98:3; 2 Thess 3:3).

Reflecting on Ps 46:2, David Dickson (1583–1663) writes that "nothing can guard the heart of God's people against the terror of possible, or imminent troubles, save faith in God; for here the Lord's people, having fixed their faith, make this inference, therefore will we not fear."[28] If you continue to sink into "sad anxiety," you may intellectually affirm God's faithfulness, but you have not internalized it enough.[29] The medicine is in your hand but you have not swallowed by meditation yet.

The theme of God's love toward believers is prominent in the Old Testament (Pss 23, 27). In the New Testament, the love of the Heavenly Father is supremely demonstrated through the gift of his self-sacrificing Son (John 3:16). Likewise, Jesus's love warms the hearts of believers chilled by the cold winds of worry. The disciples learned that when Jesus was with them, he was always protecting them, providing for them, and giving them peace. Like them, the maturing believer is learning to lean on Jesus's love and faithfulness to reassure them.

You can draw comfort from meditating on what must await you in the *future*, not what you fear might happen. As a Christian, you will meet Jesus either in death or at his descent at the second coming (1 Cor 15:51). Death, the greatest fear of human beings, enslaves many (Heb 2:15). Yet, because Christ has conquered even death, the believer should hope beyond the grave. Paul reminded us that "whether we live or whether we die, we are the Lord's" (Rom 14:8)!

You will be with your loving Lord Jesus, who guaranteed you an eternity with himself in heaven. While the Bible focuses on God's glory in heaven, it also describes heaven in vivid and beautiful language to assure you that it is a place without lack, dangers, and any reason to worry. Combat worry by regularly meditating on your eternal destiny in the presence of your great, good, and glorious God.

Revelation 21:3–4 is a beautiful passage to mark and frequently reflect upon as you think about the *future* presence of God with you and

---

28. Dickson, *Brief Explication of the Psalms*, 266.
29. Pink, *Nature of God*, 63.

for you: "And I heard a loud voice from the throne saying, 'Behold, the dwelling place of God is with man. He will dwell with them, and they will be his people, and God himself will be with them as their God. He will wipe away every tear from their eyes, and death shall be no more, neither shall there be mourning, crying, or pain anymore, for the former things have passed away.'" Robert Morgan calls Rev 21–22 the "Bible's travel brochure of heaven." Especially for worriers, it is relieving to know that "burdens cannot follow us to heaven."[30] When discouraged, meditating on heaven can be like a "heart defibrillator" for your weakening spiritual heart, jolting your heart back to life.[31]

To meditate on truths about God, use techniques such as reading aloud from the Bible and pausing to pray to God about each truth that moves your heart. You can also speak each of them aloud from memory or sing them from a song you know.[32] You could also write out God's truths verse by verse, copying relevant passages from the Bible. As you reflect on God's comforting characteristics, the Holy Spirit will move your frightened heart back toward God. J. I. Packer (1926–2020) called meditation "the activity of calling to mind, and thinking over, and dwelling on, and applying to oneself, the various things that one knows about the works and ways and purposes and promises of God."[33] You will gain strength as you remember what God has revealed about his greatness and goodness. This is preaching to yourself about God and his gospel!

May you be quickly glancing at your problems daily as part of alertness yet lingering only to gaze at God. Follow the wisdom expressed by Octavius Winslow (1808–78): "Thinking of God! Meditating upon Christ! There is no other subject of meditation that can calm your perturbed thoughts, fix your wandering thoughts, purify your sinful thoughts, harmonize your perplexed thoughts, quench your panting thoughts, soothe and comfort your sad and mournful thoughts, as thinking upon God!"[34] God will defeat your worry for you, his way, through meditation!

---

30. Morgan, *Worry Less*, 39.
31. Workman, "I Look Forward," para. 3.
32. Baxter, *Practical Works*, 274.
33. Packer, *Knowing God*, 23.
34 Winslow, *Precious Things of God*, 50.

COMBAT THE FEAR OF PEOPLE WITH THE FEAR OF GOD

The fear of people is the most paralyzing of all anxieties! Fear of other people overwhelms many and can be a problem their whole lives. Think of how many people fear public speaking or even offering their opinions in small groups, whether in school, the workplace, or even the church. How many bad decisions are made by men, women, teenagers, and children who sincerely want to do the right things but will yield and quietly do anything under the relentless force of peer pressure?

Consider how fearful Christians sometimes give into ungodly cultural pressures, disobeying the command to "not be conformed to this world" (Rom 12:2). In a similar way, that fear can lead to ignoring God's positive commands! It drives the widespread terror of sharing the gospel with others. Instead of rejoicing in opportunities to share the most wonderful news with the most spiritually needy people, many believers would rather do anything for Jesus than mention him to others evangelistically.

Usually, when combating anxiety and fear, you should focus on the positive aspects of God's goodness and faithfulness. But when you are arming yourself to fight the fear of people, focus more on God's fearsome traits! Fight against the fear of others with the fear of God! The saying goes, "Fight fire with fire." Fight the fear of finite people with the fear of your truly frightening and fiery God (Exod 24:17; Deut 4:24; Heb 12:29).

How can you diminish "people fear"? By fearing God more, remembering his greatness and glory in reverent and humbled awe. John Flavel (1627–91) put it succinctly: "Exalt the fear of God in your hearts, and let it gain the ascendant over all your other fears."[35] This is not slavish fear but an "indefinable mixture of reverence and pleasure, joy and awe which fills our hearts when we realize who God is and what he has done for us."[36] When you feel peer pressure, instead of yielding, remember his goodness to you in the *past* and his warnings about obeying him in the *future*. Remembering the fear of God will catalyze obedience, even if you face human opposition.

This is the strategy that Jesus taught to his apostles, placing the fear of God in direct conflict with the fear of people. *After* commanding them to proclaim the gospel with "openness and fearlessness," Jesus reminded them to fear the wrath of God, not the "minor danger" of "evil people or even

---

35. Flavel, *Whole Works*, 3:310.
36. Ferguson, *Grow in Grace*, 29.

Satan himself."[37] Jesus warned them: "Do not fear those who kill the body but cannot kill the soul. Rather fear him who can destroy both soul and body in hell . . . whoever denies me before men, I also will deny before my Father who is in heaven" (Matt 10:28, 33).

Isaiah confronted and comforted God's people by reminding them of the contrast between their mighty God and mere man: "I, I am he who comforts you; who are you that you are afraid of man who dies, of the son of man who is made like grass, and have forgotten the Lord, your Maker, who stretched out the heavens and laid the foundations of the earth, and you fear continually all the day because of the wrath of the oppressor when he sets himself to destroy? And where is the wrath of the oppressor?" (Isa 51:12–13). The fear of others is a sign of forgotten holy reverence for God and a failure to tremble before his words instead of the words of others (Isa 66:2).

Fearless Meditators Together

Graciously, God has placed every believer in a church, a community of believers living together as fellow time travelers. In life together, you will feel empowered and emboldened! Even the Spirit-led, Spirit-filled apostles returned from their victorious conflicts over the religious leaders to gather with fellow Christians. They praised God and prayed together for more boldness (Acts 4:23–31). They needed their community of faith, and you do, too! As you seek to win against worry, remember to stay active with your spiritual family for strength and encouragement.

Moreover, if you discover fellow Christians hunkered down and afraid, God calls you to rally them to remember God's supremacy. David did just that when he encountered the army of Israel, acting as if they did not know their God. Paul Tripp links their forgetfulness to their cowardice: "It was an army suffering from a tragic case of identity amnesia. They forgot who they were. They forgot the promises they had been given. And because they did, they drew a false spiritual equation as they evaluated the moment. It wasn't these puny little soldiers against this huge giant; it was this puny giant against Almighty God."[38] In contrast, David knew the God of Israel's *past* intimately. He fought with the confidence that his *past* deliverer (1 Sam 16:34–37) would deliver him and his nation in the immediate *future*: "For the battle is the Lord's, and he will give you into our hand" (1 Sam 17:47).

37. Morris, *Gospel according to Matthew*, 262.
38. Tripp, *Dangerous Calling*, 66–67.

Unanxious, Unyielding Jonathan Edwards

Since meditation ends anxiety, meditators are *pre*pared to weather hostility from others without bending under pressure to compromise in order to please them. Jonathan Edwards (1703–58) modeled this marvelously, as he both wrote about meditation and practiced it.[39] As a result, when he faced opposition, he showed terrific tranquility. Centuries of Christians have marveled at his peaceful reaction to his church firing him. He cared deeply for his congregation and sought the best for their souls, even though they resisted his appeals. George Marsden's biography reveals a man whose *future* hope could not be shaken:

> In the series of church meetings in 1750 at which he was rejected by his church by a vote of 230 to 23, one eyewitness, a pastor named David Hall, remarked: "I never saw the least symptoms of displeasure in his countenance the whole week, but he appeared like a man of God, whose happiness was out of the reach of his enemies, and whose treasure was not only a *future* but a *present* good, overbalancing all imaginable ills of life." Hall says this calmness on Edwards's part was "to the astonishment of" those who opposed him.[40]

How can you plan to live "out of reach" of your worries? You learn to use two types of meditation: "scheduled" and "spontaneous." When Christians speak of meditation, they usually refer to "scheduled" meditation, practiced alongside the spiritual disciplines of Bible reading and prayer. Scheduled meditation is an excellent place to start because you should *already* be spending scheduled devotional time with the Lord, and this is an add-on benefit.

Scheduled Meditation

Scheduled meditation flows through and from your regular Bible reading. In this meditative Bible reading, you not only read but reflect on what you have read, continuing to "think carefully, deeply, and diligently" about the reading.[41] You discuss what you read with yourself in the presence of God, and he changes you through it.

---

39. Whitney, "Pursuing a Passion for God," 113.
40. Marsden, *Jonathan Edwards*, 361 (emphasis added).
41. Luther, *First Lectures*, 17.

Transformative Time Travel

The meditative Bible reader ingests God's word by reflecting on it, applying it, and praying it back to him. This brings spiritual flourishing and success (Ps 1:2–3; Joshua 1:7–8). Reflecting on his own experiences of battling and defeating anxiety, J. P. Moreland concludes that "what an anxious and depressed person needs is to believe that the kinds of experiences and divine encounters that took place with folks in biblical times also take place *now*—that, in fact, they could really happen to him or her."[42]

On any given day, you read in your Bible about God's *past* work in the lives of his saints. For example, you might read that "God is our refuge and strength, a very *present* help in trouble" (Ps 46:1; emphasis added). From this truth, you can expect that the same God who always delivered his people will also deliver you. Perhaps you are *already* studying the Bible this way because you were taught to read the Bible this way, and you have heard it modeled in sermons and Bible studies. If so, rejoice and increase in your passionate exploration of Scripture. But if reading the Bible thoughtfully instead of just checking it off your daily task list is a new idea, what new joys await you! Through God's word, the Spirit changes his spiritual children.

Learning to see God's greatness, goodness, and glory in the Bible's stories means having your spiritual eyes opened to see reality as it is instead of how you *now* perceive it. You need the Holy Spirit to grant you supernatural sight to see God's control over this seemingly out-of-control and dangerous world. Until God provides this illumination, you live spiritually shortsighted, much like Elijah's anxious servant, overwhelmed by the human army surrounding their city.

Elijah prayed, but his prayer did not change anything about the situation except that God gave the servant the supernatural sight to perceive their security and, therefore, the reason not to worry: "So he answered, 'Do not fear, for those who are with us are more than those who are with them.' Then Elisha prayed and said, 'O Lord, I pray, open his eyes that he may see.' And the Lord opened the servant's eyes and he saw; and behold, the mountain was full of horses and chariots of fire all around Elisha" (2 Kgs 6:16–17).[43] May God open your eyes to behold wonderful and reassuring realities, too (Ps 119:18)!

A vital daily practice is to find a verse that impacts you and write it down. Then, take your portable portion with you into your day. It is like taking medicine along with you in case you get a headache. Whatever

---

42. Moreland and Issler, *Lost Virtue of Happiness*, 172.
43. Jamieson et al., *Commentary*, 234.

happens in the day *ahead*, pull out that Scripture prescription and ingest it again and again. It is even better to commit that verse to memory, even if just as a paraphrase. Robert Morgan testifies to the effectiveness of this method when he discovers "a phrase from Scripture to think about repetitively when fear or panic rises."[44] It is carving God's eternal word into the walls of your life and letting them change you.[45]

Before you leave your meditative Bible reading each day, pray that God will empower you to live in light of what you have reflected upon. Just ask the same Holy Spirit who authored that verse to activate its truths in your life, and he will. A healthy three-step pattern involves Bible reading, meditation, and prayer. If you prefer just two steps, it is "meditative" Bible reading that then kindles "meditative" prayer.

Not only does this practice help you *pre*pare to wipe away worry, but it slowly elevates your gaze off your life of fleeting vapor (Jas 4:14) to gaze at God's story, in which he always emerges as the victorious hero. Then we become "less concerned about ourselves and, consequently, not experience as much anxiety, worry, or fear."[46] It supercharges all Christian areas of growth not just the battle plan against anxiety. The following chapters apply the discipline of scheduled meditation to other areas of transforming time travel. But for *now*, let yourself "meditate" on the power of meditation with the strong claim of Thomas Brooks (1608–80): "It is not he that reads most, but he that meditates most, that will prove the choicest, sweetest, wisest, and strongest Christian."[47]

Spontaneous Meditation

People with asthma know when to use their control inhalers and when to use their rescue inhalers. Their daily medicine helps control their asthma, but when they have an actual attack, they use their rescue inhaler for that emergency. In the same way, your daily practice of scheduled meditation keeps your worry under control, but you must reach for the medicine of spontaneous meditation when anxiety attacks.

We all have those moments, even Christians who will not admit it. Perhaps worry grabs hold of your heart when you hear strange sounds in

---

44. Morgan, *Worry Less*, 59.
45. Weidmann. *End of Anxiety*, 91.
46. Dunlop, *Wellness for the Glory of God*, 26; see also Piper, *Desiring God*, 10.
47. Brooks, *Complete Works*, 8.

the supposedly empty house, when the late-night unexpected phone call comes, when the lab results are expected, or when there will be an upcoming confrontational conversation. What do you do in those moments? You must choose to redirect your thoughts away from the situation's urgency onto the stability of God.

This is not ignoring issues with a carefree attitude about the *future*, disregarding dangers and responsibilities while singing "Hakuna Matata," meaning "no worries," popularized by the catchy song from *The Lion King*.[48] Instead, you reach up through meditation to remember that God has promised to provide for you, his beloved child. He will take care of you, but will you honor him while you wait for his deliverance? Like that desperately needed medication, you must immediately meditate on God to fight off panic. James Boice (1938–2000) compared what we should do when we start to worry to the automatic reactions and reflexes that help us all day long: "You need to get into the habit of turning to God whenever you feel worry approaching. Your reaction in trouble should be something like a conditioned reflex."[49]

Even modern secular psychology agrees that you must redirect your thoughts when anxious. But as a secular field, it stops short, unable to appeal to supernatural help. Spontaneous meditation helps you focus on God's character and his promises in your moments of need. God will help you perceive his *past* faithfulness to you in your life, faithfulness you have *temporarily* forgotten! Paul, who commanded Christians not to "be anxious about anything" (Phil 4:6), also told them to think of good things as a framework for meditation: "Whatever is true, whatever is honorable, whatever is just, whatever is pure, whatever is lovely, whatever is commendable, if there is any excellence, if there is anything worthy of praise, think about these things" (v. 8). He intentionally used broad categories because when you meditate on the good things of God seen around you, your eyes are lifted off your situation and fixed on steady, eternal realities.[50]

Once you have your eyes on God again, pray and ask him for supernatural sight to see the situation more clearly and to settle your heart. This can be a quick process, especially if you have *pro*actively hidden God's words in your heart. If you are still struggling to connect your pain and panic to God's promises, try to take a mental freeze-frame video of your

---

48. Allcock, *Deeper Still*, 36. Allers, *Lion King*.
49. Boice, *Sermon on the Mount*, 223.
50. Fee, *Philippians*, 178.

runaway thoughts. Then, meditate on that stressful thought, examining it like the single frame of a movie reel. Analyze it! What specific lies drive that anxiety? What are you afraid of losing?[51]

Once you know what is running through your mind, it will be easier to recall a specific Scripture of promise. If nothing comes to mind immediately, use a Bible concordance or call a friend or minister to find a passage for reflection. As you engage in time-traveling meditation, you are pausing the chaotic stream of consciousness flowing from your *past* to your *future*. This allows you to examine the *present* in light of Scripture and embrace a different *future* course by faith. This is you taking yourself in hand, the very art of spiritual living.[52] "Meditative prayer" comes from meditation on God and his truth and flows back toward God.[53] It must be "meditative" because many "pray" without reflecting on the God to whom they pray. Some pray so poorly that they get more stressed as they pray! Even among Christians, too many begin by enumerating all their needs and potential dangers in an accelerating process of panicky petitions. Kevin Halloran's testimony illustrates this:

> *After* I realized that praying was making my anxiety worse, I conducted a *post*mortem analysis of what had happened—which revealed that my prayers were masking a sinful and struggling heart. God doesn't promise that any type of prayer will be a silver-bullet anxiety stopper. The content of our prayers matters. The motives of our hearts matter.... We don't get points just for trying.... We need to align our prayers with scriptural truth.[54]

Even church prayer meetings, if not first focused on the Lord with Scripture and singing, can do more emotional harm than spiritual good. The prayer requests keep piling up, and with each request, the mood and faith of the group can sink. Corporate prayer is important, but like all important things, it must be planned well! Together, we must look to God by faith *before* we pray together so that our faith is in who God is, what he has done, and what he has promised.

---

51. Moreland, *Finding Quiet*, 87.

52. Lloyd-Jones, *Spiritual Depression*, 20.

53. This is "meditative" prayer, not "contemplative" prayer, and it always anchors to God's revelation and is practiced in biblically reverent ways. Owen, *Works of John Owen*, 334–35.

54. Halloran, *When Prayer Is a Struggle*, 112 (emphasis added).

It will be easy for you to move from poor praying to powerful praying because God will help you, and he is the expert at turning evil into good (Gen 50:20; Rom 8:29). Even worry can be redeemed! Charles Spurgeon (1834–92) rhymed in his advice about worry: "Turn into a prayer everything that is a care."[55] Especially during a panic attack, "God's way of escape" is to "commune with God" and invite him to intervene.[56]

How can you help yourself hear God's word over the panicky shouts of your struggling soul? Speak God's promises aloud to yourself and turn them into vocal prayers! These meditations and prayers can flow from verses you *already* have hidden in your heart (Ps 37:31). Or, if you *pre*planned well, you could pull out *already pre*pared verses on paper or stored electronically. Vocalizing God's word has an amazing amplifying effect on how it impacts your soul and naturally launches you into praying aloud to God.[57] You can also personalize the promises as you pray, filling in your name. Just like your voice helps you hear and heed God's words, so can listening to the lyrics of biblically faithful Christian music. Like *pre*planning your go-to stress Scriptures, you should *today* develop a playlist of songs focusing on God and his character instead of gambling on whatever is on Christian radio in your *future* moments of need. Your playlist is like that first aid kit in your house that you keep for bumps and scrapes. You need never remember it until you need it, but then better be ready.

Spontaneous meditation can move from your anxiety to God's "word book" of the Bible! But God wrote another book. God's "world book" of creation is an oasis of soul-calming reassurance. Jesus taught that if you "look" and "observe" the birds and the grass (Matt 6:26, 28–30), you can reassure yourself that God will provide for you, as any loving father would (Matt 7:9–10), especially your heavenly Father (v. 11). Have you ever seen a nervous wild animal paralyzed by doubts and fears about next week? You have not! You have to be human to live so out of sync with God's care for his creatures.

ANXIETY AND OTHER FORMS OF TIME TRAVEL

Anxiety is *future*-oriented toxic time travel. It has a *future* orientation that mimics alertness. However, the spiritually alert feel God's transforming

---

55. Spurgeon, "Prayer, the Cure for Care," 110.
56. Hibbs, *Struck Down but Not Destroyed*, 154.
57. Tautges, *Anxiety*, 118.

peace, not negative thoughts and feelings. All of the aspects of time travel in this book are interrelated. So, "don't worry", even as we move on to other topics, we will keep an eye on anxiety! In *future* chapters, you will see that living with an appreciation for the *past* (chapter 4) reduces anxiety. You will also learn that the opposite, forgetting the *past* (chapter 5), worsens your worry. The spiritually healthy believer living with discipline in the *present*, with an eye to the *future* (chapter 6), has less to be worried about than those living a life of idle un*pre*paredness.

Happily, you are not time-traveling alone! You move toward the *future* side-by-side with fellow time travelers in your family and church (chapter 7), which helps immensely when worries threaten you. Then comes the end! But again, "don't worry!" Because you are developing your time-traveling skills and learning to use them to master anxiety, when you face the *last* chapters of your life (chapter 8), you will have the perfect peace of those whose minds are stayed on God (Isa 26:3).

RECOMMENDED READING AGAINST ANXIETY

Pierce Taylor Hibbs, *Struck Down but Not Destroyed: Living Faithfully with Anxiety* (Middletown, DE: Truth Ablaze, 2021).
C. S. Lewis, *Screwtape Letters* (New York: Harper Collins, 2001).
Martyn Lloyd-Jones, *Spiritual Depression* (Grand Rapids: Eerdmans, 1965).
Josh Weidmann. *The End of Anxiety: The Biblical Prescription for Overcoming Fear, Worry, and Panic* (Washington, DC: Salem Books, 2020).
Edward T. Welch. *Running Scared: Fear, Worry, and the God of Rest* (Greensboro, NC: New Growth, 2007).

MEMORIZATION PASSAGES AGAINST ANXIETY

Psalm 56:3–4
When I am afraid, I put my trust in you.
In God, whose word I praise, in God I trust;
I shall not be afraid. What can flesh do to me?

Matthew 6:31–32
Therefore, do not be anxious, saying, "What shall we eat?"
or "What shall we drink?" or "What shall we wear?"
For the Gentiles seek after all these things,
and your heavenly Father knows that you need them all.

Matthew 10:28
And do not fear those who kill the body but cannot kill the soul.
Rather fear him who can destroy both soul and body in hell.

Romans 8:38–39
For I am sure that neither death nor life, nor angels nor rulers,
nor things *present* nor things to come, nor powers,
nor height nor depth,
nor anything else in all creation,
will be able to separate us from the love of God in Christ Jesus
our Lord.[58]

---

58. Emphasis added.

CHAPTER FOUR

Toward the *Past* and the *Future*
Be Appreciative!

> Remind yourself that God deserves thanks.... Meditate on the Psalms. This book is brimming over with thanks to God. Soak it up, read it aloud; it will turn your hard heart to thanks.
>
> —Clint Archer

Your journeys to your *future* to see the benefits of alertness and the baneful effects of anxiety have focused on the *present* in light of the *future*. Being watchful and being worried are both *future*-oriented. *Now* we come to two ways of approaching your *past*: being appreciative or amnesic, remembering it or forgetting it. You must anchor appreciation in God's eternity and your *past*, and it should extend through the *present* into the *future*. Appreciation is so essential to life that people use many words to describe it, such as acknowledgment, thanksgiving, gratitude, and remembering.

People generally live more alert toward their *future* than appreciative of their *past*. Their mental time travel to the *future* is more successful than their travel to the *past*. The savvy businesswoman looks *ahead* for investment opportunities or potential problems. The kindergartner's parents hover over their child, celebrating every minor achievement and anticipating a bright *future* academic career.

Just glance at the types of books written about *future* business strategies or parenting books advising the best ways to raise your child *today* for the best *tomorrow*. There are far more books concerning what you should do to prepare for your *future* than books that urge you to look *back* reflectively and respectfully. Becoming and staying appreciative is naturally more difficult than being alert. God must develop this in you supernaturally! Only transformed people can always appreciate their *past*. They can trust that God did *then* as he does *now*, knowing that he made "all things work together for good" (Rom 8:28).

APPRECIATION HAS A *PAST*

While there is some overlap between Christian alertness and secular alertness, there is little in common between Christian appreciation and secular attempts at it. The secular world struggles to articulate why anyone should be thankful. This makes Thanksgiving Day one of the most guilt-ridden holidays! Many people can only see a cascading series of crises that overwhelm them in the *present* and threaten *future* happiness. That is because "the real difference between a Christian and a non-Christian is that the former gives thanks to God."[1]

Unbelievers know that they should be more appreciative of their *past* and make attempts at it. Still, outside of a *past* saving relationship with God, genuine appreciation of the goodness of God and his good gifts is impossible to achieve. For the atheist, gratitude is illogical! How can anyone thank the random, impersonal forces they believe are the ultimate cause of all that occurs? G. K. Chesterton (1874–1936) quipped that "the worst moment for the atheist is when he is really thankful and has nobody to thank."[2] This ingratitude, the failure to mentally travel to the *past* to appreciate God, is a root sin. Paul, prosecuting his case against humanity and pressing toward the uncontestable guilty verdict, wrote that "they did not honor him as God or give thanks to him" (Rom 1:21). Therefore, David Pao observes that "in biblical theology, the failure to acknowledge one's dependency upon the Creator is the root of all sins."[3] Christians should appreciate the *past* as they reflect on it, rejoice in it, and revere God for it. Yet sometimes Christians

---

1. Longman, *How to Read the Psalms*, 144.
2. Chesterton, *St. Francis of Assisi*, 46–47. He was repeating an unsourced insight from Dante Rossetti.
3. Pao, *Thanksgiving*, 35.

are discontent and grumble. Does that not describe you on certain days? You must stand firm against the temptation of being underappreciative of your *past*.

APPRECIATION HAS A *FUTURE*

A Christian must also appreciate the *future*. A woman rests comfortably, knowing God will fulfill all his *promises* about the *future*. She does not merely expect or wish for the realization of *future* hope. Instead, she understands that her *future* is guaranteed! Peter's glorious introduction to his first letter reminds suffering saints of this uniquely Christian hope. It is "an inheritance that is imperishable, undefiled, and unfading, kept in heaven for you, who by God's power are being guarded through faith for a salvation ready to be revealed in the last time" (1 Pet 1:4–5). Envision it as an eternal life insurance policy that guarantees not only the protection of the policy but the policyholder as well! The Holy Spirit keeps you saved by God's power and protects your reward! You are safely saved, and so are your *future* blessings.

Though admirable traits, being hardworking and diligent can hamper your thankfulness if you forget that God is the one who supplies you with the ability to work hard. A scene from a classic Jimmy Stewart movie illustrates this danger—the hardworking yet nominally religious character Charlie Anderson prays an anemic prayer over a family meal:

> Lord, we cleared this land. We plowed it, sowed it, and harvested it. We cooked the harvest. It wouldn't be here and we wouldn't be eating it *if we hadn't done it all ourselves*. We worked dog-bone hard for every crumb and morsel, but we thank you Lord, *just the same* for the food we're about to eat, amen.[4]

When you realize you can accomplish nothing significant apart from God's power working in and through you (John 15:5), you can avoid the spiritual shipwreck of the memory lapses of amnesia, forgetting the goodness of God in your *past*.

---

4. "Shenandoah—James Stewart."

EXPECTED APPRECIATION

Is deep appreciation for God really that important? It is essential! The Bible both commands and commends it. Calls to wholeheartedly thank God for his goodness permeate the "thanksgiving psalms." These include Psalm 136, which begins and ends with a call for appreciation to the Almighty: "Give thanks to the Lord, for he is good, for his steadfast love endures forever" (vv. 1, 26). God is praised for that covenant love twice more between the opening and closing verses. Four times the psalmist praises God for his acts as Creator. Eight times he is commended for his mighty acts as Redeemer. *Once* he is thanked for his perfect providence because he "gives food to all flesh" (v. 25). This psalm, called by the Jews "the Great Psalm of Praise,"[5] contains "meditations on God's *past* acts, particularly emphasizing his gracious acts of deliverance to remembrance."[6]

Even more intense than the thanksgiving psalms are the short, universal commands of Paul to give thanks always in all things. These brook no exceptions: "Giving thanks always and for everything to God the Father in the name of our Lord Jesus Christ"; "And whatever you do, in word or deed, do everything in the name of the Lord Jesus, giving thanks to God the Father through him"; "Continue steadfastly in prayer, being watchful in it with thanksgiving"; "Give thanks in all circumstances; for this is the will of God in Christ Jesus for you" (Eph 5:20; Col 3:17; 4:2; 1 Thess 5:18).

Thanksgiving is also commended through many examples in the Old and New Testaments. Think of Daniel, whose prayers included "giving thanks before his God" three times daily. He was so devoted to prayer that he continued praying even under the threat of death (Dan 6:10). He did precisely what God calls his people to do, to meditate on his mighty deeds and thus remember him reverently in prayer (Num 15:39–40; Deut 8:2; 24:9).[7] Every act of remembrance is an act of meditation, and meditating on the *past* is spiritual time travel that transforms you!

In the New Testament, Jesus exemplifies perfect thankfulness. He gave thanks over the bread *before* he multiplied it (Matt 14:19; 15:36; John 6:11). Astonishingly, even on the evening of his betrayal and the eve of his crucifixion, Jesus prayed with thanksgiving over the bread and the cup (Matt 26:26–27). He cherished his heavenly Father, even though he was *already*

---

5. Kidner, *Psalms 73–150*, 493.
6. Longman, *How to Read the Psalms*, 58 (emphasis added).
7. John Newton called this "affecting remembrance." Newton, *Works*, 535–36.

troubled by the *approaching* suffering (John 12:27; 13:21). He knew that he would be in agony again in the garden *later* yet grumbled not (Luke 22:41–44). Marvel that Jesus's sinless perfection (2 Cor 5:21; Heb 4:15; 1 Pet 1:19) meant that he never failed to appreciate God's goodness and gifts! Ingratitude never darkened his mind or fueled faithless complaining. The Lamb of God either praised his Father or endured silent suffering, honoring his Father through his obedience (1 Pet 2:23). It was not just his Father for whom Jesus was thankful. He was quick to praise the faith of others, especially when their actions brought glory to his Father (Matt 8:5–12; Luke 17:11–19).

TIME TRAVEL AND APPRECIATION

Like Jesus, our appreciation for God should span the *past*, the *present*, and the *future*. You are undoubtedly most familiar with God's blessings in the *present*. Many believers live with an appreciation for what they *currently* have. They often pray in commendable ways for God to help them in their *present* distresses and thank God for his *present* grace. That is healthy, and God's children should be increasingly grateful for God's *present* blessings. But people could too quickly miss the importance of thanking God for the *past* and the *future*. Consider what you give thanks for. Suppose you appreciate mainly what is *presently* true in your life. In that case, you need to take advantage of the deeper levels of Christian thanksgiving available to you, remembering to use the other two time periods (*past* and *future*) for thanksgiving! If you are only thankful for the *present*, you are not topping off your thanksgiving gas tank. Instead, you are driving along spiritually with just a third of a tank and may soon be running only on fumes.

People are often so rooted in their *present* circumstances that they do not think much about their *past* or *future*. This limits their capacity to be appreciative. Toward the *future*, they might be anxious. Toward the *past*, they might need help with how to view it. Not quite sure what happened in their *past* and being frightened by what the *future* could hold, they desperately try to appreciate the fleeting moments in the *present*. Every year, surveys conducted around the Thanksgiving holiday show that Americans are thankful for what they *presently* possess. In 2021, an Economist/YouGov poll asked open-ended questions about what people appreciated. Their top responses included family, health, life, job/finances, faith/religion, basic needs met, and friends.[8] These are excellent reasons for appreciation in the *present*, but if you limit thanksgiving to *present* gifts, you should be nervous. Those blessings will likely erode and disappear over time. Friends can move away, and some family members will die *before* you. Your health may last for decades, but it eventually declines, leading toward the inevitable end of physical life. Not surprisingly, many people feel less grateful as they age. With all respect to seniors, notice that the phrase "grumpy old men" rolls off your tongue more easily than "grumpy young toddlers"! However, gratitude should grow as you age, especially among heaven-bound believers. Since living appreciatively of the *past* and the *future* is *meditative* time travel, Christians should become expert appreciators.

Time-Travel to the *Past* for Increased Appreciation

Among the countless reasons for praising God, your salvation is the greatest! Engaging in meditative time travel is a terrific tool for stirring up daily appreciation. Gratitude will spring up in you as you recall your *past* sinfulness. In fact, you cannot fully appreciate God's amazing grace without remembering your awful godlessness. The idea of recalling your failures might seem negative, but when you reflect on your sins in the light of God's *past* grace, they can become a source of rejoicing in the Lord. Hear the joy of the psalmist, who thinks of his sins in the light of God's *past* forgiveness: "As far as the east is from the west, so far does he remove our transgressions from us" (Ps 103:12). Although God never literally forgets sins, not being a victim of divine amnesia, he promises never to hold them against believers. The psalmist is sure there will be no *present* or *future* consequences of *past* sins.

Because of Jesus's *past sacrifice*, God promises that "I will forgive their iniquity, and I will remember their sin no more" (Jer 31:34, quoted in Heb 8:12; 10:17). Is there a greater blessing than forgiveness? Yes, an even "richer" blessing was granted to you: adoption into the family of God.[9] Although you were *once* an enemy of God in the *past*, *now* you are in the *present*, one of his children, and in Christ, you are blessed with every spiritual blessing (Eph 1:3).

This connection between fresh awareness of your sins and lavish love for Jesus is beautifully illustrated by Jesus's commendation of the sinful woman (Luke 7:36–50). The host and his friends cannot get beyond this

---

8. Frankovic and Sanders, "Thanksgiving 2021." See Earls, "Americans Most Thankful."
9. Beeke, *Heirs with Christ*, 28.

woman's tainted *past*, but Jesus sees her in the *present*, extravagantly appreciative and acquitted. Jesus links the grace received and grateful response: "Therefore I tell you, her sins, which are many, are forgiven—for she loved much. But he who is forgiven little loves little. . . . And he said to the woman, 'Your faith has saved you; go in peace'" (vv. 47, 50).

Her affectionate appreciation in the *present* for Jesus proved her *past* forgiveness: "The woman's attitude (as revealed in her loving much) was evidence that she had experienced forgiveness in her very recent *past*."[10] Her *past*, now forgiven, prompts her appreciation for Jesus. But the cold-hearted listeners have a time-travel problem. Jesus's commending of her *present* forgiveness becomes a stumbling block for the hearers whose *pasts* had not been likewise forgiven yet and which *now* endangers their *futures*.

Time-Travel to the *Future* for Increased Appreciation

Everyone rises from bed thinking about the day *ahead* and what must be accomplished. While all can anticipate the day, good or bad, believers can go a step further and actually appreciate the day yet unlived. Only a Christian can thank God for his *future* blessings *before* they arrive. Scott Hubbard urges appreciation in advance: "Not content to praise God only on the far side of deliverance, faith teaches us to praise him *before* deliverance even comes: not only *after* he's parted the Red Sea, but while the Egyptian army still presses in; not only *after* Goliath lies slain, but as he still taunts the hosts of Israel; not only *after* the stone rolls away from the tomb but during the Sabbath silence of Holy Saturday."[11]

What guaranteed acts of God's goodness can you praise him for *beforehand*? Let us highlight the work of the Holy Spirit in your *present* and *future* life to remind you of what must be true *now* and what will be true. He *already* worked in your *past* to make you a Christian through the conviction of sin, regeneration, and adoption. But the work of the Holy Spirit in your life has just begun! His role is to glorify the Father through the exaltation of the Son in your life (John 16:13–15). The Holy Spirit blesses believers in at least six areas of life. First, the Spirit will sanctify you (Rom 8:13; 2 Cor 3:18).[12] A mark of all true believers is that they will be sanctified, even if that "appears" to be happening through unsteady growth. This

---

10. Stein, *Luke*, 237.
11. Hubbard, "Will You Praise Him," para. 2 (emphasis added).
12. Manton, *Complete Works*, 19:478.

Spirit-prompted growth will include progressive moral purification and bearing fruit for God (Rom 7:4–6; Gal 5:22–23).

Second, the Spirit will give assurance of salvation. Not all believers embrace their assurance; sadly, some lack a secure sense of that salvation. However, one of the Spirit's gifts is that he "bears witness with our spirit that we are children of God," so assurance is possible (Rom 8:16). If you still lack this blessed assurance, seek it through prayer, biblical meditation, and reading theology books: ask, seek, and knock (Matt 7:7–8). God will give it to you because a lack of confidence robs you of joy and dilutes your appreciation. If you are continually doubting if God has saved you in the *past*, how can you enjoy *today* or anticipate *tomorrow*?

Third, the Holy Spirit will intercede for you. Christians live partially in the *present* and partially in the *future*, and the Spirit works in this dynamic of your inner life through prayer. Commenting on Rom 8:26–27, Gregg Allison and Andreas Köstenberger write, "Such intercession is born out of the '*already–not yet*' reality in which Christians live. In *anticipation* of the arrival of the *age to come*, believers, like the rest of the created order, are hard-pressed in the *present* age."[13] The Spirit is *already* praying for you what you ought to be praying for yourself. How reassuring!

Fourth, as you read and hear the Bible, the Holy Spirit will illuminate your eyes, enabling you to see truths you would miss without his help.[14] Without the Spirit's *past* work to save, you could have never understood the Scriptures enough to be saved (1 Cor 2:14). Even *now*, as a believer, when you grasp what the Bible says, it is because of the Spirit's illumination, for which you should be grateful.

Fifth, the Holy Spirit will empower you for service. He gives specific spiritual gifts for serving in the church and the world (1 Cor 12:11; Heb 2:4). When used correctly, they build up the church to do God's work (Eph 4:11–12). The Spirit also empowers each believer to minister using those gifts, enabling them to serve with the "strength that God supplies" (1 Pet 4:11). And even beyond the specific gifts, Christians should trust that whatever God calls them to do *now*, he will make possible, profitable, and often even pleasurable.

Finally, your eternal *future* in heaven will arrive, securely delivered by the Spirit! Your confidence is never in yourself but in the preserving ministry of the Spirit. He is "the guarantee of our inheritance," God's seal

---

13. Allison and Köstenberger, *Holy Spirit*, 407 (emphasis added).
14. Bruce, *Message of John*, 232.

placed on you (Eph 1:13; 4:30; 1 Cor 1:22; 5:5). Both your salvation and your inheritance in the *future* will be protected by the power of God working through your faith and empowered by the Spirit (1 Pet 1:4–5). You can cheerfully count on the promising words of Jesus that his sheep "will never perish" (John 10:28). Through, over, and beyond your efforts to stand firm, you will be kept from stumbling by the blessed Holy Spirit (John 10:28; Jude 24).[15] Furthermore, his gifting and empowering provide "*partial foretastes* of the fuller working of the Holy Spirit that will be yours in the age to come."[16] Such appreciation for God's *future* grace produces joy. That joy then ignites a life of serving God by doing good for others. Further, knowing that God will work through you creates the courage to take risks in new seasons of service.

Think of the *past* when a church leader asked you to pray about serving in a ministry. What thoughts went through your head? Two negative responses likely sprang to mind instantly. The first was "I am not qualified or good at doing that." Another thought followed: "I am *already* too busy to get everything done that I have *already* committed to, so how could I even consider that?" But a more healthy hope in the *future* will overcome those knee-jerk objections. If God shows you that you should serve in a ministry, you can be confident that God will gift and empower you to function effectively and joyfully. In addition, if God calls you to a new ministry, he can lighten your other obligations or make you more efficient in using your time. Be confident that the more appreciation you have for the *future*, the more often you will step *forward* to seize opportunities to serve!

THANKSGIVING AND THEOLOGY

You can also enhance your appreciation through study. Theology helps all Christians know what to believe about God and how to live in a relationship with him. An often-overlooked benefit of formal theology, such as systematic and biblical theology, is deepened appreciation. J. I. Packer (1926–2020) explained that "theology is for doxology and devotion—that is, the praise of God and the practice of godliness."[17] The more you understand what God has done, is doing, and will do for you, the more gratitude you will feel. Then, you will reflect those feelings to God in private and

---

15. Grudem, *Systematic Theology*, 793.
16. Grudem, *Systematic Theology*, 1258 (emphasis added).
17. Packer, *Concise Theology*, xii.

public praise! For example, learning that God *fore*knew and *pre*destined you for salvation *before* the foundation of the world is perpetually a fount of unending praise (Eph 1:3–7; Rom 8:28–30; 1 Pet 1:1–3)!

Knowing sound doctrine also increases your appreciation for the *future*. The Bible teaches the *final* and *future* perseverance of the saints. All authentic believers will persevere. Jesus promised that neither he nor the Father would lose hold of any sheep (John 10:28–29). Paul could proclaim that nothing "will be able to separate us from the love of God in Christ Jesus our Lord" (Rom 8:39). Unlike unbelievers, you know what is coming for you in the *future*, descriptions of which are beyond imagination! God's kindness shown in Christ in the *past* and the *present* will continue *forever*, as it is his purpose that "in the coming ages he might show the immeasurable riches of his grace in kindness toward us in Christ Jesus" (Eph 2:7).

Christians with weaker theologies can be thankful, but their appreciation and satisfaction are limited by what they know! If you are observing the starry night sky, you can enjoy seeing many marvelous sights. But if you are becoming an amateur astronomer, how much more can you see, identify, and enjoy! In the same way, those who know more about God, including better doctrines, can appreciate so much more. Therefore, be sure you are an active member at a church where sound doctrine is taught through the careful exposition of God's word. In addition, choose to read more profound Christian books, passing over light devotional books for more substantial God-centered doctrinal books. Charles Spurgeon (1834–92) advised, "Renounce as much as you will all light literature, but study as much as possible sound theological works, especially the Puritanic writers and expositions of the Bible."[18] You will grow spiritually, and your joy through time-traveling meditative appreciation will flourish.

THANKSGIVING AND THE LIBERAL ARTS

Many other fields of learning outside and beyond your personal life are also fertile grounds for cultivating appreciation. A growing knowledge of the liberal arts can grow your appreciation. For example, God's creation shouts his intelligent design and beautiful glory, so adding to your understanding of it through the study of science will lead to awestruck thankfulness. Many of the beloved, traditional hymns celebrate God as Creator, and you can, too as you study science informally.

18. Spurgeon, "Paul," 668.

Have no fear! Studying God's creation with an appreciative heart will not lead you astray. James Boice (1938–2000), commenting on the heavens which "pours out speech" (Ps 19:2), claimed that the study of nature points us toward God:

> Whenever we do investigate them by scientific or other means, we soon find the testimony of nature even stronger than we at first surmised. In other words, the existence of a creator is not a facile but erroneous judgment naively made by the uneducated; a judgment quickly disproved as soon as one looks into the evidence carefully. On the contrary, the more one looks, the more the heavens gush forth knowledge.[19]

Studying history, language studies, music, philosophy, and other liberal arts should give you a rising appreciation for God's greatness and goodness. Just as Christians can and must study the Bible with both academic skills and meditative piety, any subject can be investigated in light of God's character and revealed truths. Read more, think more, study more, and explore more for your joy and the worship of God! The younger, wiser Solomon set a great model for you. Divinely enlightened with unrivaled wisdom, he wrote Scripture. Yet, he also investigated God's great handiworks of creation: "He spoke of trees, from the cedar that is in Lebanon to the hyssop that grows out of the wall. He spoke also of beasts, and birds, and reptiles, and fish" (1 Kgs 4:33).

ADVANTAGES OF APPRECIATION

Not only does God deserve your gratitude, but when you live with thanksgiving, other areas of your Christian life will bloom. Envision meditative appreciation as a beautiful fruit tree with many wonderful fruits hanging from it, including some of the rarest fruits of the Christian life. For example, Christian contentment is worth pursuing but hard to achieve directly. You can only get so far by telling yourself to be content. But when you recognize that appreciation increases contentment, the pathway to joyful bliss opens before you. Instead of resolving to muster up the joy to be content, seek contentment by counting your blessings, all of them, *past, present,* and *future.*

The Spirit will grow contentment in you supernaturally without you struggling to find it. Just three verses into his letter to the Philippians, Paul

---

19. Boice, *Psalms 1–41*, 163–64.

promised, "I thank my God in all my remembrance of you" (Phil 1:3). Rejoicing in chains, he declared: "I have learned in whatever situation I am to be content" (Phil 4:11). His contentment and joy were two fruits of his learned appreciation. Two more low-hanging fruits of gratitude are also within your reach.[20]

First, appreciation for God gives comforting hope in *present* distress. All that God has done in the *past* is an anchor for your *present* and hope for your *future*. That is why older Christians, having walked with God for many years, are more optimistic than aging unbelievers. The longer Christians have walked with God, the more faith they have developed. They are children of the same faith as Abraham (Gal 3:7). Despite the distressing *present* indisputable fact that he and Sarah were too old to have children, he "grew strong in his faith as he gave glory to God, fully convinced that God was able to do what he had promised" (Rom 4:20–21).[21] Like their father Abraham, God intended for Israel to take comfort by knowing and remembering their history and his goodness in the *past*. Andrew Hill notes that in 1 Chronicles, the retelling of the nation's history functioned as "retrospect (meditation on the *past*) and prospect (anticipation for the *future*)."[22] As Jews read their history, their meditative time travel allowed them to trust God and be comforted.

Second, humility blooms on the tree of appreciation. No Christian denies the importance of humility before God and others, yet achieving humility is quite difficult! Like contentment, you cannot pursue it directly. But appreciation helps because there is neither appreciation without humility nor humility without appreciation. Paul leveled the arrogant pride of the Corinthians with his piercing questions: "What do you have that you did not receive? If then you received it, why do you boast as if you did not receive it?" (1 Cor 4:7). Remembering that God has in the *past* given you all the good things you enjoy (Jas 1:17), is in the *present* working all things for good (Rom 8:28), and that your good *future* depends on his faithful promises, will guard you against foolish self-confidence.

This humility honors God, and it will bless others. For example, deciding not to take vengeance proves that you are leaning on God's *future* promises to provide for you and reward you.[23] You will lack nothing you

---

20. Ussher, *Body of Divinity*, 377.
21. Challies, *Aging Gracefully*, 17.
22. Hill, *1 & 2 Chronicles*, 110.
23. Challies, "It's Better to Suffer Wrong."

need for your ultimate good in your *future*, so you can open your hands to give to those with *present* needs and even respond gently to aggressors (Matt 5:38–42). Moreover, even if you give away what you need to have, as you humbly and prayerfully wait on God, he will give you what you need back again.

STRATEGIES FOR INCREASING APPRECIATION

Your life is both scheduled and spontaneous. You follow patterns and plans every day, yet there are moments of unplanned thoughts, emotions, and activities. Appreciation should spring up in the heart of a believer naturally in unprompted ways, but having scheduled plans to increase appreciation is wise. Just as your battle plan against anxiety involves scheduled strategies and spontaneous reflections, so does the approach to increase appreciation.

Strategy: Scheduled Appreciation

Make expressing appreciation to God a goal for your daily devotional time. Then, look *back* periodically and ask if that is happening. If not, what is hijacking that time? Shockingly, a child of God can be self-centered in quiet times! Yes, typically, you will gain personal blessings through your time with the Lord, like the wonderful gifts of joy, peace, and hope. But what you gain from God should not be your primary focus. Your purpose is, first and foremost, to know God by learning to love, appreciate, obey, and worship him. Jesus quoted from Deut 6:5 when he clarified that the greatest commandment was to "love the Lord your God with all your heart and with all your soul and with all your mind" (Matt 22:37). With that goal firmly in mind, how can you be more appreciative during devotional times?

First, you should take conscious steps to engage in meditative reading. The adjective "meditative" means that you do not read the Bible passively like you might the newspaper. Proficient Bible readers *already* naturally read reflectively, pouring over this love letter from God. However, since anyone can fall into the habit of reading inattentively, it helps to be clear by calling this engaged approach "meditative" Bible reading. That reminds you of the goal over, above, and beyond the mere collection of information. You move from and through the information toward transformation.

You must reflect as you read instead of rushing. Ironically, the Bible passages that you *already* know the best (which lend themselves most readily to meditation) are the ones that are the easiest to hurry past. God wants you to let the words of the Bible light your heart on fire. Amazon chose precisely the right word, Kindle, for their e-reader. Books with human authors can kindle thoughts, warm hearts, and start revolutions. How much more powerful is God's supernatural book for igniting a flame in you! It always accomplishes God's will in those who muse over it: correcting (Jer 23:29), comforting (John 16:33), or conforming to his image.

When one of God's truths you read warms your heart, keep blowing on that flame by meditation until a great fire of affection and appreciation roars.[24] Donald Whitney wrote, "Meditation works like bellows on the fire of Scripture. As it does, both spiritual light and spiritual heat increasingly emanate from the fiery word."[25] Ponder what you are learning about God. If it describes people's lives, what did God show them about himself? Should they have trusted God, or did they trust God in some particular way? Then, thank God for his faithfulness in revealing himself to these people, often in saving ways. Or if the passage contains a universal promise that God will do something in response to human actions, thank him for his faithfulness since "not one word has failed of all the good things that the Lord your God promised" (Josh 23:14).

For example, Prov 15:8 tells you that God knows the hearts of those who pray to him. You could find a twofold reason to thank God: the "sacrifice of the wicked is an abomination to the Lord, but the prayer of the upright is acceptable to him." First, you could prayerfully rejoice and thank God that the wicked cannot get away with deceiving the all-knowing God. Even though wicked people sometimes hijack religion for personal gain, God knows. He will judge them! Second, thank him for accepting your prayers from a purer heart, made cleaner only by his amazing grace. It is not the prayers of the "perfect" that he accepts but those of his children, justified in the *past* and in the process of being sanctified in the *present*.

Whenever you are reading the Bible, you need to be *pre*pared to stop in the middle of a passage or pause at the end to think about what God wants you to learn from it. That will lead you to pray and praise. You might be reading in Exod 14:10–14 that Moses trusted God on the bank of the Red Sea, remembering God's *past* power and faithfulness and not fearing the approach of Pharaoh's army. His memory of God's *past* mighty power gave him more faith than the absent-minded Israelites who panicked: "The

---

24. Piper, *Desiring God*, 144. See Calamy, *Art of Divine Meditation*, 21.
25. Whitney, *Simplify Your Spiritual Life*, 66–67.

sight of hundreds—perhaps thousands—of approaching chariots apparently drove all memory of God's assurances through Moses to the Israelites in 14:1–4 out of their minds."[26] But God did hear their frightened pleas and carried out his *pre*planned rescue for them despite their doubts. You could pause here and thank God for the many times he rescued you against the odds. Then, continue praying by asking that he keep protecting you and giving you greater faith to trust him more.

George Whitefield (1714–70) loved meditative Bible reading, and he practiced "praying over every line and every word."[27] Even if you pause less than he did, choosing to read your Bible meditatively will take you more time than regular Bible reading, but it will profit you so much more![28] This is "meditative prayer," connecting God's words to you and your words back to God. This is the best way to pray, with a full head and heart, instead of lifeless, empty-headed, cool-hearted praying.

Strategy: Spontaneous Appreciation

Thanking God at regularly scheduled intervals opens the door to a more spontaneous appreciation of him each day. Like newlyweds who spend every available hour together and then spend their time apart thinking of each other, so you must leave your precious moments alone with God and go into your day, but he can always be on your mind. Filled with those spontaneous thoughts all day long, obedience is easy when God puts unplanned opportunities in your path. William Perkins (1558–1602) wrote that when you leave your time of prayer, you must practice what you prayed: "*Now this thankfulness must not be only in word but in deed, testified by due obedience in life and conversation.*"[29] You tell God you are thankful for him and then live a life demonstrating that spirit of gratitude.

To pursue spontaneous appreciation, stay alert to recognize moments of spare time in your life. Think of the different reactions of people around you when they encounter typical delays: an extra-long line at the checkout in the store, an unusually long wait at a traffic light during "rush" hour, or a longer than reasonable wait in the "waiting" room. As fast as it is, modern life can be repeated patterns of "hurry up and wait!" Some people get

---

26. Stuart, *Exodus*, 335.
27. Dallimore, *George Whitefield*, 25.
28. Hubbard, "Set Your Mind on Things Above."
29. Perkins, *Works*, 413 (emphasis added).

anxious, allowing their minds to jump *ahead* to the bad things that might happen from their interrupted schedule. You can see their nervous, fidgety energy; unfortunately, you often hear it in grumbling or profane words. Some even perversely swear in frustration, invoking God's name in irreverent anger instead of worship.

Others calmly whip out their cell phones and zone out of the *present* time, wasting time by ignoring the passing time. They mentally check out of their *present* life, becoming detached from what is happening in their here-and-*now*. They scroll and scan along, oblivious to eternal realities, thinking only of trivial, *temporal* things. Surely Satan smiles at the worldliness displayed in wasted time. The screen's glow blocks their view of the glory of God glowing all around them in creation and through circumstances. John Piper observes that "one of the great uses of Twitter and Facebook will be to prove at the Last Day that prayerlessness was not from lack of time."[30]

As an alert Christian, redeem such spare, unplanned moments! Pause to pull out the passage of Scripture you are carrying around to memorize or meditate on. Perhaps you are *already* wisely *pre*pared in your *past* for just such moments! You can even meditate on good things around you (Phil 4:8). The adage is to turn life's lemons into lemonade. That is good! Do better and praise the God who makes everything, including lemons and unexpected "waits." There are no actual "idle" moments in God's plan for your day! Linda Allcock encourages envisioning your daily tasks and activities that must take place as the text on the page of a book. Everyone has the "white space around the edges."[31] Turn the white spaces of your days into space for prayer, especially appreciative prayer.

Many leaders have described the dangers of having social media and technology at our fingertips, which can allow the flitting away of every idle moment with news feeds, cat videos, and friend updates. Those are indeed modern dangers, but the tendency to relieve boredom with daydreaming, unproductive thoughts, and discontentment is as ancient as humanity. Blaise Pascal (1623–62), writing in the seventeenth century, attributed human unhappiness to the inability to sit quietly and be content in the circumstances. Instead, humans are too often driven to divert themselves from their *present* condition. Looking at lives *today* and the tendency to be discontent, Pascal would still conclude that "all the unhappiness of men arises from one single fact, that they cannot stay quietly in their own

---

30. Piper (@JohnPiper), "One of the great uses."
31. Allcock, *Deeper Still*, 117.

chamber."[32] What a better course for a Christian to consciously choose to redeem these newly discovered moments *before* they pass by (Eph 5:16)!

Spontaneous Appreciation Applications

You can stop and appreciate God in many ways, all of which are in-the-moment mirrors of what you have been doing in your scheduled times. The simplest option is to begin praying and thank God for what has been "wasting" your time. Those time-wasting annoyances of modern life often tempt others to think wicked thoughts. Instead of yielding to those temptations, you could pray praises that arise from those delays, like "Thank you, God, for medical doctors, comfortable waiting rooms, and insurance that pays most of my bill." Or you could even say "Thank you, Lord, for traffic lights that will help us all reach our destinations more slowly and safely."

You might not feel like praying, so instead of forcing it, fuel up your heart to pray by drawing upon *past* Bible memorization or meditation. You could pull out your *preplanned*, "go-to verses" to memorize. Did you know that you have enough spare transitional time in the next five years to memorize a short book of the Bible? Pick up that passage in those otherwise "lost" moments and work on it. You can even listen and recite it on your phone's audio player or Bible app. It does not matter if it takes you years to finish that passage because there is no rush! God delights *now* in your efforts as much as in your eventual *future* arrival at your goal.

Those moments would have been wasted, but *now* you have recycled them from the trash bin of time waste. God will honor that! If you are not ready to memorize spontaneously, use spare moments to read Scripture. Sarah Zylstra and Megan Hill calculate that in a thirty-second gap, you can "read a Bible verse aloud," in three minutes, you can "read (or listen to) Philemon, 2 John, or 3 John," in five minutes that reading could be all of "Obadiah or Jude." By the ten-minute mark, you could read "Jonah, Nahum, Habakkuk, Zephaniah, Haggai, 2 Thessalonians, Titus, or 2 Peter."[33]

Instead of memorizing or reading Scripture, you could meditate in those moments. Direct your mind upward toward God and think of his glorious characteristics, time-travel *back* to the *past* to appreciate what he has done for you, or time-travel *ahead* to the *future* to see what he will do for you. By mental time travel, you can pray "Thank you, Father, for saving

---

32. Pascal, *Pensées*, 49.
33. Zylstra and Hill, "Build Spiritual Habits."

me and guaranteeing me a *future* with you where boredom cannot even exist. And I appreciate that you are enabling me to grow in contentment and patience, even as I wait!"

In addition to meditating on Scripture directly, you can mentally review something profound you read in the Bible this morning or heard in *last* Sunday's sermon at church. Since all songs are themselves meditations (good or bad), you can sing to yourself that inspiring hymn or praise chorus from your church last Sunday. Some Christians find it helpful to carry along with them their church's bulletin from the previous Sunday, especially if it is chock-full of sermon notes, prayer lists, and song lyrics.

You can even grab your cell phone and use it for devotional purposes rather than distractions. Do you want to encourage someone? Think of people in your life. Pause to thank God for them, and text them that you thanked God for them! If you are thankful for someone, let them know that you thank God for them, just as Paul told the Philippians, "I thank my God in all my remembrance of you" (Phil 1:3). Surely, if Paul were alive *today*, he would leverage all forms of modern technology and social media to build up others!

As you grow more appreciative of God in the calm times of scheduled devotions, you also *prepare* for chaotic days. Chapter 3 emphasized that you must combat worry by reining in your runaway thoughts and directing them toward God and his word. In the same way, when pain and pressure build in your life, you must choose thankful thoughts toward God. God expects that along with your frantic petitions, you will also include thanksgiving.

Paul twice commanded prayer with thanksgiving, connecting the need for God's help to being appreciative for it, even in advance: "Do not be anxious about anything, but in everything by prayer and supplication with thanksgiving let your requests be made known to God" (Phil 4:6); "Continue steadfastly in prayer, being watchful in it with thanksgiving" (Col 4:2). Rarely will you find unbelievers appreciative in times of trouble. But Christians, empowered by the Spirit of God, can supernaturally direct their thoughts upward to God with both petitions and praises. This pattern of thanking God as you seek his strength also works for battling a whole range of temptations that attack you through your emotions, such as the heat of anger, the chill of envy, the allure of lust, and the attraction of worldliness.

God has given you biblical models of appreciating and imploring him during extended emotional and spiritual battles. The pages of the Bible are full of stories of men and women facing problems and the temptations "common to man" (1 Cor 10:13). The lament psalms help in particular. God has given you many models of believers learning to shepherd their emotions. The honest words of the writers may strike you as a bit embarrassing. Still, those saints were telling God exactly how they felt: "How long, O Lord? Will you forget me forever? How long will you hide your face from me?" (Ps 13:1). But *after* being breathtakingly honest, the writers then remember God, trust God, and often praise God. These inspiring journeys, from agony to appreciation, are models for you! John Calvin (1509-64) advised using the Psalms as a directory for understanding and shepherding your emotions. He wrote,

> I have been accustomed to call this book, I think not inappropriately, "An Anatomy of All the Parts of the Soul;" for there is not an emotion of which any one can be conscious that is not here represented as in a mirror. Or rather, the Holy Spirit has here drawn to the life all the griefs, sorrows, fears, doubts, hopes, cares, perplexities, in short, all the distracting emotions with which the minds of men are wont to be agitated.[34]

In addition to the Psalms, praise God's characteristic that you most need at that moment. When you are perplexed, thank God that he is omniscient (all knowing); therefore, he is not perplexed like you! On that sure foundation, ask for guidance. When you are powerless, thank God that he is not because he is omnipotent. With confidence restored, ask for his intervention. Hear this example of a Puritan prayer of praise arising from emotional pain: "O God Most High, Most Glorious, the thought of thine infinite serenity cheers me, for I am toiling and moiling, troubled and distressed, but thou art for ever at perfect peace."[35]

APPRECIATION AND OTHER FORMS OF TIME TRAVEL

Alert Christians look to the *future* and watch for all God has promised to be fulfilled in this life or *after* it. While aware that dangers will come, they see their *future* as brighter than the *past*. Therefore, alertness and appreciation fit together like a pair of hands. The opposite is true, too. Attempts to be

---

34. Calvin, *Commentary on the Book of Psalms*, xxxvi–xxxvii.
35. Bennett, *Valley of Vision*, 130.

alert without being appreciative will inevitably end in despair. To contemplate the *future* without remembering God is dismal.

Chapter 6 calls for discipline in the *present* in light of the *future*. That discipline is necessary for appreciation. Frantic, disorganized, and overly busy people cannot appreciate their *present* moments, much less their *past*. But creating space in your schedule to travel *back* in time opens the door to increased thankfulness. Chapter 7 focuses on how you should time-travel together with others in your biological and spiritual families. Those relationships can encourage you to be more appreciative as you see their models of thankfulness.

The ultimate test of appreciation comes when your life in all its physical glory fades away (Jas 1:10–11). Yet, appreciative heirs of God can even then rejoice in their coming *future* life! True believers cherish God more than the sum of their entire *past* experiences. Paul exhibited that kind of faith even as his body faded: "Therefore we do not lose heart. Though outwardly we are wasting away, yet inwardly we are being renewed day by day. For our light and momentary troubles are achieving for us an eternal glory that far outweighs them all" (2 Cor 4:16–17).

RECOMMENDED READING ABOUT APPRECIATION

Sam Crabtree, *Practicing Thankfulness* (Wheaton, IL: Crossway, 2021).
Mary K. Mohler, *Growing in Gratitude: Rediscovering the Joy of a Thankful Heart* (Charlotte, NC: The Good Book Company, 2018).
David W. Pao, *Thanksgiving: An Investigation of a Pauline Theme* (Westmont, IL: IVP Academic, 2002).

MEMORIZATION PASSAGES ABOUT APPRECIATION

Psalm 136:1
Give thanks to the Lord, for he is good,
for his steadfast love endures forever.

Romans 8:28
And we know that for those who love God
all things work together for good,
for those who are called according to his purpose.

Toward the Past and the Future

Ephesians 5:20
Giving thanks always and for everything to
God the Father in the name of our Lord Jesus Christ.

Colossians 3:17
And whatever you do, in word or deed, do everything in the
name of the Lord Jesus,
giving thanks to God the Father through him.

CHAPTER FIVE

Toward the *Past* and the *Future*
Don't Be Amnesic!

We fight amnesia by remembering. Sin makes us forget;
Christ helps us remember.

Deepak Reju

When people often forget human history, failures frequently follow! That is why the adage is so popular: "Those who cannot remember the *past* are condemned to repeat it"![1] Yet the greatest tragedies happen when we forget our own personal *pasts*! This is the opposite of appreciating the *past*. We all have moments when we forget *past* experiences and live in the *present* as if the *past* never happened.

The medical condition of amnesia, actual memory loss, is a helpful analogy for this tragedy of living without the *past*. For example, the famous mystery writer Agatha Christie experienced her own real-life mystery when she lost her memory for an eleven-day period in which she went missing. Her memories of those lost days never returned.[2] As terrifying as this mental condition is for its sufferers, the spiritual amnesia of forgetting your *past* and *future* can cost you much more. It is as toxic toward the *past*

---

1. Santayana, *Life of Reason*, 103 (emphasis added).
2. Mosse, "Eleven Days."

as anxiety is toward the *future*. Yet, its cause is the opposite: a failure to time-travel instead of overdoing it. Instead of living in the *future* anxiously or remembering the *past* with *appreciation*, the spiritual amnesiac's mind never leaves the *present*, causing cascading problems. It is not good to live alone in the *present*!

God repeatedly warned his people not to forget him or his blessings! Israel was to actively remember the *past* and pass that history to *future* generations: "Only take care, and keep your soul diligently, lest you forget the things that your eyes have seen, and lest they depart from your heart all the days of your life. Make them known to your children and your children's children" (Deut 4:9). Deuteronomy contains five more sets of instructions to "not forget" (Deut 4:23; 6:12; 8:11; 9:7; 25:19), a warning of the dire consequence if they "forget" the Lord (Deut 8:19), and an ominous *pre*diction that they will become prideful and "forget" God (Deut 8:13–14). But Deuteronomy also has a positive, reassuring promise that, unlike humans, God never suffers amnesia and will not forget his promises (Deut 4:31). The *pre*scription to guard against forgetfulness is to stay alert, practicing the skill of remembering. Through remembering, forgetfulness and fear will flee.

FINITE FORGETFULNESS

Why do we suffer from amnesia? Because we are finite and fallen! As a finite creature, you experience innumerable sensory experiences, relational dynamics, and news sources that flood your mind. You cannot focus on everyone and everything simultaneously, and some information must be set aside. The information you continually ignore begins to slip from memory. You can get that information back through *recall*, but that requires intentional effort. If you drift through life, caught up in the *present* right before you, you lose your anchors to your *past* and will fail to reach your best *future*. Chapter 2 emphasized the importance of being alert toward the *future*. Yet, you must also be alert toward your *past* and make wise decisions based on what you *once* knew.

Fallen Forgetfulness

Our fallen spiritual condition also makes amnesia much worse. As sinners whose natures have been corrupted, we forget because we do not want to remember anything that would limit our freedom for self-expression.

Because of "inherited corruption" and "inherited tendency to sin," we were likely to forget God, his goodness, his warnings, and his grace in the *past*.[3] Paul reminds us that *before* conversion, we were those who "by their unrighteousness suppress the truth" (Rom 1:20). Human parents can witness this amnesia in their children and teenagers. How quickly they "forget" how to act! It is as if they were never taught manners. Their attenuated attention, diminutive desire to obey, and fast forgetfulness produce all sorts of disobedience. But *once* regenerated, Christians have "the Spirit of God dwelling in them, which leads them to crucify the flesh, and to strive after complete conformity to the image of God."[4]

Yet, spiritual amnesia remains a significant problem. Even if you are a seasoned saint, sin can darken your mind and deaden your heart. As you seek to "put off your old self daily" (Eph 4:22), your old nature hangs around like a *pre*existing medical condition ready to present itself as amnesia if you do not keep an eye on it. Commenting on 2 Pet 1:9, Thomas Schreiner observes that Christians lacking knowledge, self-control, steadfastness, godliness, brotherly affection, and love "have *forgotten* their baptism and their forgiveness of sins. In other words, they are not living as forgiven sinners. They are behaving like unconverted people."[5]

But Christian maturity develops as you regularly allow the Holy Spirit to take God's *past* words in Scripture and apply them afresh to your *present* life. You learn to see yourself in the mirror of God's word and walk away from it, committed to change. James warned against mere hearing: "For if anyone is a hearer of the word and not a doer, he is like a man who looks intently at his natural face in a mirror. For he looks at himself and goes away and at *once* forgets what he was like" (Jas 1:23–24). In contrast, those who hear, remember, and act upon God's word "receive with meekness the implanted word" (v. 21).

Relationships and institutions can also suffer from amnesia. Couples take solemn religious vows before God and in front of their family. Yet time can fade their commitment to each other. Too often, a *future* divorce will reveal that they have decided to risk the possibility of better divergent *futures* than a continued joint *future* together. While not all ailing marriages can mend, many can be reconciled through counseling. Such marital intervention is particularly powerful if the counselor can direct

---

3. Grudem, *Systematic Theology*, 625–26.
4. Hodge, *Systematic Theology*, 248.
5. Schreiner, *1, 2 Peter, Jude*, 304 (emphasis added).

the couple to remember *past* joys together and begin again to envision a better potential future one.[6]

Children will likely remember the Christian teachings of their parents and enjoy the blessed life of obedience (Prov 1:8–9; 3:1–2). However, some will reject their family's *past* moral training and strike out on their path toward an unknown *future*. This often leads first to unwise decisions, eventually to immoral ones, and often to spiritually unsuccessful *futures*. Large organizations and institutions can experience amnesia, too. Businesses, governments, and academic institutions may lose sight of their original, *past* goals and values, experiencing what experts call "mission drift" and "mission creep." Nations, too, can drift from their founding principles and identities.

Sadly, churches also can forget the priorities of the great commission and feeding the flock of God, getting caught up in numerous well-intended but distracting causes. But a church's vitality is linked to its appreciation of God's *past* grace and alertness toward the *future*. This is why some churches lose their spiritual power: "If challenged to give an answer for why we've lost a great deal of our power as the Church, one of the major reasons we'd give is this: our misunderstanding about what the gospel actually does. We seem to have developed gospel amnesia, forgetting that the gospel not only creates and sustains the Church but also deeply shapes the Church."[7]

Spiritual amnesia lies at the root of some of the most perplexing sins in the Christian life. Christians sometimes admit they struggle with sins such as anxiety, discontentment, grumbling, prayerlessness, pride, and disobedience. But progress in the battle against such sins can seem too overwhelming. What good does it do to worry even more about whether you can remember the tips for defeating worry? How do you battle pride without becoming proud of it? What if these sins had common causes and a standard solution?

The solution is appreciative *remembering* of all about God that you *already* know. Temporarily "lost" knowledge of God makes you more likely to sin. Remembering what you have forgotten is part of repentance, turning to head back home to God. Like the prodigal who came to his senses and remembered his father's generosity (Luke 15:17), you begin the road home

---

6. Through decades of pastoral counseling, it became apparent that a key to overcoming many of the challenges of discipleship and relationship issues was having more biblical views of the *future* and the *past*. That insight contributed to the writing of this book.

7. Chandler et al., *Creature of the Word*, 17.

from these sins when you turn back to God's faithfulness: worries cease, contentment springs up, grumbling becomes praising, pride gets pruned, and disobedience disappears.[8] Prone to wander away from what they have forgotten and remembered *before*, Christians must recover from amnesia repeatedly. A frustrated "forgetter" quipped that his Christian life was "a combination of amnesia and déjà vu: 'I know I've forgotten this *before*.'"[9]

THE PRACTICAL ATHEISM OF AMNESIA

Spiritual amnesia is "practical atheism." Christian leaders have observed that believers, at times, can live as if God does not exist. Naturally, unbelievers are without God since they suppress truths about God (Rom 1:18–19), but this is perversely unnatural for believers.[10] Practical atheism develops like heart disease when affections are "not set on God":[11] At moments, you forget the *past* and are caught up in "pride and self-sufficiency, forgetfulness of God and practical atheism."[12]

When God and his ways are temporarily forgotten, believers are capable of frightening transgressions! Launching out on our own, we lean on our understanding and not his grace. King David fell prey to such sinful, forgetful lapses in judgment. Seventy thousand men died from a plague when God disciplined him for the grave error of taking the census, thinking assuredly to himself, "I shall never be moved" (Ps 30:6; 2 Sam 24:1–17).[13]

His dynamic spiritual life could exemplify both the burning intensity of a heart after God and the disasters of a hardened heart. David's cold-hearted response to the news of Uriah's death, a death he had planned to cover up his adultery, was purely secular. When David said, "The sword devours *now* one and *now* another" (2 Sam 11:25; emphasis added), in actuality "David is saying that God doesn't exist. People die by the sword randomly and there is nothing that kings, generals, or soldiers can do about

---

8. "He had forgotten much, but he had not forgotten his father's love." Hughes, *Luke*, 142.
9. Clair Davis, quoted in Ryken, *Exodus*, 335 (emphasis added).
10. Charnock, *Existence and Attributes*, 90.
11. Manton, *Complete Works*, 5:84.
12. Plumer, *Studies in Psalms*, 379.
13. Plumer, *Studies in Psalms*, 379.

it. God is not sovereign! This is typical talk for unbelievers but not for a writer of Scripture" and a man of God's own heart.[14]

ADDLED AMNESIA

All of us have had this experience! When we reflect on a wrong *past* decision, we ask ourselves, What was I thinking? That sounds like the right question, but the better question is, What was I not thinking? You likely had temporary amnesia and you were not thinking straight. You engaged in decision making without engaging in mental time travel to your *past* to access your wisdom. Such decision making is as successful as backing out of a parking spot in a crowded parking lot without looking in your rearview mirror. Perhaps it works a couple of times *before* ignoring what is behind you reminds you never to rush again.

In *hind*sight, you can *now* see your mistake. What kept you from accessing the information that you needed? Likely, you got distracted and your brain was addled. Because of things flooding your senses and gushing emotions at the moment of that *present* decision, you could not recall what you needed from your *past* to make the best decision. That is a gracious take on it! Perhaps, though, you knew what you wanted and, for a *moment*, did not care about *past* knowledge and warnings or *future* consequences! But *looking back now*, as the fog of confusion has cleared, you see the decision more clearly. What chaotic thoughts, processes, and feelings lead to such dreadful decisions!

Addled amnesia occurs when you feel so absorbed in *present* pleasures or pain that you detach from your *past*. This leads to poorer decision-making than you could be doing, and you start piling up *future* regrets. These are not ignorant mistakes but a culpable inability to recall what you needed at that moment, especially God's words of wisdom and warning. God still holds you responsible for your mistakes because you allow yourself to get distracted. Even human judges and juries hold drunk drivers responsible for anyone they harm *after* choosing to abandon control of themselves and their vehicles.

---

14. Standridge, "King David," paras. 8–10. John Gill observed that "David's heart being hardened by sin, made light of the death of his brave soldiers, to which he himself was accessory; his conscience was very different *now* from what it was when he cut off the skirt of Saul's robe." Gill, *Exposition of the Old Testament*, 608 (emphasis added).

Addled Amnesia Is a Modern Problem

Those alcohol-fueled temporary losses of memory and skills destroy lives. Since alcohol impairs both driving skills and language skills (learned in the *past* and hindered in the *present* when drunk), one German company is creating the world's first "audio library of alcohol-addled speech," hoping to develop technology for car manufacturers. The goal is that in the *future*, intoxicated drivers who have temporarily forgotten how to speak clearly will not be able to start their car since they likely cannot remember how to drive safely either.[15]

That is possible *future* technology, but many programs and phone apps are available *today* to prevent drunk people from sending emails and texts while inebriated.[16] The development of such technology demonstrates that people are well aware of the dangers of addled amnesia in their physical lives. Just thinking through how someone would plan to use those products is a time-traveling roller coaster! *Today*, while sober, a man recognizes that because of his *future* plans to become alcohol-addled, he should *now*, in the *present*, purchase technology that will prevent him, in the *future*, from making mistakes. He *now* dreads those mistakes in *advance* and would *later* regret making them but would not care about them in the *near future* while drunk!

Addled Amnesia Is an Ancient Problem

Because humans are so irrepressibly creative in their evil and expert at distracting themselves, there are many ways of getting addled amnesia beyond the obvious issue of getting drunk. Moreover, there is an element of spiritual warfare in addled amnesia. Commenting on Ps 39 and its call to consider the brevity of life, James Boice (1938–2000) noted there is opposition to remembering the eternal:

> The world, by contrast, does not like us to think much at all, especially about such things as life, death, and eternity. Thinking about them spoils the world's fun and makes us harder to manipulate. The flesh cannot think about eternal matters, at least not in spirit and truth. It cannot understand them because "they are spiritually discerned" (1 Cor. 2:14). The devil hates us to think and does

---

15. Braga, "Inside the First Audio Library."
16. Goldman, "Solution for Drunk Dials."

everything he can to keep us from thinking, especially about the meaning of life and the fact that we must spend an eternity either with God in heaven or without him in hell. Therefore, the world, the flesh, and the devil conspire to keep us amused or entertained.[17]

Sometimes, Christians distract themselves with God's beautiful blessings to them and forget to enjoy God himself. This is a form of functional forgetfulness. How tragic to come to love the gifts more than the giver! To enjoy this world without thinking of eternal matters and the eternal God ignores and offends the Father of all good things (Jas 1:17).

Israel showed a similar pattern across the centuries and was warned repeatedly not to forget God. Even *before* they entered the promised land, they were warned not to forget him, yet they did (Deut 6:10–12). *Later* in Nehemiah, the leaders confessed Israel's corporate *past* sins. They acknowledged that *after* enjoying all of God's great goodness in the land of abundance, the people were "disobedient and rebelled against you and cast your law behind their back and killed your prophets, who had warned them to turn them back to you, and they committed great blasphemies" (Neh 9:26).

For the rest of Israel's history, the prophets lamented this pathetic pattern of enjoying God's blessings while ignoring God: "Israel's sin represents theological amnesia."[18] How terrible and treacherous was the behavior that stirred up these words of indictment from God: "But when they had grazed, they became full, they were filled, and their heart was lifted up; therefore they forgot me" (Hos 13:6). Like God's ancient people, when we are *full* of God's blessings and *filled* with satisfaction, it is easy to *forget* God.

Good Things Can Cause Amnesia

The list of good blessings that can be misused is probably innumerable, but common ones include movies, music, and other forms of entertainment. These are forms of modern "noise" defined as "external information and entertainment that block our ability to be silent and reflective."[19] Without reflection, you cannot remember the *past*, much less appreciate it or act based on it. Think of the man who professes Christ but regularly

---

17. Boice, *Psalms 1–41*, 339.
18. Butler, *Hosea, Joel, Amos*, 94–95.
19. Raynor, *Redeeming Your Time*, 53.

binge-watches movies all weekend. He is so spiritually addicted and amnesic that he "forgets" to go to church on Sunday morning.

Examples like this are tragically easy to multiply. There are families so committed to their children's sports, anglers so obsessed with fishing, and workaholics so driven to perform that church is optional at best and abandoned at worst! If believers cannot remember to gather with God's people publicly, how much more dismal must their private devotional lives be? A Christian who lives this way has vision problems, so "nearsighted that he is blind, having forgotten that he was cleansed from his former sins" (2 Pet 1:9). He lives as if no *past* grace saved him and without sight of the *future* grace to come. He is at least temporally lost, caught up in the *present*, missing the joy of God's daily sustaining and satisfying grace.

Even for devoted disciples, technology can enable listening to streaming music, podcasts, or talk radio almost from dawn to dusk, whether at home in the morning, during work commutes, or throughout the evening. Many even hear music in the background at work. Describing both the pervasiveness and generic nature of the instrumental music like Muzak heard almost everywhere, a communications professor lamented that "it's just a kind of amniotic fluid that surrounds us, it never startles us, it is never too loud, it is never too silent; it's always there."[20] While the moral content of some music may also be a problem, the greater danger is that the lack of silence limits the ability to hear God speaking through conscience and circumstances.

Thomas Watson (1620–86) wrote about such entertaining distraction: "The world's music will either play us asleep or distract us in our meditations."[21] Other distractions can be as traditional as printed books. The history of publishing unhelpful books has plagued humanity since the invention of the otherwise marvelous printing press. For example, some in the nineteenth century contained worthless fiction, which Charles Spurgeon (1834–92) labeled as "stuff which only addles the brain and does the soul no good."[22] Overindulging in practically anything can dull the memory. All kinds of things limit the meditative time travel you desperately need and impoverish your life: overeating, overexercising, oversleeping, overspending, or "over-anything"!

---

20. Gary Gumpert, quoted in Hulyer, "Inside the Booming Business," para. 12.
21. Watson, *Christian on the Mount*, 2.
22. Spurgeon, "Incomparable Bridegroom," 283–84.

Though you cannot spend your days solely in solitude with God, you can seek as many silent moments as possible. You can open up these "spaces" to hear God reminding you of himself and your relationship with him. Moreover, since God truly controls everything, you can pray that God will pry open more sacred spaces for you each day. Jesus was incredibly active, but he often opened up times in his schedule, especially early mornings and late nights, to be with his Father in secret.

Amnesia Causes Idolatry

There is a shocking link between distractions and idolatry! *Once* people start dazzling their minds through excesses, it is just a short step to depending on those activities, objects, or people for joy. James attributed conflicts to idolatry and warring over desires and evil cravings (Jas 4:1–4). How can you identify hidden idols in your life and the lives of others? Just ask what absence of a person or thing in life immediately makes someone particularly angry, irritable, sad, moody, fearful, or anxious. That can't-live-without-it idol might be as simple as morning coffee or watching the news!

Idolatry is not new, as a sixteenth-century definition of idols demonstrates: they are "something else on which to place our trust."[23] Instead of reaching *back* by faith to anchor to God and God alone, idols distract and, therefore, harm your faith. Idolatry and amnesia combine to create devastating, destructive power. Any good thing can grab your affection too strongly, and God, the source of all goodness, is forgotten. May we heed John's last words in his letter, a call to *future* alertness: "Little children, keep yourselves from idols" (1 John 5:21).

If morally positive things can distract you by dulling your memories, how much more can inherently sinful attitudes and actions? Drinking alcohol to excess, abusing prescription medications, taking illegal drugs, and having illicit relationships are just a few of the many causes of addled amnesia. Even worse, such forgetful sins can fuel more forgetfulness. The sin of willfully forgetting God fuels a downward spiral of sins that increase forgetfulness.

---

23. *Heidelberg Catechism*, 102.

Anger and Pain Make Amnesia Attractive

Some slip unintentionally into addled amnesia by not being alert or cautious! But others seek it intentionally, desiring to block out emotional or physical hurt. Pain drives some to embrace the mind-numbing, memory-fading effects of overindulging. Just listen to any sampling of country music songs about broken hearts, and you will soon hear the call to hit the bar and drown the sorrow. But suppressing whatever pain one eventually faces will worsen it and delay healing. What a cataclysmic mistake to repeatedly turn to temporary means of escaping the pain instead of bringing that pain to God in lamenting prayers, Bible reading, private worship, and meditation!

Life is challenging and pain arises, sometimes sharp and piercing. What should you do if the circumstances of your life seem to contradict your profession of God as mighty and merciful? The best response is to expand your understanding of God, to grow through the pain, and to trust that in God's sovereignty "all things work together for good" (Rom 8:28)! God allows, even encourages, you to cast your burdens on him. The psalms repeatedly model turning heartfelt lamentations into heart-healing meditations on God's character and care for you.

Those who follow God through dark seasons may, in the *future*, be able to declare that their suffering had good purposes. Did you know that the saints in heaven, looking *back*, *now* see God's good purposes in their earthly journeys, including the seasons of shadows? How remarkable is the psalmist's declaration that looked to his *past*: "*Before* I was afflicted, I went astray, but *now* I keep your word.... It is good for me that I was afflicted, that I might learn your statutes" (Ps 119:67, 71; emphasis added).

Fanny Crosby (1820–1915), the famous blind hymn writer, exemplified this high view of God throughout her life. Reflecting on the doctor's mistake that blinded her as an infant, she wrote in her autobiography stunning words. Hear her appreciation, not her anger, as she remembered her injury in light of God's character:

> I have heard that this physician never ceased expressing his regret at the occurrence and that it was one of the sorrows of his life. But if I could meet him *now*, I would say, "Thank you, thank you—over and over again—for making me blind, if it was through your agency that it came about!"... Although it may have been a blunder on the physician's part, it was no mistake of God's. I verily believe it was His intention that I should live my days in physical darkness so as to be better *pre*pared to sing His praises and incite others so to do.

> I could not have written thousands of hymns—many of which, if you will pardon me for repeating it, are sung all over the world—if I had been hindered by the distractions of seeing all the interesting and beautiful objects that would have been presented to my notice.[24]

Her faith in God's omnipotence helped her rule out any possibility of a divine mistake and made her alert to look for the good God intended through it. She had such an appreciative heart that living in physical darkness was worth writing new songs to praise God and to "incite others so to do." She also knew that "all the interesting and beautiful objects" could have distracted her if she had possessed sight. Her blindness kept her from soul-numbing distractions!

SYMPTOMS OF AMNESIA

Since any believer can forget God in the flow of daily life, examine whether the symptoms of amnesia appear in your life. Spiritual amnesia's symptoms are subtle and hard to spot! You can remember if you encountered an anxious person in the last month, whether across the plane or the church aisle. Likewise, the stench of a particularly ungrateful and entitled person does not soon fade. However, you have probably never looked at someone's life and said, "There goes a spiritually forgetful person!" Closer to home, it has likely been a long time since "forgetting God" made your prayer confession list: "Lord, this week, I lived as if you did not exist or care for me, bringing pain to myself and dishonor to you." Since amnesia is an absence of something good, it is harder to spot. Just as medical professionals call high blood pressure "the silent killer," spiritual amnesia is easily undiagnosed. A subtle symptom of amnesia is anxiety, *already* covered in the last chapter. But there are two other sneaky amnesic symptoms, which are discontentment and disobedience expressed in immoral and idolatrous amnesia.

Discontent Amnesia

Discontentment comes from forgetfulness. It often grows in your heart from fearing that how you live in the *present* and may live in the *future* does not fulfill what you envisioned for yourself. When you start skipping mental time travel to the *past* of God's grace and *future* promises, this fear

---

24. Crosby, *Fanny Crosby's Life*, 13–14 (emphasis added).

of missing out (FOMO) can grow. In the *present*, you are imagining all sorts of better circumstances in which you could or should find yourself. In its worst form, this discontentment develops into an entitlement mentality.

Depreciating any day God has given is dangerous. Disregarding any day as worthless or wasted is passing a verdict on a day of God's goodness in your life. As a terribly time-bound transgression, it is a complete failure to engage in transformative time-travel. For mere creatures to *pre*sume to know what has happened, will happen, and should happen is offensive to God (Isa 29:16; Rom 9:20). In moments of pain and pessimism, people mentally displace him from his role as the blessed and only Sovereign, who alone knows best and does best. This reverses the roles of Creator and creature so much that you might be tempted to pray at your worst moments, as it has been quipped, "Father, I forgive you; you know not what you do"![25]

Short-term sorrow in light of painful problems is understandable. God is compassionate and cares for your pain. But in those moments, God wants the best for you, which is to pursue him and the superior circumstance-defying joy of his presence and promises. Wherever you find yourself *presently* in life, you have not somehow escaped from the loving hand of God. Nor have you been overlooked and accidentally left out of his grand plans. Even in deep valleys of grief, Paul encouraged believers not to "grieve as others do who have no hope" (1 Thess 4:13). Perhaps there is also some anger in your pain. In seasons of discontentment, have your eyes drifted off God and to others, thinking that they have it better? Instead of rejoicing with those who rejoice (Rom 12:15) and being happy for those who prosper, have you drifted into envy? Envy is a warning that you are discontent: "How can we tell when we've drifted off the path of contentment? One way is when we experience envy."[26]

The model of Nanci (1953–2022) and Randy Alcorn shows how to respond to *present* distress *before* discontentment sets in:

> Nanci and I give each other permission to experience sadness when we hear bad news. We don't pretend all is well. But knowing God's commands to rejoice in him through his all-sufficient power, we meditate on his Word and call on him to impart his gladness to us. In time, God exchanges our natural responses with his supernatural, joy-giving presence. Sometimes sorrow and joy

---

25. Ware, *God's Lesser Glory*, 171.
26. Chappell, *Grace at Work*, 91.

do battle; sometimes they coexist, but when our hearts and minds are on Christ, joy is never far away."[27]

When the Alcorns shift their focus from their *present* circumstances to Jesus, their emotions follow. That is the only way to escape discontentment! Using the spiritual disciplines of Bible reading, meditation, and prayer, you must fight against having your "horizons of hope constricted to the here and *now*."[28] You will not always live in this hard season or this broken world! A better world is coming quickly, and everything bad will be gone. God himself will put an end to death, mourning, crying, and pain forever (Rev 21:4).

Discouraged and discontented silence would still be sinful. But what is within always comes out. The lips will speak what is in the heart, and discouragement will eventually escape the lips as slanderous murmuring. Jesus taught that "what comes out of the mouth proceeds from the heart, and this defiles a person. For out of the heart come evil thoughts, murder, adultery, sexual immorality, theft, false witness, slander" (Matt 15:18–19).[29] Murmuring against God is a terrible sin, which Thomas Brooks (1608–80) called "the mother-sin."[30] It is "profanity against God."[31] Although such grumbling is a native language for unbelievers, Christians can, by the Spirit, overcome it and even praise God in the darkness as they remember him and his goodness (Acts 16:25).[32]

Immoral Amnesia

Amnesia can quickly lead to even more severe acts of disobedience, such as sexual immorality and idolatry. As soon as one forgets God, yielding to temptation soon follows! In hard seasons, a believer may fall into amnesia, from amnesia into discouragement, and then from discouragement into overt disobedience. A pouting Christian may soon become a prodigal!

How can spiritual amnesia lead to immorality? A believer first forgets his new, *present* identity in Christ, God's purpose granted to him from

---

27. Alcorn, *God's Promise of Happiness*, 19.
28. Johnson, *Philippians*, 217 (emphasis added).
29. Morris, *Gospel according to Matthew*, 399.
30. Brooks, *Complete Works*, 335.
31. Prince, "Different Kind of Profanity," para. 9.
32. Piper, *Lessons from a Hospital Bed*, 44–45.

eternity *past* (2 Tim 1:9). Then he forgets the new requirements for holy living in light of the *past* purchase price and the *future-oriented* upward call of God in Christ Jesus (1 Cor 6:20; Phil 3:14). Finally, he forgets to heed God's commands. This was a recurring problem for the Corinthian believers: "There is a crisis of identity—a case of gospel amnesia—which leads to us acting like non-saints/unrighteous."[33]

Think of the tragedy of marital unfaithfulness. A man who commits adultery has "forgotten" his *past* love for his wife that led to marriage, his marriage promises before others, and the good they have experienced and accomplished together. He leaves all that *behind* for fleeting pleasure. This man should have meditated on *future* costs, such as the possible loss of his marriage, the damage to his children, and the diminishing of his social reputation.

If that man is a Christian, he should have added even worse consequences to that list of things tragically forgotten that will happen to him in the *future*,: the betrayal of his vow to God (Heb 13:4), the belittling of an image of the church's relationship to Christ (Eph 5:25–32), the breakdown of his peaceful conscience, and the breakup of his church membership when he falls under church discipline. The *future* will also play out differently from what he mindlessly assumed. At best, God will chasten and discipline him, bringing him back with a godly, grief-producing repentance (2 Cor 7:10). But something far worse could happen! His hardened heart may not bend under God's discipline, and he could perish if he continues to resist. Randy Alcorn advises that "if we would rehearse in advance the devastating consequences of immorality, we would be far less prone to commit it."[34]

Idolatrous Amnesia

Could spiritual amnesia even lead to idolatry? Yes, it is a frighteningly swift journey! God created people as worshipers, and everyone will worship someone or something. Forget God, and you will worship something or someone else. Israel forgot God and his servant Moses at the foot of flaming Mount Sinai, yet they did not strike out on their own without a god. Instead, they sought the creation of an idol to worship and follow. Aaron declared to the people, "These are your gods, O Israel, who brought you up out of the land of Egypt." He even planned a feast for their newly recreated

33. Um, *1 Corinthians*, 105.
34. Alcorn, *Purity Principle*, 89.

Yahweh (Exod 32:4–6). Israel still needed a god to explain their *past* and to lead them *forward* into the *future*. Even if they had to replace the forgotten true God with a re-created god, they could not live without one. The nation "still looks for a god who acts, even if it be a false god."[35]

Israel's history continued to show that idolatry frequently follows forgetfulness. In one of its tragic summary verses, Judg 2:12 makes this connection explicit: "And they abandoned the Lord, the God of their fathers, who had brought them out of the land of Egypt. They went after other gods, from among the gods of the peoples who were around them and bowed down to them. And they provoked the Lord to anger."

LEARNING QUELLS AMNESIA

Some Christians who have to fight against amnesia are stuck in churches which fail to feed them spiritually. Sometimes these churches do excellent evangelistic work, introducing people to saving relationships with the Lord, but then they tragically neglect those people *after*ward. The focus of such churches is often commendable, as they emphasize outreach and evangelism. Yet there is little prominence given to teaching and training believers. Church-based evangelism is essential, but starving newly born spiritual children cannot be right! Reaching the lost cannot be more important than the equipping of "the saints for the work of ministry, for building up the body of Christ" (Eph 4:12). Believers who are being fed a steady diet of God's word have a growing knowledge of their great God and are moving in the opposite direction from amnesia, gaining instead of losing knowledge of God. They are partially immunized against forgetfulness! Further, they are more effective at evangelism. When they remember God all day long, they are eager and excited to introduce others to him.

Christians who are not being fed enough spiritually must seek more spiritual food individually and privately through personal spiritual disciplines and from gifted teachers outside their anemic church. This will usually mean changing churches to find more mature and intentional teaching. The healthiest churches feed their people through the expository preaching of God's word and stir them up to study the Bible with other hungry believers in small groups.

---

35. Cole, *Exodus*, 224.

PREVENTING AMNESIA

People naturally love their marvelously created minds, and as they age, they often fear losing their mental acuity and memories. They will go to great lengths to hold onto their minds, doing things like taking vitamins, exercising, playing mind-stimulating games, completing puzzles, and trying anything else to *prevent* memory loss. How much more should believers be zealous to retain their spiritual memories? How can you *proactively prevent* spiritual memory loss?

Prevention: Encountering God Daily in the *Present*

Returning to a theme of this book, spiritual health and mental time travel are linked. When you are forgetful, your connections to your *past* and *future* have grown weak. God's ordinary means of grace, such as Bible reading, hearing the public preaching of God's word, prayer, and meditation, are the best prevention! In your fellowship time with God, you are reconnecting your mind with his greatness and goodness. "Awe amnesia" cannot coexist with intimate encounters with the Almighty.[36] The next chapter encourages you to practice the daily spiritual disciplines that keep you connected with your *past* and *future* with God.

Prevention: Recording and *Recalling* Memories

If you are a wise Christian, you read, meditate, pray, and then take active measures to record what God has done for you in the *past*. Then, thankfulness for all God has done in your *past* can be carried into every day of your *future*. The longer you live, the more you can be thankful as you *re*read and rejoice in *past* mercies. John Flavel (1627–91) recommended keeping such a record of God's *past* mercy: "It hath been the pious care and endeavour of the people of God, to preserve and perpetuate his mercies, by using all the helps to memory they could."[37] Following his advice, write down or type God's mercies in a journal and *re*read it periodically to strengthen your *re*collections.

You need to do more than *recall* God's faithfulness to you individually! God also intends for you to benefit from the experiences of other

---

36. Tripp, *Awe*, 60.
37. Flavel, *Works*, 5:409–10.

Christians. Innumerable other brothers and sisters in the faith have walked with God *before* you. Their testimonies still live on through hymns, biographies, autobiographies, and books they purposely penned to bless their generation and *future* generations.[38] Keeping connected with your *past* will protect you from dreaded "dyschronometria"! That is James Smith's word for what ails contemporary Christianity:

> A lot of contemporary Christianity suffers from spiritual dyschronometria—an inability to keep time, a lack of awareness of what time it is. Too many contemporary Christians look at history and see only a barren, textureless landscape. We might think of this as the temporal equivalent of color blindness—a failure to appreciate the nuances and dynamics of history. We can't discern why when makes a difference. We don't recognize how much we are the products of a *past*, leading to naivete about our *present*. But we also don't know how to keep time with a promised *future*, leading to fixations on the "end times" rather than cultivating a posture of hope. This temporal tone deafness is a feature of the view from nowhen that characterizes too much of contemporary Christianity.[39]

NOW ARRIVING: THE *PRESENT*!

What an extraordinary ability we have, as people created in the image of God, to travel by imagination to the *past* and the *future* by meditation. God wants you to orient your heart toward the *future* in alertness and the *past* in appreciation. But you must choose each day in the *present* to engage in such time travel. To live in light of the *past* and the *future* requires a disciplined *present* life to which we are *now pre*pared to turn. Believers who have a fully graced *past* and a fully guaranteed *future* are truly free to live boldly in the *present*.

RECOMMENDED READING AGAINST AMNESIA

Jeremiah Burroughs, *The Rare Jewel of Christian Contentment* (Moscow, ID: Canon Press, 2020). Free public domain versions are available online from ministries such as monergism.com

---

38. "This is pushing back against the world's 'ahistorical/existential *now*' mindset." O'Donnell, *Matthew*, 439 (emphasis added).

39. Smith, *How to Inhabit Time*, 5 (emphasis added).

Erik Raymond, *Chasing Contentment: Trusting God in a Discontented Age* (Wheaton, IL: Crossway, 2017).

Paul David Tripp, *Awe: Why It Matters for Everything We Think, Say, and Do* (Wheaton, IL: Crossway, 2015).

MEMORIZATION PASSAGES AGAINST AMNESIA

Numbers 15:40
So you shall remember and do all my commandments,
and be holy to your God.

Deuteronomy 4:9
Only take care, and keep your soul diligently, lest you forget the things that your eyes have seen, and lest they depart from your heart all the days of your life. Make them known to your children and your children's children.

Psalm 63:5–6
My mouth will praise you with joyful lips,
when I remember you upon my bed,
and meditate on you in the watches of the night.

Psalm 77:11–12
I will remember the deeds of the Lord;
yes, I will remember your wonders of old.
I will ponder all your work, and meditate on your mighty deeds.

CHAPTER SIX

In the *Present* for the *Future*
Be Disciplined!

> We should always be disciplining ourselves.... We should always be holding the reins tightly upon ourselves, we must always be in a disciplined condition in every respect.
>
> MARTYN LLOYD-JONES (1899–1981)

Almost everyone wants to be disciplined and move successfully toward their *future* goals. Yet many soon realize that they lack the discipline to reach those goals and are confused about why they lack it. Think of the many people who make New Year's resolutions. They intend to strive for a year of better fitness, financial restraint, career advancement, stronger family relationships, and spirituality. They are so close to success, yet many fail. They were alert enough about their *past* lives to see that they needed *future* improvement and excited enough about the *future* to envision *future* change. But they are missing the *present* skills required to succeed.

THE STRUGGLE FOR NATURAL DISCIPLINE

Usually, the problem with natural discipline is that visions of *future* achievement are not connected to daily discipline. A lack of daily meditative time travel leaves each day disconnected from that hoped-for *future*! But to the degree that some can *fore*see their success and the *present* steps to get there, they will have the energy to *propel* themselves *forward*. Not everyone loses their way *forward*. Some secular people are skilled mental time travelers, anchoring to *future* goals, building on *past* successes, and showing remarkable discipline in the *present*. Successful coaches of athletic teams, whether believers or unbelievers, know that they must continually renew the team's vision of victory, which will motivate the effort to follow that path *forward*. Dallas Cowboys coach Tom Landry (1924–2000), a devout Christian, knew that the role of the coach was to force players to reach for their *future*: "To make men do what they don't want to do in order to achieve what they've always wanted to be."[1] Because so many need a vision for their potential *future* lives cast and *re*cast again, there is a vast market of motivational speakers, books, and courses, all promising to help the undisciplined reach their desired *futures*.

Many people commit to improvements only to slide *back* into *former* habits. The statistics about the success of New Year's resolutions may depress you. Most will fail at their resolutions by January 19. By February, the percentage of abandonment reaches over 80 percent.[2] Shockingly, by the end of the year, only 8 percent will succeed in reaching and keeping those resolutions![3] Even medical professionals routinely see patients with shocking inabilities to change. A 2019 study discovered that "less than 10% of heart failure patients comply with advice on salt and fluid restrictions, daily weighing, and physical activity." Considering that those numbers are self-reported, the levels of failure to change are likely higher than that![4] More than 90 percent of these patients, with their lives at stake, will not or cannot make simple life-saving physical changes! Obviously, people need supernatural help to overcome such struggles against being undisciplined!

THE NEED FOR SUPERNATURAL DISCIPLINE

When the Holy Spirit ignites the desire to conform to Christ's image, this is the beginning of a lifelong journey toward a better *future*. It is a *future* for which we must make every effort: "Strive for peace with everyone, and

1. Landry, quoted in Whitney, *Simplify Your Spiritual Life*, 20.
2. Haq, "This Is the Day."
3. Diamond, "Just 8% of People."
4. "Lonely Patients with Heart Failure."

for the holiness without which no one will see the Lord" (Heb 12:14). More directly, Paul commands Timothy to "discipline yourself for the purpose of godliness" (1 Tim 4:7 NASB). The term "spiritual disciplines" is derived from this passage because pursuing spiritual discipline is the human *prerequisite* for God granting the godliness being pursued.

You need to discipline your spiritual life more than any other area of your life. Christian happiness in this life largely depends on it.[5] Martyn Lloyd-Jones (1899–1981), both a pastor and a medical doctor, noted, "If we are unhappy and depressed Christians, it is more than likely that it is all due to that lack of discipline." Moreover, spiritual disciplines provide the means to *prepare* for both "the *present* life and also for the life to come" (1 Tim 4:8; emphasis added). Having been justified by grace through faith, we *now* must "work out our salvation" in sanctification.[6] A fruit of the Spirit, flowing from the process of sanctification, is increasing "self-control" (Phil 2:12; Gal 5:23).

OPPONENTS OF SPIRITUAL DISCIPLINE

The disciplined Christian life is delightful and difficult. There is joy in serving God and other people. Yet, a disciplined life is difficult to maintain because Christians face additional challenges from oppressive opponents. If you ask Christians why they struggle with spiritual disciplines, their answers are often inaccurate or incomplete. They blame surface issues such as life circumstances, scheduling, and pressure. Although those can hinder you, God wants you to recognize that your real opponents are spiritual and sinister: the world, the flesh, and the devil.[7]

The "world" is the antagonistic supernatural order set against God, his children, and their holy pursuits. Committing to a disciplined life of living for God and not for the world's approval places Christians at odds with the prevailing views of human society. Being transformed is always more costly than being conformed to the world (Rom 12:2). You need little effort if you intend to "go with the flow"! Closely linked to the "world" is

---

5. Lloyd-Jones, *Spiritual Depression*, 216. We are bodies and souls, so medical conditions can also contribute to depression. Start by applying more time-travel discipline to your soul, but also consult medical professionals.

6. "Believers are to accomplish their salvation, and yet ultimately it is God who does the work. He gives the strength to do the work." Schreiner, *Paul*, 256–57.

7. Ryle, *Fighting for Holiness*, 30–34.

your old sinful "flesh," definitively defeated since regeneration. Yet it clings to life within you and is still quite capable of rearing its ugly head. Finally, Satan himself directly opposes anything that benefits your soul. The famous missionary Hudson Taylor (1832–1905) knew this from his experiences of having prayer opposed by the evil one. He wrote, "Satan will always find you something to do . . . when you ought to be occupied about that if it is only arranging a window blind."[8]

THE MASTER OF SELF-MASTERY

Just as Jesus modeled a life without worry, you can look to Jesus to see an utterly disciplined life. For example, Jesus committed himself to the spiritual disciplines. He withdrew to pray either all night (Luke 6:12) or in the early morning hours (Mark 1:35), showing "the example of a disciplined life" in terms of prayer.[9] Further, Jesus learned the Holy Scriptures, beginning in childhood, in ways that exceeded those of his contemporaries, even putting time alone with God above public ministry (Mark 1:35; Luke 4:42; John 6:15).[10] He both memorized his Father's words and meditated on their meanings, including learning which verses *predicted* his suffering.[11] His intimate walk with his Father sustained through Bible intake, meditation, and prayer, led to a life of Spirit-empowered, scripturally-grounded decision-making.

Jesus proved his lifetime of meditative memorization through his victory over Satan during his temptations in the wilderness. Though all alone in the wilderness, Jesus was not apart from the internalized Scriptures he carried inside his soul. John Piper observes that "the Lord Jesus memorized Scripture verbatim. We know he did, because when he was fasting in the wilderness there were no libraries or books, and with every temptation of the devil he quoted a passage of Scripture to defeat the devil" (Matt 4:4, 7, 10).[12] That discipline of applying God's words to his situations sustained him through his darkest hours on the cross, where he was still quoting

---

8. Taylor, *Hudson Taylor's Spiritual Secret*, 141.
9. Chambers, "Approved unto God," 21.
10. Mathis, "Time Alone for God."
11. Ware, *Man Christ Jesus*, 53–54.
12. Piper, "Thy Word I Have Treasured."

Scripture: "My God, my God, why have you forsaken me?" (Matt 27:46; Ps 22:1).[13]

TIME TRAVEL AND THE SPIRITUAL DISCIPLINES

Christians have traditionally labeled the interpersonal activities of spending time with God as "spiritual disciplines" or "means of grace." The term "spiritual disciplines," derived from 1 Tim 4:7, emphasizes that you "must work" to practice and maintain them.

Time Travel Motivates the Spiritual Disciplines

Imagine an ordinary married Christian couple, Michael and Michelle. They love the Lord Jesus Christ, are committed to a local church, and desire to build their lives and the lives of their *future* children on the faith. Yet they have two starkly different experiences in their quiet times. Both know they should pray and read their Bibles, and both sincerely try, but one is thriving spiritually while the other's devotional life is wilting. Michelle rises in the morning, anticipating a joyous time with the Lord, and sees each time as an opportunity to enjoy the Lord's presence and end any worries about the day *ahead*. She eagerly *prepares* spiritually for whatever comes their way. Confident in the power of God's word and based on her *past* experiences of God's grace, she earnestly pursues the Lord and enjoys the time alone with him in secret (Matt 6:6). She agrees with Richard Baxter (1615–91) about the joy of those contemplating heaven while still on earth: "None on earth live such a life of joy and blessedness."[14]

Michael's experiences are surprisingly dismal. In the morning, he has difficulty focusing on reading the Bible, plagued with regrets about *yesterday's* failures and pondering the problems that this day will bring. He wishes he could confess sins as smoothly as Michelle describes, but he is also still a bit uncertain about God's grace. Maybe God gets tired of his failures like his earthly parents often did. Praying through his prayer list frustrates him, too. Michelle recommends that he *begin* with Bible reading *before* praying, but he still tries to pray first. He is getting bored, though he will not admit it, with saying the same things the same way to God daily.

---

13. Perkins, *Works*, 658.
14. Baxter, *Practical Works*, 338.

Even worse, his nagging questions from college are resurfacing. Is God's word relevant to all of *today*'s current issues? Is it really inspired and without error? If God knows everything in advance, why pray? His heart tells him he should enjoy praying, but he knows that his time with the Lord is becoming stale. He knows that his spiritual disciplines can move from seemingly "needless, unprofitable, impossible, and burdensome" to "exceeding beneficial, delightsome, and easy." But he needs to learn how to move in that direction.[15]

Observe some differences in how Michelle and Michael do or do not anchor their *present* disciplines to the *past* and *future*. Toward the *future*, Michelle is alert, not anxious, choosing to battle through her worries, even letting them drive her to prayer. From her *past*, her informed decision to trust the relevance and authority of the Bible and her memory of God's *past* grace fuels her enthusiasm for enjoying time with the Lord. Michael, however, lets *past* pain and *present* pressures interfere with focusing on the Lord; therefore, he feels no freedom. In addition to that pain, he often allows the ongoing uncertainty about how much God cares for him unconditionally to hamper his time alone with God.

Learning to embrace God's overwhelming love in the *present* would help him link prayer, peace, and God's love more readily. Remembering, instead of forgetting, divine love would encourage him to pray more. If Michael could trust that God's *future* for him is spiritually prosperous, his pursuit of that *future* through the disciplines for the glory of God would be empowered. Peter describes prayer as "casting all your anxieties on him because he cares for you" (1 Pet 5:7). Michael will pursue the *present* disciplines to the degree that he develops greater clarity about the *future*. Donald Whitney's well-known caution applies: "Discipline without direction is drudgery."[16]

Time Travel and the Foundational Spiritual Disciplines

This book focuses on the four "foundational" spiritual disciplines, those most essential for the spiritual life: Bible intake, meditation, prayer, and memorization. Three of them provide the basic means for communing with God, generally following a pattern: Bible intake, meditation, and prayer. William Bridge (1600–1670) suggested this sequence: "Read or hear first;

15. Ball, *Treatise of Divine Meditation*, 23.
16. Piper, *Desiring God*, 12.

then meditate; and then pray upon both."[17] Likewise, David Brainerd (1718–47), the famous missionary, advised his brother to "fill up your time in reading, meditation, and prayer."[18]

The fourth one, memorization, is an essential *supporting* discipline. It supports and extends the others, making them profitable and portable into the *future*. Countless Christians have testified how memorizing a verse of Scripture at some point in the *past* has *pre*pared them for unexpected *future* events, allowing them to *re*call their Bible in their moment of need and to apply it to that situation through meditation and prayer. The focus will not be directly on memorization, but you will see that Bible intake, meditation, and prayer become much more fruitful when memory is added! Honor the Spirit who inspired the Scriptures by storing them in your heart, and he will unleash his power in and through them.

Planning in the Present for Future Spiritual Disciplines

The success of your devotional life will depend on the quality of your planning. Just as many New Year's resolutions to "get fit" or "lose weight" will fail without specific planning of the details, so many who sincerely intend to read the Bible and pray will fail because they do not plan well. Right *now*, in the *present*, you must plan for the *future*.

When will you spend time with God? Take simple but powerful advice. Right *now*, in the *present*, plan to set aside time in each *future* day to be with the Lord. Reflecting that biblical emphasis, Edward Reyner (1600–1668) advised believers to think of gathering up spiritual supplies for the day: "Make your provision of strength and grace from Christ, every morning fetch from him so much as you shall have occasion to use all the day long."[19] Not only do vain thoughts rush to fill your mind in the morning if you do not fill it with God's truth, but your concentration probably wanes as the day wears down.[20] C. S. Lewis (1898–1963) opined against evening prayer: "No one in his senses, if he has any power of ordering his day, would reserve his chief prayers for bedtime—obviously the worst possible hour for any action which needs concentration."[21]

17. Bridge, *Sweetness of Divine Meditation*, 68.
18. Brainerd, "Remains," 435.
19. Reyner, *Precepts for Christian Practice*, 9.
20. Goodwin, *Vanity of Thoughts*, 27.
21. Lewis, *Joyful Christian*, 88–89.

Try mornings first to start or restart your devotional time. If you categorize yourself as a "morning person," you can spend extended time in the morning with the Lord: Bible intake, meditation, and prayer. Then, come *back* at brief moments *later* for quick, spontaneous moments of seeking him, perhaps a few minutes at lunch or spare moments in the evening. In those moments, meditate spontaneously on what you have *already* read and in response to the events and emotions of the day. Your aim should be to keep your soul close to the Lord all day. King David loved God deeply, seeking him in the morning (Ps 5:3), evening (Ps 8), and continually (Ps 55:16–18).

Since personal spiritual disciplines are just that, *personal*, it is fine if morning does not work for you. Some are more alert at other times or their family and work commitments free them up to have more time *later* each day. You, "night owls," should not be ashamed to plan most of your disciplines in your best evening hours! Making these decisions is part of the freedom of servants seeking to please their Master (Rom 14:4–5). For example, famous church leaders such as Richard Baxter (1615–91) and Joseph Hall (1574–1656) found the evening the most beneficial time for their extended meditations.[22] Isaac also demonstrated an evening pattern of meditation and prayer (Gen 24:63). If you fit in this category, then rise and pray briefly to dedicate the day to the Lord and *later* engage in the more set disciplines. Schedule your "set" spiritual disciplines at your best time of day while planning to use other spare moments for more "spontaneous" times with God. Regardless of your choice, communicate with God throughout your day. Just as you eat throughout the day, so seek to satisfy your hunger for God (Matt 5:6) by feeding on his word and in prayer.

The Best Sequence of Spiritual Disciplines

Why have centuries of Christians found that a regular pattern of Bible intake *before* meditation and then prayer *after* meditation provides the most help? The answer is that this sequence enhances spiritual time travel! Read George Müller's (1805–98) testimony about a revolutionary change he made in his morning devotional routine:

> *Before* this time my practice had been, at least for ten years previously, as an habitual thing, to give myself to prayer, *after* having

---

22. Baxter, *Saints' Everlasting Rest*, 195.

dressed in the morning. *Now I saw, that the most important thing I had to do was to give myself to the reading of the Word of God and to meditation on it, that thus my heart might be comforted, encouraged, warned, reproved, instructed; and that thus, whilst meditating, my heart might be brought into experimental communion with the Lord . . . so that though I did not, as it were, give myself to prayer, but to meditation, yet it turned almost immediately more or less into prayer.*[23]

Müller's reading of God's word fed his soul and provided food for meditation. Then, those biblical truths he had chewed on supplied him with truths about God and his promises from which to pray. The specific pattern that yields the best spiritual fruit is Bible intake, leading to meditation, which then launches prayer. Just as a "threefold cord is not quickly broken" (Eccl 4:12), the intertwining of Bible intake, meditation, and prayer makes for a robust devotional life.

Read first, then meditate. For Thomas Watson (1620–86), reading the Bible without meditating content is unfruitful, and meditation detached from reading is downright dangerous.[24] Remember the image of the hot air balloon of meditation. Meditation provides the hot air to lift the balloon of your daily reading into the air. If you do not plan the time to meditate *after* reading, then do not read at all. Alternatively, you could use your memorized scripture as the spark for the fires of meditation leading to prayers ascending to God.

What about prayer? Can you not pray effectively and joyfully without beginning with the Bible? It is almost impossible! When believers pray, they *rely on what they* know about God, whether aware of it or not. How could you even begin a prayer to God without something in your mind *already*? The child sings, "Jesus loves me, this I know," an excellent summary of the Bible message for little ones, and then prays to the God who loves her. The maturing Christian is learning God's characteristics and, with more theological maturity, can pray more age-appropriate prayers to the God who is also holy, all-knowing, and eternal. The mature believer brings Scriptures *just* read or a lifetime of *past* Bible knowledge to his prayers. The "freshest" prayers are the ones prayed out of the Scriptures that have been read or called to mind. Thus, the Bible-soaked Christian is always *pre*pared to pray anywhere, anytime, drawing biblical truths about God from memory.

---

23. Müller, *Autobiography*, 152–53 (emphasis added).
24. Watson, *Christian on the Mount*, 72.

So, the question is not really whether you need knowledge about God *before* praying. Knowledge must *precede* prayer! Only God creates from nothing! Consider what Paul wrote regarding the need of lost souls to call out for grace: "How then will they call on him in whom they have not believed? And how are they to believe in him of whom they have never heard? And how are they to hear without someone preaching?" (Rom 10:14). You cannot believe in God or pray to him if you do not *already* know him or know about him. The real question is how much you remember from the *past* about God when you start praying.

Beginning with Bible intake ensures you have heard from him through his word. God *just* spoke to you if you had ears to hear (Matt 11:15). *Now*, speak back in prayer and worship! But failure to ingest God's word *before* speaking to him relies too much on your fallible memory of him and his word. Why not refresh your encounter with him *before* you talk with him? W. H. Griffith Thomas (1861–1923) expressed it as two-way communion: "God speaks to the believer, and the believer speaks to God. This reciprocal communion is obviously summed up in the Bible and Prayer; for it is through the Bible that God speaks to us and through Prayer that we speak to God."[25]

Where does meditation fit in this process? It forms the middle step of chewing on and pondering what God's word says, sandwiched between Bible intake and prayer. The experienced Christian probably passes through meditation so seamlessly that she does not think, "I am *now* moving on to meditation." Imagine the Christian woman whose morning Bible reading includes Rom 8:38–39, "For I am sure that neither death nor life, nor angels nor rulers, nor things *present* nor things to come, nor powers, nor height nor depth, nor anything else in all creation, will be able to separate us from the love of God in Christ Jesus our Lord" (emphasis added). Prompted by the Holy Spirit, she grasps through meditation the beauty and breadth of this promise.

She no longer reads this passage as just an ancient apostle's writings but as suddenly alive. The Spirit enlivens her soul as she begins to "consider" and "reflect" on this truth. She "muses" on her *past* and knows that God has brought her safe thus far, and she realizes that she has never been in danger of perishing. That gives her a new perspective on her *past*, driving away any spiritual amnesia and filling her with fresh appreciation. Then, she "contemplates" the challenges *ahead* of her in the *future*, releases her

---

25. Thomas, *Life Abiding and Abounding*, 5–6.

anxieties to God, and praises him in prayer for this invigorating reassurance. All those words, such as "consider" (Prov 6:6; Rom 4:19), "reflect" (Prov 20:25), and "muse" (Ps 39:3), are words for the activity of meditation. The Bible uses a whole palette of words to paint pictures of the "activity of holy thought" applied to biblical truth.[26] Meditation is so vital that your devotional success depends on it. Fail to meditate, and the rest will flop, because all the other disciplines are improved by meditation.[27]

Segmented Time or Sequential Time?

People only do well what they plan well. You must make decisions *now*: how, when, where, and for how long? There are two equally helpful ways to plan. Either schedule a segment of time or a sequence of disciplines. If you use a segmented approach, you will begin every day at this specific time and end at a particular time. Those with packed schedules and limited time benefit from this approach because they know exactly when and to how much time they are committing.

On the other hand, the sequential approach is less defined. Those with more flexible schedules will find it helpful. This approach involves planning what you will do, such as reading several chapters, meditating at the end of each chapter, and concluding with prayer without setting strict time boundaries. It is *pre*planning a sequence instead of *pre*planning the time.

On most days, you will complete that sequence in about the same amount of time, but this "untimed" sequence approach gives you leeway to spend more or less time in different disciplines on different days. On stressful days, you will likely need to pray longer than usual. Or, if you have begun a chapter with a captivating story in the Bible, you can read a bit more to learn what will happen next. Likewise, if meditation has loosed you from this physical world and freed your soul to "soar up to our heaven in meditation,"[28] then stay there as long as you like, something more possible with this sequenced approach. If the segmented approach is like eating from a restaurant's meal-deal menu every day so that you get the same amount of food every day, then the sequential approach is a buffet, where you can eat anything you want for as long as you want.

---

26. Packer, *Knowing God*, 56.
27. Baxter, *Practical Works*, 310.
28. Calamy, *Art of Divine Meditation*, 123.

Always Take Time to Read Aloud!

You should begin with Bible reading *after* a quick whispered prayer for enlightenment. The Bible contains verses from which to prayerfully launch your reading, including many verses of Ps 119. To start, use the famous verse 18, "Open my eyes, that I may behold wondrous things out of your law." Or pray Ps 19:14, "Let the words of my mouth and the meditation of my heart, be acceptable in your sight, O LORD, my rock and my redeemer." Whatever verse or passage you use, you are humbling yourself as a servant before your Lord, asking for him to speak to you through the Spirit.

Read your daily passage aloud, seeking to read it with clarity and diction. This will bless you in four time-related ways. First, it will slow you down, "costing" you more time, and that is a great price to pay for the payoff! Many Bible readers are more Bible browsers than investigators because they move too fast. They take the "express train" through the Bible stories' countryside instead of slowly perusing the town's shops and homes.[29] Be careful! The modern breakdown of healthy reading habits means you are more familiar with scanning than studying. Surveying the Bible to get the "big picture" has its place and value, but not during your meditative Bible reading.

Second, reading aloud also helps your mind ponder what individual words and phrases mean to you *now*. Hearing yourself read aloud will *prepare* you to meditate well. Martyn Lloyd-Jones (1899–1981) wrote, "When we read our Bibles, nothing is more important than that we should look at every word and question it as to its meaning." He cautioned that if you do not carefully think about the words, you might as well skip reading them.[30] But if you read and meditate on them, God will fill your heart with his words. These will be the fuel for praying at the moment and then for meditation throughout the day. The Bible, even if it is not open in front of you, will still be open in the front of your mind.[31]

Third, vocalizing your reading will also help you remember it accurately over time. Instead of just your eyes, you have added your lips and ears to the process. In his last interview *before* his death, J. I. Packer (1926–2020) showed the end-of-life zeal commended in chapter 8 ("Time Travel Tested by Decline and Death"). He desired to read the Gospels more

---

29. Spurgeon, *Barbed Arrows from the Quiver*, 162.
30. Lloyd-Jones, *God's Ultimate*, 36.
31. Allcock, *Deeper Still*, 8.

often and more aloud. He looked *forward* to this adventure even though it would require using a magnifying glass to overcome the effects of macular degeneration: "I want to read the Gospels a good deal more than *once* a year. I do find, again and again, that passages come to life when I read them aloud, in a way which they didn't do when I read them silently."[32] Hearing your own voice speak God's word aloud will also help you obey. There is a long tradition of hearing God's oracles aloud and being blessed by obeying them (Rev 1:3). Join that tradition and bless your Bible reading *today*!

As a fourth and final benefit, you will be *pre*paring to speak God's word aloud to someone. That might be a word of comfort spoken to the grieving at just the right instant, a gospel word spoken to an interested unbeliever, a word of public prayer, or even a word of gentle rebuke to a spiritual brother or sister. In your *past*, you may remember another believer who spoke just the right verse from her heart for your need at the moment (Eph 4:29). Read aloud to *prepare* yourself to speak God's words, which to your hearers can be richer "than thousands of gold and silver pieces" (Ps 119:72).

Sources of Daily Meditation

Your daily meditation flows from the Scriptures. So, you need to consider your options for finding the Scriptures for that meditation. You could meditate on key Bible passages: the Ten Commandments (Exod 20:1–17; Pss 1, 8, 19, 23, 27, 32, 46, 51, 91, 119), the Lord's Prayer (Matt 6:9–13), Jesus's High Priestly Prayer (John 17), Rom 8, Eph 1, Phil 2, Jas 1, etc. Chewing on many of these passages will prompt meditative time travel. For example, in the Lord's Prayer, you are to pray, "Your kingdom come, your will be done, on earth as it is in heaven" (Matt 6:10). Reflecting on this verse will transport your mind *forward* in time. While in the *present*, you are part of God's kingdom gathered together in the local church, you are praying in revolutionary ways for the *future*, God's complete establishment of his kingdom on earth.[33]

Instead of using the same verse or passage for a while, you could also meditate slowly through a longer passage or book, day by day. But be sure to pick a leisurely pace. For example, if you want to meditate on the Beatitudes, a great pace is two verses a week for a month. Two verses of

---

32. Brant and Strong, "Catechism of Knowing God," 22 (emphasis added).
33. Mohler, *Prayer That Turns*, 86.

Philippians (104 verses) digested each week for a year would fill you with joy! You can also select something each day you have read aloud in your daily Bible reading. Find a verse that warms your heart and is "profitable for teaching, for reproof, for correction, and for training in righteousness" (2 Tim 3:16).

God also intends for you to encounter his word with others. Be an active church member in a Bible-loving church led by a pastor who preaches from God's word. That preaching can be another source of profitable meditation. Take a passage you recently heard preached, listened to attentively, and took notes on. *Now*, return to that passage and reread it for a week, asking the Holy Spirit to apply it to your life. You only receive the full benefits of those sermons if you reflect on them, respond to them, and apply them in the *upcoming* week. That is how you digest sermons.[34] Why not write down one thing spoken that pierced your heart or brought you joy and reflect on it daily for the week? Let that truth, drawn accurately from the Bible and applied skillfully to your life, fill you with joyful prayers of thanksgiving and renewed passion to pray for yourself and others.

When you meditate, remember that it is a slower but more intense process than reading. Take time to reflect on each phrase and sentence, responding to it depending on how it applies to you (e.g., rejoicing, repenting, recommitting, releasing pain and anxiety to God). The longer you can take to suck the nourishing juice from the fruit of every verse, the more you get from it.[35] There is no race or pace in meditation! You are directing your prayers to God from your word-based encounters with him. How greatly that honors him! As you grow better at reading and meditating, the distinctions between Bible reading, meditation, and prayer will blur together, a sign that you are becoming skilled at taking the jewels of God out into the sunlight to view the dazzling sparkle of the things of God.[36] You will read, meditate, and pray so naturally and smoothly that you would be hard-pressed to know when you did each separate one. Encountering God's supernatural truths and being transformed by them is becoming "natural" to you!

---

34. Calamy, *Art of Divine Meditation*, 124.
35. Witsius, *Economy of the Covenants*, 51.
36. Calamy, *Art of Divine Meditation*, 125.

IN THE PRESENT FOR THE FUTURE

DEVOTIONAL TIME TRAVEL RESOLUTIONS

To maximize your benefit from time travel, you should make some devotional resolutions. Consider the nature of personal resolutions like the ones you might make for the New Year *ahead*. You promise yourself that you will do or not do certain things in the *future*. Are such resolutions not vehicles of meditative time travel? You say to yourself, "Standing here *now* at this point in the *present* time, I commit that at *future* times, I will or will not . . ." Further, since resolutions can create a better-envisioned *future*, they are usually made because *past* experiences have led you to make commitments to ensure that your *future* is better than the *past*. Successful resolutions link *present* motivations to the *future*. Why should you do something? You should take daily steps because you *foresee* the *future*. Deciding on your goal's specific steps is less critical than the overall goal set before your mind! If you are highly motivated enough, you will accomplish your goal.

As you keep resolutions, they grow stronger. Resolutions keep *reinforcing* themselves as *past* successes propel *present* discipline. Think of a happy couple on the day of their wedding. They make vows about the *future* to each other based on their *past* and *present* love. Yet, that love is never static. If they live together harmoniously in committed ways, their love and corresponding commitment to each other will also deepen. Keeping their head commitments will sew their heart emotions ever closer together.

The famous resolutions of Jonathan Edwards (1703–58) demonstrate a most remarkable set of commitments to live a disciplined life and how they involve time travel. Among the 70 resolutions, some show *precommitment* to how he would approach the spiritual disciplines. For example, in number 28, Edwards resolved "to study the Scriptures so steadily, constantly, and frequently, as that I may find, and plainly perceive, myself to grow in the knowledge of the same."[37] His *present* love for God's word drove this commitment to studying God's word. Encouraged by Edwards's example, I offer five related time-travel-linked resolutions that will make you a savvy, spiritual time traveler for your joy and God's glory.

---

37. Edwards, *Works*, 1:lxiii.

Two Resolutions about the *Past*

1. Resolved: To Remember God's Character and Count on It

Resolve that you will remember the greatness and goodness of God as you read, meditate, and pray. If you forget God's greatness, you may develop a mistaken mindset that thinks of the disciplines as *pre*payments to God, for which he will grant you whatever you ask. Too often, you encounter believers who barely pray *now*, claiming that *after* praying for years and years, God never gave them what they needed! Audacious enough to be bitter at the Almighty God of the universe, they conclude that although they made a good-faith attempt to barter with him, he failed them. How foolish to try "bartering" with God since he is self-sufficient, having no "need" to which you could appeal.

Any such form of irreverence toward God in prayer comes from a lack of appreciation for his majesty *before* beginning to seek him. Ecclesiastes 2:1–2 warns about rashly rushing into prayer and just letting go of gushing, borderline irreverent words toward God: "Guard your steps when you go to the house of God. To draw near to listen is better than to offer the sacrifice of fools, for they do not know that they are doing evil. Be not rash with your mouth, nor let your heart be hasty to utter a word before God, for God is in heaven, and you are on earth. Therefore, let your words be few." Remembering the God whom you approach will *pre*pare you to listen more than you speak.

This is remembering his *past* grace so that you can joyfully anticipate his ongoing *future* goodness. Paul was confident that you can rely on God to provide all you need: "He who did not spare his own Son but gave him up for us all, how will he not also with him graciously give us all things?" (Rom 8:32). Coming to God with a refreshed reassurance that he provides everything good for your soul will make it possible to follow this command: "With confidence draw near to the throne of grace" (Heb 4:16). Your *past* patterns of human relationships may make trusting God's goodness harder for you than for others. But be assured that your good God knows those pains and will never neglect or abandon you. This confidence in God's goodness and reliability should also help you trust the Bible's authority, reliability, and truthfulness. J. I. Packer (1926–2020) wrote about the tragic effect of the modern loss of confidence in God's word: "These things were understood *once*; but liberal theology, with its refusal to identify the written Scriptures with the word of God, has largely robbed us of the habit of meditating on the promises, and basing our prayers on the promises, and venturing in faith in our ordinary daily life just as far as the promises will take us."[38]

There are many resources available if you need to examine the reliability of the Bible for yourself and reach a point of greater assurance that God's words are "pure words, like silver refined in a furnace on the ground, purified seven times" (Ps 12:6). Some Christians never have to deal with doubts about God's word, but if you do, check out the evidence for yourself and get the reassurance you need.[39] What you believe about God's word in *advance* will affect how much you benefit from it because what you do not fully trust cannot fully transform you. Centuries of skeptics and scoffers have found that the meaning of God's word eludes them. Not only do they read it with hardened hearts, but God often hides his precious truths from those who are too wise in their own eyes (Matt 11:25).

Trusting the goodness of God as you practice the spiritual disciplines will also protect you from unrealistic pessimism and performance anxiety. You might need to improve how you read the Bible, meditate, or pray, but do not feel guilty or ashamed. Satan seeks to discourage you, casting accusations at you and questioning your ability to please God. Often, you will find discouraged Christians who have convinced themselves that they cannot pray or read well. If they approach God with a mindset like "Well, God, here I am to fail again! I will surely disappoint you with meager prayers and confused Bible reading," it is not surprising that they gain so little benefit from it. What is the solution? Trust that God loves you and wants to commune with you *now* and forever. He will help you, not hide from you! His voice will come to you as gentle as a breeze (1 Kgs 19:12).

2. Resolved: To Remember Your Sins and Confess Them

Commit to spending time with God with as much personal holiness as possible. This is not an impossible requirement for perfection. Believers are "positionally" wholly holy before God based on their *past* justification. But through God's *present* and *future* grace, the Holy Spirit sanctifies them "progressively" in incremental ways.[40] There is danger in trying to seek God's face for blessing while holding onto unconfessed or hidden sins. Just

---

38. Packer, *Knowing God*, 115 (emphasis added).

39. Those believers who supernaturally trust the Scriptures as they read them are not naive or gullible. "Scripture indeed is self-authenticated." Calvin, *Institutes*, 80.

40. Demarest, *Cross and Salvation*, 407–8.

as God loathes the prayers of the wicked (Prov 15:8), he will not bless the spiritual disciplines of unrepentant children. This applies to Bible intake, meditation, and prayer. Joseph Hall (1574–1656) wrote that "the hill of meditation may not be climbed with a profane foot: but, as in the delivery of the Law, so here, no beast may touch God's hill, lest he die; only the pure of heart have promise to see God."[41]

Three Resolutions about the *Future*

As you come to be alone with God, make three resolutions in the *present* about what you will do in the *future*. You are spending time with God in order for him to reshape and refashion you. To a certain degree, the amount of benefit you will receive for your soul will depend on your hunger for change (Matt 5:6). Come hungry and show that through these commitments, you "watch at wisdom's gate, with a humble, hungry soul, and God may fill thee with good things."[42]

1. Resolved: To Worship God from Future Learning

Pledge to respond to what God shows you with appreciation and adoration. Higher than any other goal, you should want to "see God, and to aim at glorifying of God above all."[43] Reading and praying over passages that contain precious promises or stories of wonderful deliverance will make this easier. Rejoice in God's promises to his children and apply them to yourself personally. Even in difficult passages, thank God for challenging warnings or descriptions of his judgments. They will stretch your ability to give thanks for *all things* (1 Thess 5:18).

Biblical meditation will increase your healthy fear of God and a desire to live holy before him. That is the opposite direction that secular meditation moves you. A dark and destructive abyss lies along that path that focuses solely on the self in the *present*. In the words of one writer who *once* practiced it *before* discovering its errors, "Secular meditation anesthetizes me so that I can keep on living my life away from God."[44]

---

41. Hall, *Art of Divine Meditation*, 4.
42. Swinnock, *Works*, 216.
43. Ranew, *Solitude Improved*, 39.
44. Allcock, *Deeper Still*, 31.

2. Resolved: To Pack Up Food for the Day Ahead

Commit that from each day's harvest of biblical truths, you will continue to meditate on some portion of it. When you enjoy a fabulous meal at a restaurant or someone's home, you are eager to take leftovers with you for *later*. You can enjoy *today's* feast *tomorrow*, which may taste even better as the flavors have more time to blend. The spiritual morsels you pack up from your quiet time for the day *ahead* are just what you need to feed your soul for the day. God knows your day *ahead*, and as you let him pack a lunch for it, it is always exactly what you need.

Leave a few minutes at the end of your scheduled devotional time to write out a key verse, something you can carry with you. You can do that electronically, but there is something extra efficient about writing it out and toting it along physically. John Piper even penned a poem about it:

> I know not how the light is shed,
> Nor understand this lens.
> I only know that there are eyes
> In pencils and in pens.[45]

Charles Stanley (1932–2023) also modeled this discipline for many years, carrying along little cards of handwritten scriptures that pertained to his life situations.[46]

3. Resolved: To Memorize for Your Future

Enhance this daily meditation practice further by memorizing the verses of your meditation! Taking into your *future* a firm grasp of what God has said word-for-word will exponentially expand your meditation's power! Whether you need a verse to combat Satan's frequent ploy of asking, "Did God actually say?" or a verse to encourage you in moments of tired discouragement, every believer can memorize. Just be sure to plan a slow enough pace for that memorization. All of us have a personal memorization speed limit! Adjust your pace to your natural ability and stage of life.

Sometimes, the *past* memorization you had to do for school or Sunday school may have left you feeling like you cannot memorize well. That was "memorization on demand" or "rushed memorization," not memorization

---

45. Piper, *When I Don't Desire God*, 124.
46. Stanley, *10 Principles for Studying*, 35.

of a precious word to you. Just as you did not have to work hard to memorize your best friend's name, you will not have to exert much effort to remember God's words that you have *already* come to love. Or perhaps you memorized something zealously but too rapidly, and *now* it is "lost," and your effort was apparently "worthless." Tragically, both mindsets, the "could-never-do-that" and the "been-there-done-that," are prevalent among Christians. In that regard, Satan has *prematurely* cut off many from a powerful spiritual discipline. If you have memorized a passage or a book of the Bible and then lost it, you did it wrong, likely much too fast and with mixed motives.

As you memorize, let the words roll off your tongue, hearing the words in your voice so that you benefit from them in the *present*, even as you memorize for the *future*. God will bless the process of learning it as much as any finished feat of recitation. Edmund Clowney (1917–2005) noted that memorization was an invaluable tool for meditation: "So simple a technique as actually repeating the words of Scripture may seem too rudimentary for one seeking the transports of meditational joy, but there is no better way to begin real meditation."[47]

Once you have found a verse or passage that impacts you, pray to God about it, asking God if he wants you to memorize it and then promising him that you will.[48] You will have certainty that as you memorize, you are leaning *back* in time to his calling for you. Take courage that whatever God calls you to do, he will empower you to do, even obeying the sometimes-daunting task of memorization. The disciples forgot that when Jesus started them on their stormy nighttime journey across the water, he would come to them to guarantee their arrival on the other side. Wherever God tells you to head in your memorization journey, he will come to your aid and enable you to cross the uncertain seas of muddled memorization!

DISCIPLINE AND OTHER FORMS OF TIME TRAVEL

Meditative time travel to your *future* to be alert (chapter 2) and not anxious (chapter 3) and to your *past* to be appreciative of your *future* (chapter 4) will empower you to be disciplined in the *present*. This means that you will put time with God first in your schedule, seeking to know him better, to enjoy him, and to become more like him. Just like athletes often train better together as a team than individually, so God has given you communities

---

47. Clowney, *Christian Meditation*, 23–24.
48. Davis, *Approach to Extended Memorization*, 13.

of faith, fellow time travelers alongside you and *ahead* of you to encourage your faith. They multiply our joy, increase our spiritual stamina, and will help us even more in the *later* portions of our lives (chapter 8).

RECOMMENDED READING ABOUT DISCIPLINE

R. Kent Hughes, *Disciplines of a Godly Man*, 2nd ed. (Wheaton, IL: Crossway, 2019).
David Mathis, *Habits of Grace: Enjoying Jesus through the Spiritual Disciplines* (Wheaton, IL: Crossway, 2012).
J. I. Packer, *Knowing God* (Downers Grove, IL: InterVarsity, 1973).
David W. Saxton, *God's Battle Plan for the Mind: The Puritan Practice of Biblical Meditation* (Grand Rapids, MI: Reformation Heritage Books, 2015).
Donald S. Whitney, *Spiritual Disciplines for the Christian Life* (Colorado Springs: NavPress, 1991).

MEMORIZATION PASSAGES ABOUT DISCIPLINE

Philippians 2:12–13
Work out your own salvation with fear and trembling,
for it is God who works in you, both to will and to work
for his good pleasure.

1 Timothy 4:7–8 (NASB)
On the other hand, discipline yourself
for the purpose of godliness;
for bodily discipline is only of little profit,
but godliness is profitable for all things,
since it holds promise for the *present* life
and also for the life to come.

Romans 12:1–2
I appeal to you therefore, brothers, by the mercies of God, to
present your bodies as a living sacrifice, holy and acceptable to
God, which is your spiritual worship. Do not be conformed to
this world, but be transformed by the renewal of your mind, that
by testing you may discern what is the will of God, what is good
and acceptable and perfect.

CHAPTER SEVEN

In the *Present* for the *Future*
Time Travel Together!

> It was the prayers of his uncle, not his measly faith that saved him. Lot was not saved on his own merits but through Abraham's intercession.
>
> GORDON WENHAM

THE CHRISTIAN LIFE AS AN INDIVIDUAL IN COMMUNITY

A challenging dynamic in the Christian life is that you must be willing to live for the Lord regardless of others, even though you need them. You relate to the Lord individually: being justified and sanctified individually and then persevering to the end. We receive no group admission passes to heaven! Ultimately, the success or failure of your spiritual life depends on no human being but you. You could not save yourself or even contribute to your salvation. But God's gifts of saving grace and faith were given to you individually. You must follow Jesus, even if that means doing so with only family beside you (Josh 24:15) or even alone, apart from family (Luke 14:26).

However, you will not find yourself alone! God will give you other believers alongside you, perhaps ones you do not yet know about, like the remnant of at least seven thousand in Elijah's day (1 Kgs 19:18). God will grant you a loving community apart from which you cannot make it. Even if you feel alone for a season in your journey, remember that the message of gospel salvation came to you through Christian communities across the centuries, who preserved God's word for you and proclaimed it from generation to generation.

Imagine an extreme situation in which a desperate man, having never heard about Jesus, discovers a Bible in his hotel room. Reading it, he is supernaturally saved in a room by himself! Was he not saved all alone? No, the Gideons, a wonderful community of believers from across many denominations, sacrificed their time and money to place that Bible, along with more than two billion other Bibles, in the path of the spiritually needy.

THE THREE COMMON *PASTS* OF YOUR TIME-TRAVELING RELATIONSHIPS

You *already* know you need other believers in your life and appreciate them. Strengthen that appreciation by considering how you are related to them as fellow travelers. Every relationship you currently have has a *past*. You met someone at some point, and your common history with them began then and continues *now*. You have probably known your best friends for many years, and you have shared many wonderful experiences with them in the *past*. However, your Christian relationships have so much more background than that! When you think about fellow Christians, you share three aspects of *past* experiences with them.

A Common Redemptive *Past*: New Birth

To enter the kingdom of God, you must be "born again" (John 3:3; 1 Pet 1:3, 23). Hearing the saving words of Jesus through the gospel brings one from death to life and from judgment into grace (John 5:24)—not a process but an instantaneous change. The life of Zacchaeus paints a beautiful picture of someone who *began* a day of this life without spiritual life but *then* encountered Jesus. Read the happy pronouncement of Jesus to the grumbling crowds: "*Today* salvation has come" (Luke 19:9; emphasis added). He moved from death to life! So have all who belong to Jesus and also belong to you in Christian relationships. You share with them an essential unifying bond of a common spiritual birth. You are time travelers together, moving from a common redemptive *past* toward God's great *future* for all of you!

A Common Intermediate *Past*: Church History

At the moment of spiritual birth, the Holy Spirit connected you to billions of other Christians, most of whom live *now* in heaven. Your spiritual *fore*fathers and *fore*mothers stretch *back* through all of church history and biblical history to Pentecost (Acts 2:41) and even further *back* to Abel (Heb 11:4). Just as the ancients gained approval by faith in God (Heb 11:2), so have you (Rom 5:1). You *now* belong to that greatest of all families, the family of God extending across all time. The Spirit knitted your heart in love into the "household of God" (Col 2:2; 1 Tim 3:15). Previous chapters have urged you to learn church history to increase your appreciation for God's marvelous grace across the centuries and to be inspired by models of alertness, appreciation, and discipline.

A Common Eternal *Past*: Chosen

Regardless of how your theology leads you to interpret the many verses about believers being "chosen" (Matt 22:14; John 13:18; Rom 11:7; Col 3:12; 1 Thess 1:4; 1 Pet 1:1; 2:9, 5:13), "elected" (Matt 24:22, 24, 31; Luke 18:7; Rom 8:33; 9:11; 11:7; 2 Tim 2:10; Titus 1:1; 1 Pet 1:1; 2 Pet 1:10), "*fore*known" (1 Pet 1:2), and "*pre*destined" (Rom 8:28, 30; Eph 1:5, 11), the Bible clearly teaches that when a person in the *present* chooses to become a Christian, that *present* decision is linked to God's eternal *past*. Moreover, the frequency of such language shows that God wants you to appreciate that *before* you responded to his grace, he extended it to you individually and even particularly. That humbling realization serves to bring you into his family on equal footing with all other spiritual beggars (Matt 5:3) who have also received undeserved saving grace.

CATEGORIZING YOUR TIME TRAVEL RELATIONSHIPS

You can think of all your relationships under three general categories: family, close friends, and church family (members and ministers). Tragically, some of your closest relationships are with loved ones not saved yet. For example, your relationship with your children is important, but until they become Christians, they are not yet time-traveling alongside you toward a blessed *future*.

If some of your beloved people have not accepted a relationship with Christ *yet*, be concerned but not anxious! God can save anyone: "Everyone who calls on the name of the Lord will be saved" (Rom 10:13, quoting Joel 2:32). There is still *time*! Keep praying for them and pursuing them with the gospel. After all, the very nature of meditative time travel allows you to express *future* hope that those not saved in the *present* can be saved in the *future*. Instead of sitting passively on the sideline or anxiously worrying about their souls, be alert for opportunities to reach out to them with the gospel. Remember that just as Jesus reached you in the *past*, he can reach them in the *future*, especially as you pray in the *present*.

Family as Time Travelers Together

Marriage is the original institution, the only one created *before* the fall. God established and blessed this unique relationship that arose from human need (Gen 2:18). Couples maintain their relationship in needy, mutual interdependence (1 Cor 11:11). The idea of marriage is so familiar to the human experience that both its time-traveling nature and its symbolic meaning (Eph 5:32) often elude people. However, the truth that God created marriage to endure from the *present* into the *future* is evident even in traditional marriage vows, which often include phrases like these: "To have and to hold from this day *forward*, for better, for worse, for richer, for poorer, in sickness and in health, to love and to cherish, till death do us part." Notice that it is a commitment in the *present* about the *future*, come what may!

In marriage, no partner knows what life events, positive or negative, the *future* may *hold*. Still, the bride and groom make a lifelong commitment to each other regardless of who they might become over time. John Piper writes, "When you marry a person, you don't know what they are going to be like in thirty years. . . . You don't know what this person will be like in the *future*. It could be better than you ever dreamed, or worse. Our hope is based on this: We are chosen, holy, and loved. God is for us, and all things will work for the good of those who love him (Rom 8:28; Pss 23:6; 84:11)."[1]

---

1. Piper, *This Momentary Marriage*, 58–59 (emphasis added).

When entering Christian marriage, your eyes should be firmly fixed on the God of *future hope*, trusting him to provide the grace to move *forward* together in time from a joyful *present* to the happy *future*. A Christian couple believes that God brought them together to live a life together that will bring him more glory and them more joy than continuing to live apart.

Most married couples have children, introducing yet another aspect of time travel into their lives. In God's plan, marriages firmly grounded in *past* commitments produce children. Parents enjoy them in the *present* and help them mature into the *future*. That ideal family life provides emotional and spiritual maturity for raising children. God's plan is for a Christian couple's *past* to guarantee their ability to love children in the *present* and into the *future*.

Furthermore, children change over time as they grow, becoming more functional in the *future* than they were in the *past* and changing the nature of their relationships with their parents. How great a dynamic shift for children, who begin in the *past* as entirely dependent to reach a *present* adult moment of parity with their parents. Eventually, they can tenderly care for their parents through the *later* senior years of increasing dependence until the end of life! The roles of independence and dependence reverse! As dynamics change radically over time, they require alertness, appreciation, and discipline.

Family Goals in Time Travel Together

If God has given you a spouse or spouse and children, God has increased your ability to live alertly! Just as two eyes are better than one, four or more eyes are even better. Your family members can be more insightful time-travel companions. Not only can your spouse see more, but they also bring a different personality, background, concerns, and, most importantly, an intimate knowledge of you as they help watch over your soul. Answer these questions:

- Who knows your strengths and weaknesses better than your spouse?
- Who can share your private burdens and lighten them better than your spouse?
- Who can support you more in extraordinary seasons of testing better than your spouse?

- Who can pray more specifically and diligently for you than your spouse?
- Who can remind you about the Scriptures better than your spouse?

Similarly, who knows your children better than you, their parents? Who anticipates their inborn and learned weaknesses and their gifts, both inherent and developed? Unless they have grown cynical in the battles to raise their children or live blinded by love to any shortcomings, most parents are excellent *predictors* of their children's *futures*. Painful seasons occur when godly parents aspire for a better *future* for their children than the direction they seem *presently* headed. Parents can still pray for a better *future* than their child deserves, for God abounds in *future* grace. Parents with relentless faith are following the pattern of the highly-commended Canaanite woman, so desperate for her daughter's *future* to be better than her *past* or *present* that she "pestered" Jesus to get the grace she needed for her child (Matt 15:21–28). Jesus commended such persistent faith *then* and hears such prayers *today*.

Setting Family Goals for Time Travel Together

If you do not plan for your family's spiritual growth, their growth will be limited. Think *ahead* and plan goals for your family's spiritual and emotional development. You need to prayerfully determine how you want to see your family life in the *future* and proceed *now* toward those scriptural goals. You could choose any key passage of Scripture. Then, as a family, memorize it, meditate on it, and pursue it in your family life.

For example, your family could pursue the fruit of the Spirit (Gal 5:22–23): "Love, joy, peace, patience, kindness, goodness, faithfulness, gentleness, self-control." Those godly traits are the most valuable *present* and *future* goals. When your family members move toward them consistently, this is a sure sign of the kind of faith that saves—"faith working through love" (Gal 5:6). Remember to pray together for those goals because those types of *future* traits are borne only by the Spirit of God, working through your family's pursuit of godliness. Or a family could pursue the blessed values of the Beatitudes (Matt 5:3–12) or the Lord's Prayer (Matt 6:9–13). All these goal-oriented passages overlap and work together seamlessly in the Bible, so you could set one as a goal each year and rotate through them.

Transformative Time Travel

Pursuing Family Goals for Time Travel Together

How in the *present* can your family work toward their best spiritual *future*? Three alliterated words will help you remember the path *forward*: encouragement, entreaties, and enforcement. In your marriage, knowing another person so intimately places you in a position to be the greatest blessing to them. God's good plan for marriage includes helping the other partner to grow spiritually. God may have also blessed you with children to be raised for his glory. Wise parents, informed by the Scriptures, set goals for their spiritual development. Most parents have many goals for their children, but the most important goal is for them to have a vibrant relationship with God. Jesus asked this piercing question: "What will it profit a man if he gains the whole world and forfeits his soul?" (Matt 16:26). So it is with families! What does it profit a family to gain all successes and all material goods in the *present* age, yet forfeit their souls in the *future*?

Parents should be ambitious in building the best *future* life for themselves and those they love, but that begins with making spiritual life the highest priority. Godly spouses and parents see beyond mere physical, social, academic, and financial goals and seek to influence their beloved family members to grow in godliness "as it holds promise for the *present* life and also for the life to come" (1 Tim 4:8; emphasis added). Those steps toward growth start with encouragement!

Family Time Travel Encouragement

In your marriage and family life, you can pursue goals of transformative time travel like alertness, appreciation, and discipline by using your words to encourage. Timely words of reminder about God's goodness and faithfulness can move a conversation from the realm of anxiety to patience, waiting on the Lord to provide. Almost all conversations in the home about the stresses of the day resolve themselves in one of three ways: mutual "venting" leading to more anxiety together than apart, mutual reassurance of self-sufficiency leading to *future* failures, or honest admission of needing God's grace leading to calmness and trust. What pattern pervades in your household? What can you change to shift the direction of the evening conversations in a more Godward direction?

Spouses should ask each other about and encourage each other to practice the spiritual disciplines. That encouragement will often be verbal, but do not underestimate the power of your example to encourage. Even if your spouse seems stuck in anxiety, cynicism, or a lack of discipline, continue living in righteous ways. God may surprise you with how he uses your up close, living example to persuade them to change! Since even stubborn unbelievers can sometimes be "won without a word" (1 Pet 3:1), so much more can godly models influence believing spouses!

Especially when walking through hard seasons that test you, a godly wife or husband can help you avoid anxiety by refocusing you on God and his goodness. Hardships can lead to dangerous forgetfulness, but your marriage partner can repeatedly point to God's goodness when you doubt. Your spouse is likely also affected by what troubles you, either directly because they live in the same situation or indirectly out of concern for you. Their modeling of godly trust and supernatural calmness will point you toward God.

Katharina von Bora (1499–1552), the wife of Martin Luther, showed great skill in the "marital art" of encouraging her husband when he battled depression. She helped connect his feelings with faith: "Once, when Martin was so depressed that none of Kate's counsel would help, she put on a black dress. Luther noticed it and asked, 'Are you going to a funeral?' 'No,' Kate replied, 'but since you act like God is dead, I wanted to join you in your mourning.' Luther got the message and recovered."[2]

For couples, this could mean choosing spiritual disciplines to pursue together, like memorization.[3] It also means supporting your spouse's devotional times by protecting their time and space with God against other household demands. Christopher Ash observes that the husband must think of marriage in terms of sacrificing himself: "At the heart of this pattern is the husband who consciously reminds himself again and again that he is called to be like Christ going to the cross in his marriage: to lead by serving and loving and caring, whatever the cost to himself."[4] That includes the commitment to "zealously give himself to the duties laid upon him, and, in this regard, to promoting his wife's spiritual welfare."[5]

The same patterns of encouragement also work wonderfully with children. They are generally more impressionable than your adult marriage partner. Plan *ahead* for *future* conversations with your children, but know

---

2. Markwald and Markwald, *Katharina von Bora*, 139–40.
3. Plummer and Haste, *Held in Honor*, 129.
4. Ash, *Married for God*, 95.
5. Beeke and LaBelle, *Living in a Godly Marriage*, 194.

they will often start conversations spontaneously. Be ready to teach when sitting in your house, walking by the way, and lying down (Deut 6:7). How will you handle their load of anxious thoughts from their school day? You could teach them to wait to unload emotionally until *after* they are home from school and feel safe, relaxed, and fed. Then, encourage them to share their concerns and also the positive things that happened that they have *already* forgotten. As Christian parents point their children to God's faithfulness amid their little tumults, they are guiding them into healthy lifelong patterns.

Family mealtimes provide a strategic opportunity for everyone to share their struggles and practice encouraging one another. As a family, cast the day's stresses on the Lord (1 Pet 5:7). In families that regularly pray at the table together and have family devotionals, each person's heart can rise above the *present* day's strains and pains. Celebrating special days also encourages one another. Just as God called Israel to remember his care for them and their commitments to him through special festivals of remembrance, so families can mark special days with celebration, joy, and reflection. That shows appreciation for each other on a horizontal level and for God on a vertical level. Study after study shows that appreciation in families provides the foundation for stronger relational bonds.[6]

In addition to physical birthdays, your family could add other days, such as the anniversaries of professions of faith and baptisms, special days for significant family events such as recovery from illnesses, household moves, and church calendar seasons like Advent. So many possibilities give you abundant opportunities for creativity. Balance joyous celebrations and solemn reflections on these dates, anchoring to the *past*, anticipating the *future*, and recommitting to the *present*. William Plumer (1802–80) wrote, "Very few days of man's appointing are more fitly observed in a serious, religious way, than the anniversary of one's birth, which was a wonder second only to the new birth."[7]

Family Time Travel Entreaties

Even more important than words of encouragement to your family members is your prayers for them. Speak grace to them, but even more, seek grace for them. Pray with your family regularly. Those prayers will be effective and

---

6. Webb, "Function of Gratitude in Marriage."
7. Plumer, *Studies in the Book of Psalms*, 698.

also serve as models. Think about how you learned to pray. Few Christians *first* learned to pray through a book or sermon on prayer. Instead, most Christians learned to pray by hearing family members' prayers. Parents must show confidence that your heavenly Father also welcomes their asking, seeking, and knocking (Matt 7:7) and will answer (v. 8).

Pray for them, and be humble and honest enough to let them pray for you! John Stott (1921–2011) noted that we must share our burdens for others to bear them! "The general principle is supplied in Galatians 6:2: 'Bear one another's burdens, and so fulfill the law of Christ.' Notice the assumption behind this command: we all have burdens, and God does not mean that we carry them alone. Some people try to. They think it a sign of fortitude not to bother others with their burdens. Such fortitude is certainly brave. However, it is more stoic than Christian."[8] Be open with your family, telling them your burdens so they can pray for you as you pray for their burdens. Let them learn from you the value and vulnerability of prayer.

You must pray more for your family when you are away from them than when you are with them! That is precisely when your family needs your prayers the most. How much more does a child need spiritual alertness while away from parents than when home with them? How much more discipline does a husband or wife need to practice when away from the family on business travel than when safely home? The times when you must be physically absent from your loved ones are hopefully measured in days, not weeks or months, but those extended absences sometimes occur. May you pray for your family so intently that you could say to them, as Paul said to others, "Though I am absent in body, yet I am with you in spirit" (Col 2:5).

For what can you pray for your family? Entreat God that they might live appreciative of the *past* and disciplined in the *present*. Above all, petition God for them to live alert toward their *future*. God honors prayer, and your fervent prayer for your partner or child can protect them in countless ways; some of them you might not even know about this side of heaven. Stand vigilant in prayer that they might live vigilant spiritually. Sometimes, you might even have to pray about dangers they cannot see yet. Undoubtedly, the prodigal son's father devoted daily time to pray for him to come to his senses (Luke 15:17–19)! Was it not part of the great joy of the reunion that God had answered his prayers? When you cannot remind them of anything, you can "remind" God about them, asking him to "remember" them

---

8. Stott, *Message of Galatians*, 157.

graciously. Genesis 19:29 concludes that the rescue of Lot out of Sodom happened because "God remembered Abraham." "It was the prayers of his uncle, not his measly faith that saved him. Lot was not saved on his own merits but through Abraham's intercession."[9]

Even if you could be present physically all the time with family, there will still be things you must pray for them without their knowledge. What is the fine line between nudging toward godly habits and nagging? What is the thin line between encouraging your children and exasperating them (Col 3:21)? When should you speak to them, and when should you stay silent? You can ask God for help discovering where those lines lie, and he will show you what to say and what to pray!

Especially when you cannot continue to speak to a family member about their spiritual needs, godly goals to set, or sins to avoid, you can pray for them! Wise husbands and wives maintain private prayer lists about each other before the Lord. You can pray to the Lord about what you would dare not speak more about to a spouse (out of tender love or because of their exasperated frustration). How much healthier will families be when men and women go vertical with those issues in prayer instead of venting to friends about family strife? Indeed, "your Father who sees in secret" will be inclined to intervene (Matt 6:6). When you get it right and pray for the best things for their spiritual life, you have gotten in step with the Spirit who is interceding for them (Rom 8:26–27)!

Regarding specifics of what to pray for family, you can adapt Paul's prayers for his spiritual children into prayers for your family (Rom 1:8–9; 1 Cor 1:4; Eph 1:15–19; Phil 1:3; Col 1:3; 1 Thess 1:2; 2:13; 3:9–10; 2 Thess 1:3, 11; 2:13–14; 2 Tim 1:3; Phil 4). If you read through these slowly, you will notice that Paul practiced all the transformative time-travel techniques and avoided the toxic time-travel traps. He was always disciplined (chapter 6), alert (chapter 2), and prayed without being anxious (chapter 3), which flowed from appreciation (chapter 4) instead of forgetting God's work in their lives (chapter 5).[10]

When your family knows that they are being prayed for, it is a comfort for them. You show your love for them by praying for them. Sadly, the opposite is true, too. Too little love leads to too little prayer. Your personal pain is multiplied when others fail you by not praying for you! Jesus had to face that awful night in Gethsemane alone, for who but he knew what weighed

---

9. Wenham, *Genesis 16–50*, 59.
10. For a helpful study of Paul's prayers, see Carson, *Praying with Paul*.

on his heart. However, he did request that his inner circle of apostles, Peter, James, and John, stay alert and pray: "And taking with him Peter and the two sons of Zebedee, he began to be sorrowful and troubled. Then he said to them, 'My soul is very sorrowful, even to death; remain here, and watch with me'" (Matt 26:37–38).

Their friend Jesus encouraged alertness and prayer. Why? Explicitly, he warned them to pray in the *present* so that they would not yield to temptation (v. 41). They should have obeyed his warning because he had just announced *in advance* what would happen to them (v. 31). However, his command to watch and pray also implied that they should intercede for him in prayer.[11] He who had always prayed for and guarded them (John 17:8) *now* asked for their spiritual assistance! Shockingly, they failed him three times, "leaving Jesus unsupported in his distress."[12] Pause and reflect on this story! If Jesus needed prayer, how much do your family members?

The Bible gives examples of wise men and women who encouraged and entreated. Abigail appears in David's life just at the right time. Aware of the impending danger, she cannot speak to her husband, Nabal, the fool. He will not listen to others (1 Sam 25:17), and his drunkenness ends all hope of responding to her warning about looming disaster (v. 36). Surely, she entreated the Lord for wisdom about the situation since she could not force her foolish husband to sober up physically and spiritually to do the right things. Then, she placed herself in harm's way and encouraged David not to take vengeance (vv. 30–31). God honored her influence on David and fulfilled her desire, asking him if he would, in the *future*, remember her faithfulness in the *present crisis* (v. 31).

Though David and Nabal could not see the *future* clearly at the moment, Abigail could by faith (vv. 28, 31; Heb 11:1). God rewarded her faithfulness by releasing her from her foolish husband through his imminent death (v. 38) and allowing her to marry David (v. 42). God rewarded David for responding to her insightful wisdom instead of despising her veiled correction (Prov 9:8). Surely, in her marriage, she continued to advise and encourage him as she prayed behind the scenes, and as he moved toward his *future* destiny as Israel's godliest king.

---

11. Carson, *Matthew*, 545.
12. France, *Gospel of Matthew*, 1004.

Family Time Travel Enforcement

Just as the husband and wife encourage each other and their children, both parents work to teach their children all Christ commanded (Deut 6:7; 11:19; Ps 78:4; Prov 22:6; Matt 28:20). The husband as the head of the family has the primary role to both teach the children and correct them when necessary, ensuring that children follows the family's pattern of pursuing godliness. Ephesians 6:1 clarifies the husband's calling in this area as responsibility above and beyond the wife's role: "Fathers, do not provoke your children to anger, but bring them up in the discipline and instruction of the Lord."

Wives can and should enforce the rules, with discipline, as necessary, but the husband should lift that difficult and often discouraging task off his wife's shoulders. Memorization can *prepare* the husband for speaking words of correction and encouragement at the right moments. From memory, he should be able to seize positive teachable moments and use the "strongest and sweetest words for ministering to others in need."[13] The husband, not the wife, stands more accountable to the Lord for the spiritual *future* of his children. In this serious calling, if a man cannot keep his children under control, he does not qualify for spiritual leadership (1 Tim 3:4, 12; Titus 1:6). He must practice his faith domestically *before* preaching it publicly.

Family Spiritual Disciplines Are Linked

Whatever God designs, he designs perfectly! God calls you to your pursuit of him through the spiritual disciplines. Then, they improve the spiritual health of your family and friends. Likewise, as family members and friends seek the Lord through grace, they can love you more. As a master craftsman, God fits together your private and family devotional lives so that they dovetail.

When he heard that his young son had established a pattern of reading the Bible devotionally, President John Quincy Adams (1767–1848) wrote to commend him: "The *earlier* my children begin to read it, the more steadily they pursue the practice of reading it throughout their lives, the more lively and confident will be my hopes that they will prove *useful citizens* to their country, respectable members of society, and *a real blessing to their parents.*"[14]

13. Piper, "If My Words Abide."
14. Adams, *Build Upon the Rock*, 6–7 (emphasis added).

In the Present for the Future

Family Life as Vanishing Vapor and Rejoicing Reunion

If you view your family members as fellow time travelers, there are many benefits. First, remember that they are on "loan" to you for a time, and you do not know for how long; this will change your view of them and the intensity of your investment in them. Charles Spurgeon (1834–92) saw family relationships as leases: "Hold them with a loose hand; do not count that to be freehold which you have only received as a leasehold; do not call that yours which is only lent you, for if you get a thing lent you and it is asked for back, you give it back freely; but if you entertain the notion that it was given you, you do not like to yield it up."[15]

Holding on to your family lightly truly frees you in the *present*. For example, the *present-tense* knowledge that you could lose them will motivate you to pursue their spiritual well-being above all. You actually do have enough time to encourage your spouse, pray for your children, seek the Lord together as a family, attend church, and enjoy fun in your home. Knowing the shortness of time you might have left with them will increase your passion for sharing the gospel with them. You will pray for the best things for them instead of praying mostly about worldly things.

James Boice (1938–2000) urged prayers for the highest priorities. "When you pray for your children, pray that they might do well in school, that they might be kept from sin, that they will develop winsome personalities and make worthwhile contributions in life. But do not fail to entreat God for their salvation. They can gain all these other things. Yet, if they are not saved, they will lose it all."[16]

Second, since you may die *before* some family members, your final words to them can bless them significantly! What adult child does not remember that last conversation with a parent and their final words? You can tell them how to move *forward after* your death, trusting God just as you have. Jonathan Edwards (1703–58) knew his death was imminent and wrote tender words to his daughter, giving her and the family final comfort, knowing they could not be with him at this death. In particular, he wanted Lucy to shift her spiritual gaze to the Father, who would never leave her:

> Dear Lucy, It seems to me to be the will of God that I must shortly leave you; therefore, give my kindest love to my dear wife and tell her that the uncommon union, which has so long subsisted

---

15. Spurgeon, "Last Enemy Destroyed," 647–48.
16. Boice, *Romans*, 1152–53.

between us, has been of such a nature, as I trust is spiritual, and therefore will continue for ever: and I hope she will be supported under so great a trial, and submit cheerfully to the will of God. And as to my children, you are *now* like to be left fatherless; which I hope will be an inducement to you all, to seek a Father who will never fail you.[17]

Third, as some family members go *before* you to heaven, their passage should make you long for that realm of reunion even more! Truly, the bliss of heaven is seeing the glory of God, to which everything else is secondary: "If Christ were not there, heaven would not be heaven to the believer."[18] However, being gathered to one's ancestors (Gen 25:8), parents, spouse, child (2 Sam 12:23), and other relatives is part of God's restoration of all things. Edwards knew he was not saying a final goodbye because he knew that in heaven there would be "the Christian father, and mother, and wife, and child, and friend, with whom we shall renew the holy fellowship of the saints, which was interrupted by death here, but shall be commenced again in the upper sanctuary, and then shall never end."[19]

Church Family as Time Travelers Together

God also gifts believers with a second family. He places each one in a local church to serve and be served. You choose to live in a faith community with others because God expects it and because you cannot make it to heaven without them. As you continue to think more about your time travel from the *past* to the *future*, you will realize how desperately you need a larger, gifted group of fellow time travelers along the way.

Only Christians whom a malfunctioning church has hurt resist committing in the *present* to charge into the *future* alongside their God-given spiritual family. If that describes you, and you are resistant to active church membership, return to the pages of Scripture. Read about the beauty of God's good design for the church. Consult some helpful books on church membership and seek from the Lord more grace to let go of the *past*.

If you cannot forgive and move *forward* from *past* pain, you have a toxic time-traveling disease present in your *present* life. Just as you would not excuse anyone from abandoning their relationship with Jesus because

---

17. Edwards, *Works*, 1:ccxx (emphasis added).
18. Boston, *Whole Works*, 254.
19. Edwards, *Ethical Writings*, 372n1.

another Christian hurt them, do not give yourself an excuse to live a dangerously detached spiritual life away from a local church. Seek a new, better church, grounded in the *past*, in "the faith that was *once* for all delivered to the saints" (Jude 3) living together in happy holiness awaiting the *future* return of her bridegroom (Rev 19:7–8; emphasis added).

Members and Ministers Together for Time Travel

Notice the choice to discuss church members and church ministers together. You might initially think of them as very different types of people. However, the biblical view of believers, restored through the Protestant Reformation, is called the doctrine of the priesthood of believers. Upon receiving new spiritual life, God makes each believer a priest, with the privilege of direct access to God and the ability to minister God's grace to other Christians! No Christian is self-sufficient or able to live alone spiritually, but when the church gathers, its members live "full of goodness, filled with all knowledge and able to instruct one another" (Rom 15:14).

God does give some special gifts to lead and feed, such as men qualified to be elders (1 Tim 3:1–7; 5:17; Titus 1:5–9). Nevertheless, they serve differently, not with a different quality than others. In a sermon, Charles Spurgeon (1834–92) emphasized that everyday, ordinary service is as precious to Jesus as ministerial service: "Why Mary, you can serve Christ as much in making beds, as I can in making sermons; and you can be as much a true servant of Christ in dusting a room, as I can in administering discipline in a church."[20]

The unique responsibilities of ministers are joyful and weighty. Yet the Bible elevates the importance of the work of fellow members in your church, who can minister to you even as you minister to them. Even the great apostle Paul expected to be blessed by the faith of Christians he would meet in the *future*, but who were *presently* unknown to him: "We may be mutually encouraged by each other's faith, both yours and mine" (Rom 1:12). He even appealed for urgent entreaties for himself *now* well *before* they had met him face-to-face (Rom 15:30).

---

20. Spurgeon, "Christ's Estimate of His People," 463.

The "So Much the More" of Ministers

God requires of ministers what you assume about them, that they should be mature Christians (1 Tim 3:6). Your ministers should have walked *ahead* of you in time-travel sanctification, being a little farther down the road of transformation. Additionally, since God empowers those he gifts, you can expect ministers to excel in the roles of spiritual feeding and leading beyond those of the average layperson. By modeling maturity and explaining God's words to you, they point *forward* as time travel guides on the same journey as you. They know from Scripture and personal experience what may lie *ahead* of you and how you should respond when you encounter challenges.

Let the phrase "so much the more" remind you that ministers should be more mature than their church members and able to assist them. For example, it falls primarily to ministers to enforce healthy spiritual practices in the church instead of just using encouragement and entreaties. They must lead in practicing biblical discipline for the souls that have gone astray. The whole church may have to get involved (Matt 18:17; 1 Cor 5:4–5; 2 Cor 2:6), but leaders should be directing such redemptive rescue attempts.

Members Together for Mutual Alertness for the Future

For many reasons Christians must watch over their souls and stay alert toward the *future*. Among them is the responsibility to care for fellow members and meet their specific needs, something you cannot do well while hindered by unrepentant personal sin.[21] You expect that your surgeon will do an excellent job, assuming he will not be drunk! But showing up at church intoxicated with sin and stumbling along spiritually is spiritual malpractice toward others. If you have repented of sins, then you are extra *pre*pared to help others, but if you are trying to cling to Jesus and sins at the same time, you cannot save yourself, much less others.

Paul wanted the Christians in Thessalonica to respond to each other's needs: "And we urge you, brothers, admonish the idle, encourage the fainthearted, help the weak, be patient with them all. See that no one repays anyone evil for evil, but always seek to do good to one another and to everyone" (1 Thess 5:14–15). Meeting the different needs of different types of people requires discernment. You are not to get it backward by encouraging the idle while admonishing the fainthearted! Mutual soul care will require

---

21. Challies, "Against Yous, Yous Only Have I Sinned."

that you were walking in the Spirit in your recent *past* when you appear in members' lives in the *present* to point them toward the *future*.

While the ministers in Thessalonica would be caring for believers, Paul intentionally appealed to the whole church for whole-church soul care: "This pastoral responsibility is not placed solely in the hands of the leadership but delegated to all the church members. Although the leaders played an important role within the congregation (v. 12), maintaining the well-being of the Christian community did not fall to them exclusively."[22] Church members who live in spiritual peace are *pre*pared for opportunities to minister peace to one another.[23] Further, staying spiritually alert to dangers to yourself and others will free you from apathy, an "unholy contentment with the status quo" in yourself and others.[24]

A sensitive awareness that others need "to wake up" may lead you to speak directly to them; at other times, you will privately pray to God for them. Often, God will call you to both, first vertical prayer for others followed by verbal prodding. Dietrich Bonhoeffer (1906–45) contrasted the compassion of a loving rebuke with the cruelty of silence, adding that "nothing can be more compassionate than that severe reprimand which calls another Christian in one's community back from the path of sin. When we allow nothing but God's word to stand between us, judging and helping, it is a service of mercy. Then it is not we who are judging: God alone judges, and God's judgment is helpful and healing."[25]

Those words of ministry may include both encouragements in seasons of sorrow and exhortations to resist the deadly soul-hardening effects of sin (Heb 3:11–12; Jas 5:19–20). That watchfulness *"today"* in the *present* will keep others from failing spiritually in their *future*. On your part, even as you exhort others, you must remain teachable. When you correct a Christian, be gentle (Matt 5:5)! John Newton (1725–1807) encouraged remembering that in the *future*, both you and the one you correct will soon live together in heaven forever.[26] That *future-oriented*, heaven-bound view of other believers in the *present* will calm your heart and temper your words with love.

---

22. Green, *Letters to the Thessalonians*, 252.
23. Lloyd-Jones, *Healing and the Scriptures*, 71.
24. House, *Community*, 201.
25. Bonhoeffer, *Life Together and Prayerbook*, 105.
26. Newton, *Works*, 269.

Not only will you have words for others, but they will have words of instruction and even correction for you. God will test your humility when that happens, and your positive or negative response to correction will demonstrate your wisdom or foolishness. Will you be mature enough to receive as love hard but healing words (Prov 27:6)? Lessen the sting of constructive criticism by continuing to think about spiritual time travel. Scott Sauls writes, "Because we are not *yet* what we are meant to be, we need people to remind us that we have not *arrived*. We need honest voices helping us see the sin in ourselves that we cannot see and to confront us when we need confronting."[27] Accepting the words of others will keep us alert spiritually and on the path of growth.

Members Together for Mutual Appreciation in the Present

In a world that rushes toward the *future*, wanting to build bridges toward *tomorrow* but willing to forget the *past*, members can help one another cultivate appreciation. Steer conversations from negative things in the current news to "anything worthy of praise," including positive things God has done in the world (Phil 4:8). Come together *pre*pared for mutual meditation, sharing what positive things you have been reading in God's word and how God has answered prayers. This will help you replace negative discussions of world events and politics with edifying, eternal things.

Speaking such spiritual words to others will come naturally from your thoughtful meditations on God's word. In fact, if you do not regularly share the joy of Scripture with others, perhaps you should reevaluate whether you are engaging enough with God's word. Linda Allcock links private meditation to public conversations: "Biblical meditation is talking to yourself about God's commands. It is only natural that this will overflow into talking to other people about them."[28] Ask yourself what dominates your conversations with other Christians. Are less helpful topics like sports, politics, and entertainment consuming those conversations? Commit to steering conversations so that you and others become more appreciative and less stressed. You can even help others get excited about their devotional opportunities!

Sharing God's golden words (Ps 19:10) with others will invigorate you and them. You bless others by telling of God's *past* works for you and

---

27. Sauls, *Gentle Answer*, 121 (emphasis added).
28. Allcock, *Deeper Still*, 102.

his great *present* faithfulness. This is the power of a Christian's testimonies to grace! How a Christian, just diagnosed with cancer, needs to overhear others in the church testifying to God's goodness through the valleys of the dark shadows of death (Ps 23:4)! How greatly do Christian newlyweds, beginning to encounter the un*fore*seen challenges of marriage, need to hear the joy of the couple testifying to God's faithfulness in carrying them along to their 50th anniversary!

It is not just the older and more seasoned saints called to encourage! The zeal of new Christians is a spark that can ignite the flames of faith again in others. Whatever your season of life and experiences, when you gather with others, be an encourager, intentionally increasing appreciation in others! Be quick to speak God's praises to others. Be slow to share about the negatives of your life, and when you do, share about them to be encouraged, not pitied! In Christ, the church is a community that calls to each other: "Through him then let us continually offer up a sacrifice of praise to God, that is, the fruit of lips that acknowledge his name" (Heb 13:15).

Members Together for Mutual Discipline in the Present

When you see other believers at church, realize that they are demonstrating discipline by simply showing up. Satan works overtime to convince Christians that church ranks less important than other activities and that there is no urgent need to be physically present. We have all heard the subtle but sinister otherworldly whispers, "Just skip church or catch it online from your couch! You could go to church *today*, but take it easy! You deserve it!"

The author of Hebrews repeatedly made perseverance and discipline in the Christian life a joint project. He wisely warned against the ancient temptation of skipping church. This temptation is still alive *today*: "And let us consider how to stir up one another to love and good works, not neglecting to meet together, as is the habit of some, but encouraging one another, and all the more as you see the Day drawing near" (Heb 10:24–25). This verse is a gold mine of transformative time travel. With an eye to the *future* coming of Christ ("the Day"), you should, in the *present*, keep motivating one another to disciplined lives of loving and doing good deeds. This is moving in the opposite direction of those who have, in the *past*, developed an undisciplined pattern of neglected gathering.

Neglecting the regular gatherings of your church family is dangerous for every believer. As long as God gives you the physical strength to get out of the house, go to church! If your strength fails, then you keep up with your forever family from home. Even homebound members can stay informed about their church's ministries and pray fervently for members and ministers. Paul's letter writing and prayer life demonstrated that you can choose to stay connected with other believers in spirit even when absent in the body (Col 2:5).

You cannot fully help others live alertly or obey many of the Bible's many other "one another" commands if you regularly miss church gatherings.[29] You can hear or watch excellent teaching from home. However, how can you observe others and act at the right moment to encourage or exhort those in need? There is a primacy of physical presence required for effective ministry, whether that is to with "one voice glorify" God (Rom 15:6), to learn together, to rejoice together, or to weep together (Rom 12:15). Even an apostle, writing an inspired letter to a church, could long to be physically present with the recipients rather than to just write to them. Complete joy could only come for John when he could be with believers: "Though I have much to write to you, I would rather not use paper and ink. Instead, I hope to come to you and talk face to face so that our joy may be complete" (2 John 2:12). The intimacy of that face-to-face interaction was necessary for full fellowship and his complete joy.[30]

When you gather with members for worship and study, God magnifies himself more, you are more sanctified, and others are more encouraged. Likewise, watching others worship, give, and serve inspires you to stay disciplined. You are joining together with believers *ahead* of you in their spiritual walk with the Lord and those *behind* you, perhaps struggling and lagging far *behind* you. You are worshiping with those suffering yet faithful and others living in abundance yet still faithful. You stir up each other's faith: "Have not you been stirred up by hearing the singing of others? Others will therefore also be stirred up by your singing."[31] Then, together, you sit under the teaching of God's word and learn from God's gifted and called teachers. The Holy Spirit also uses this time to stir up your generosity through the patterns of others (2 Cor 9:2).[32] The apostles likely never forgot the example of the widow's "two small copper coins" (Mark 12:41–45). She

---

29. Lloyd-Jones, *Christian Soldier*, 91.
30. Barker, "2 John," 366.
31. Brakel, *Christian's Reasonable Service*, 4:36–37.
32. Kistemaker and Hendriksen, *Second Epistle to the Corinthians*, 305.

had given all she had, just as they would someday when called to lay down their very lives for their Jesus.

Thinking about others during the Sunday sermons will make you a better listener and learner, too! If you are concerned about all members in your church instead of just your soul, you will pay attention to sermons that do not pertain to you *yet* or any longer because they apply to others right *now*.[33] Think of the young single woman in her twenties listening to a sermon on marriage roles. She can obviously pray about those truths regarding her *future* marriage and how she might live in godly ways in the *future*. However, right *now*, in the service, she can *immediately* pray in the *present* for the married couples in the church. Her intercession for them *now* works powerfully. *Later*, when she gets married, their models of faithfulness will minister to her!

Picture an elderly widower on Father's Day hearing yet *again* what used to apply to him: the biblical admonitions for raising young children in the fear of the Lord. Instead of grumping about a sermon that means nothing to him, preached to him by a younger preacher still struggling to raise his children, he can pray for young families in the middle of the battle to raise children for the Lord. How self-absorbed and arrogant it would be for any Christian on any Sunday morning to assume that since the sermon did not stir them, it must not have been a timely message for the congregation!

Ministers Entreating for Their Member's Futures

Godly ministers watch over their members' souls like they do their own. Paul exhorted the elders of the Ephesian church to "pay careful attention to yourselves and to all the flock in which the Holy Spirit has made you overseers, to care for the church of God, which he obtained with his own blood" (Acts 20:28). Like members, ministers offer private words of encouragement to members, especially in challenging seasons of life. They also frequently entreat God for the sheep over which he keeps watch (Heb 13:17).[34] What a wonderful but weighty responsibility for a minister to entreat God for his people.

When ministers intercede for members, they follow the *past* model of the Good Shepherd. Jesus prayed for the alertness and safety of his sheep in exclusive, intimate, and effective ways (John 17:9), even for those who

33. Gundersen, "Why You Need Sermons."
34. Spurgeon, *Lectures to My Students*, 47.

would *later* be sifted and found wanting (Luke 22:31–32). Peter was restored spiritually only through the effectual prayer of the Shepherd who prayed for him. Solely "because of Jesus's prayer, Peter's denial did not turn into apostasy."[35] Not just the apostles but all genuine believers *now* benefit from the Good Shepherd who prays for them. In the *present* and *forever*, he is their advocate (1 John 2:1), who always lives to intercede (Heb 7:25).

Just as a minister prays for his people, they should be praying for him. Remember that no matter how gifted, your pastor is a time traveler like you. They also walk through seasons of success and painful struggles. Remembering their human weaknesses will help you view them as those in need of prayer. Staying alert is a community project, and pastors need the prayers of their people, too.[36] Sometimes, praying for a minister and private encouragement of him may not be enough! Like Archippus (Col 4:17), a minister may need a public exhortation from the congregation to fulfill his duties!

Ministers Encouraging Members through Teaching

Ministers encourage members primarily through teaching, a role to which they are uniquely called and gifted. At their best, they engage in spiritual time travel in their teaching, moving *back* into the *past* through diligent study to discover the author's *original* intent for the *original* audiences and then bringing that message *forward* to apply it to their members' *contemporary* situations. They meditate both on Scripture and on their members as they seek to apply Scripture accurately to their listeners' lives.

Writing to preachers about preaching, John Stott (1921–2011) envisioned preaching as building a bridge between the *past* and the *future*, between the biblical world and the modern world. He wrote, "Our task is to enable God's revealed truth to flow out of the Scriptures into the lives of the men and women of *today*."[37] John Flavel (1627–91) referred to this preaching skill as prudence and urged its practice: "Ministerial prudence discovers itself in the choice of such subjects, as the needs of our people's souls do most require and call for. A prudent minister will study the souls of his people more than the best human books in his library."[38]

---

35. Stein, *Luke*, 52.
36. MacArthur, *Different by Design*, 115.
37. Chester, *Stott on the Christian Life*, 138 (emphasis added).
38. Flavel, *Whole Works*, 6:571.

This "expository" preaching carefully applies the text's "main points and subpoints" to members.[39] Through such teaching, God directs people to make many different U-turns—turning from anxiety to alertness, from amnesia to appreciation, and from undisciplined to disciplined living. Ministers work toward Paul's goal of "warning everyone and teaching everyone with all wisdom, that we may present everyone mature in Christ" (Col 1:28). Pastors teach by more than words, for they travel through different seasons of their own lives, all in front of watching eyes.[40] God has planned for the authority of their spoken words and the authenticity of their lives to blend beautifully.

God demands that pastors preach and model God's truths repeatedly, even to those who have heard it *before*. Just as Christians need to preach the gospel to themselves every day individually, leaders must "stir up" their people by patient reminder (1 Pet 1:12–14; 4:11). Called not to innovation but *re*iteration, a pastor must *re*member, as Peter did, that "believers know the gospel, and yet they must, in a sense, relearn it every day."[41]

Ministers and Members Encouraging Each Other

Even during public preaching, members should participate in time travel together! They can contribute to the preaching of God's word by responding. When the pastor begins preaching God's word, the responsiveness of the congregation should lift his preaching even higher.[42] They can pray for themselves to receive the words with humility for the profit of their souls. Indeed, the window of time to respond to God is short: "Therefore, as the Holy Spirit says, '*Today*, if you hear his voice, do not harden your hearts as in the rebellion, on the day of testing in the wilderness'" (Heb 3:7–8). Alert believers can pray for others around them, even *first*-time unknown visitors. Is not eternity at stake each Sunday? Surely it is! Sadly, too many preachers stare out over congregations with expressions that show spiritual dullness and disinterest! Be careful! Boredom while listening to sermons reveals a time-travel issue as the uninterested person does not *yet* think about the *future* regarding God's *present* word to them from the *past*.

---

39. Chappell, *Christ-Centered Preaching*, 129.
40. Spurgeon, "Why Lay Aside?"
41. Schreiner, *1, 2 Peter, Jude*, 309.
42. Lloyd-Jones, *Preaching and Preachers*, 83–84.

Ministers Driven by Future Alertness

What should keep a minister committed to intense and careful study week *after* week? Those who stay motivated have an eye on the *future* eternity! They regularly time travel, thinking about the quickly perishing souls to whom they preach, alive in the *present* and not guaranteed a *tomorrow*. Awareness of quickly approaching eternity motivates energetic ministry. They seek to pour out their very lives in preaching that changes their people. Tom Nettles writes that "meditation, prayer, right motives, right spirit, holy fervor—an incorporation of truth into the very soul—must all precede and gush forth in the task of preaching, for the preacher must 'send forth all his soul.'"[43]

TIME TRAVEL TOGETHER AND OTHER FORMS OF TIME TRAVEL

Having established time-traveling goals and the proper attitudes toward the *future*, *past*, and *present*, which are alertness, appreciation, and discipline, and *now* recommitted to traveling *forward* in communities, we are *p*repared to investigate what lies *ahead* of each of us, the ultimate testing and triumph of our faith through decline and death.

RECOMMENDED READING ABOUT TIME TRAVEL TOGETHER

Christopher Ash, *Married for God: Making Your Marriage the Best It Can Be* (Wheaton, IL: Crossway, 2016).

Dietrich Bonhoeffer, *Life Together and Prayerbook of the Bible*, Dietrich Bonhoeffer Works, vol. 5, trans. Gerhard Ludwig Müller and Albrecht Schönherr (Minneapolis: Fortress Press, 2002).

Matthew D. Haste and Robert L. Plummer, *Held in Honor: Wisdom for Your Marriage from Voices of the Past* (Christian Focus: Ross-shire, Scotland, UK, 2015).

Jonathan Leeman, *Church Membership: How the World Knows Who Represents Jesus* (Wheaton, IL: Crossway, 2012).

John Piper, *This Momentary Marriage: A Parable of Permanence* (Wheaton, IL: Crossway Books, 2009).

---

43. Nettles, *Ready for Reformation?*, 109.

MEMORIZATION PASSAGES ABOUT TIME TRAVEL TOGETHER

Proverbs 27:6
Faithful are the wounds of a friend;
profuse are the kisses of an enemy.

1 Thessalonians 5:14–15
And we urge you, brothers, admonish the idle,
encourage the fainthearted,
help the weak, be patient with them all.
See that no one repays anyone evil for evil,
but always seek to do good to one another and to everyone.

Hebrews 3:12–13 (emphasis added)
Take care, brothers, lest there be in any of you
an evil, unbelieving heart,
leading you to fall away from the living God.
But exhort one another every day,
as long as it is called *"today,"* that none of you
may be hardened by the deceitfulness of sin.

Hebrews 10:24–25
And let us consider how to stir up one another
to love and good works,
not neglecting to meet together, as is the habit of some,
but encouraging one another, and all the more
as you see the Day drawing near.

CHAPTER EIGHT

Time Travel Tested by Decline and Death

> No man would find it difficult to die who died every day. He would have practised it so often, that he would only have to die but *once* more; like the singer who has been through his rehearsals, and is perfect in his part, and has but to pour forth the notes.
>
> CHARLES SPURGEON (1834–92)[1]

Charles Dickens (1812–70) began *A Tale of Two Cities* with the famous words, "It was the best of times, it was the worst of times, it was the age of wisdom, it was the age of foolishness."[2] What perfect descriptions of the last seasons of life: decline and death. This finale of our time-traveling melody may be the best or worst, depending on our transformative

---

1. Emphasis added.
2. Dickens, *Tale of Two Cities*, 13.

time-travel skills. Will we *pre*pare to approach it with wisdom, or will we fall into despair in our *last* days? People move inexorably toward death, but they tend to recognize this reality *later* in life than in their "prime" years. Pondering mortality usually begins for people when they have significant birthdays or experience sobering transitions like a midlife crisis, an empty nest, retirement, the death of parents, or a health crisis.

DECLINE, DESCENT, AND DEATH

Typically, people experience a slow decline with a descent steepening over time, followed by a short season of rapid decline into death. We will look at the decline, typically through middle age into the senior years, and the shorter season of death as separate life stages. Some live a very long time and remain healthy. Still, death comes for us all, the inevitable penalty for sinners (Rom 5:12). James reminded his readers not to *pre*sume by planning what they expected would happen, reminding them that "you do not know what *tomorrow* will bring. What is your life? For you are a mist that appears for a little *time* and then vanishes" (Jas 4:14). The uncertainty of how much time anyone has left shows the awful error of people who *pre*-plan to live it up *now* and repent in old age. That is sinfully *pre*sumptuous *now* and will prove to be supremely foolish *later*.

Present Avoidance or Anticipation

For the unbelievers, the season of declining health begins the worst season of their lives, ending with their worst days on earth, the gradual loss of everything good *forever*. In contrast, believers live in victory over anxiety, maintain alertness, increase appreciation, and strive for discipline while time traveling together with others in their community. Therefore, they can enjoy the *last* seasons as the best of times. Their lives will cumulate with the best day, completing the race of faith and entering into an eternity of joy, described in the famous words of Paul: "My desire is to depart and be with Christ, for that is far better" (Phil 1:23).

Looking at the *past* and into the *future*, Paul could write to Timothy in his *last* letter *before* his martyrdom about the happy completion of his earthly journey: "The time of my departure has come. I have fought the good fight, I have finished the race, I have kept the faith. Henceforth there is laid up for me the crown of righteousness, which the Lord, the righteous judge, will award to me on that day, and not only to me but also to all who have loved his appearing" (2 Tim 4:6–8). Content with his *past* and contemplating his *future*, Paul's declaration has inspired saints for centuries as they *pre*pared for the end of earthly life.

However, a good *beginning* in the Christian life does not guarantee an equally successful *ending*. Realize that the fight of faith ends only at your *last* breath. You cannot coast to the end of the Christian life. No one gets *early* retirement from the daily battle for sanctification. No one earns a sabbatical from the practice of the spiritual disciplines. Consequently, your decisions *today* about embracing meditative time travel will determine the kind of spiritual stamina and resources you have when the winter of your life comes.

Will you have enough spiritual resources accumulated to make it to the end? Financial advisors work to ensure that their clients accumulate enough money for their senior years. Similarly, wise pastors motivate believers to store up spiritual wealth for the challenges of *later* life. Listen to their teachings carefully and strengthen yourself for the *last* lap of the race. Be careful! If you are a careless believer who never thinks much beyond your daily life, your final leg of the journey to heaven may be a failure, an "age of foolishness."[3] With so much at stake, Christians should think much about their *future* life. Due to greater exposure to sudden deaths around them and perhaps greater faith, there were times in Christian history when death frightened Christians less than *today*. John Wesley (1703–91) and Charles Spurgeon (1834–92) both liked to proclaim that because of the gospel, "our people die well."[4]

Because they live for their worldly passions, unbelievers naturally ignore decline and death as long as possible. When it finally approaches them, it brings terror. The affluence of the Western, developed world amplifies that avoidance even more. Even as far *back* in American history as the 1830s, one could detect a shift from thinking about death to maximizing the *present* life exclusively. Instead of living with a sobering awareness of approaching death, Alexis de Tocqueville (1805–59) wrote about the functional but fictitious immortality of Americans:

> The inhabitant of the United States attaches himself to the goods of this world as if he were assured of not dying, and he rushes so precipitately to grasp those that pass within his reach that one

---

3. Dickens, *Tale of Two Cities*, 13.
4. Wesley and Eayrs, *Letters*, 414; Spurgeon, *Farm Sermons*, 326.

would say he fears at each instant he will cease to live *before* he has enjoyed them. He grasps them all but without clutching them, and he soon allows them to escape from his hands so as to run after new enjoyments.... Death finally comes, and it stops him *before* he has grown weary of this useless pursuit of a complete felicity that always flees from him.[5]

Death is a curse for those who intend to live comfortably only in this *present* life. They are consumed with pursuing physical pleasures and believe their destinies are determined by mere chance.[6] Why would unbelievers not fear the end? However, for Christians, God reverses death's curse. Through the grace of the gospel, Jesus has made death the doorway to heaven. It is the "last gasp of a defeated enemy who opens a door to paradise."[7] At death, God's children will see that His grace extended across the whole span of their lives, from the womb to the tomb. Therefore, even *now*, Christians can develop their meditative time-travel skills, contemplate death in *advance*, and rejoice.

Spiritually minded seniors can thrive through the years of decline and sometimes even celebrate their deaths. For example, Billy Graham (1918–2018) liked to speak of his *forth*coming death as a triumph by invoking humor to make this point. Envisioning what would be said when he died, he said, "Someday you will read or hear that Billy Graham is dead. Don't you believe a word of it. I shall be more alive than I am *now*. I will just have changed my address. I will have gone into the presence of God."[8] The "*already*-not yet" blessings of the Christian life will give way to the blessed condition of beholding God in the face of Christ (Matt 5:8).

INTENSIFYING TESTS OF FAITH

The whole Christian journey includes a series of tests of your faith. God designed this process to purify you, bring him glory, and result in your *eventual* honor in Christ: "In this you rejoice, though *now* for a little while, if necessary, you have been grieved by various trials, so that the tested genuineness of your faith—more precious than gold that perishes though it is

---

5. Tocqueville, *Democracy in America*, 512 (emphasis added).
6. Calvin, *Commentary to the Hebrews*, 72–73.
7. Piper, *Taste and See*, 273.
8. Lindgren, "Someday You Will Read," para. 3. Graham was quoting D. L. Moody (emphasis added).

tested by fire—may be found to result in praise and glory and honor at the revelation of Jesus Christ" (1 Pet 1:6–7).

Ahead of you, tests will start coming more frequently and more intensely. For example, anxiety can worsen through middle age into old age. But as people age spiritually, they can grow in the appreciation that kills anxiety! Christian children, teens, and adults have many reasons to be thankful! Yet how much more should senior adults filled to the brim with memories of God's goodness reflect and rejoice? That appreciation for God will support them, as the recollection of *past* blessings arms them to fight against *present* troubles. Even negative experiences have built their faith. In hindsight, they can see that God even used challenging things for good. This strengthens them to believe that "for those who love God all things work together for good, for those who are called according to his purpose" (Rom 8:28). God never abandons his children or his long-term plans for them.

Until your last breath, God has planned and will bring to completion his good works through you (Eph 2:10). Many of these good works you will complete despite mounting physical problems. Martyn Lloyd-Jones (1899–1981) concluded that "the most difficult period of all in life is the middle period,"[9] and then comes the end when "old age tests us."[10] But empowered by the grace of God and striving to run your race, you will prove your faith's genuineness to yourself and others, bringing God glory through your trials.

INTENSIFYING TEMPTATIONS

Since trials intensify toward the end, you must expect to encounter more temptations. John Flavel (1627–91) warned that you must always watch over your heart, especially as you near the *end*:

> When the child of God draws nigh to eternity, the adversary makes his last effort; and as he cannot win the soul from God, as he cannot dissolve the bond which unites the soul to Christ, his great design is to awaken fears of death, to fill the mind with aversion and horror at the thoughts of dissolution from the body. Hence, what shrinking from a separation, what fear to grasp death's cold hand, and unwillingness to depart, may sometimes be observed in the people of God.[11]

---

9. Lloyd-Jones, *Spiritual Depression*, 192.
10. Lloyd-Jones, *Expository Sermons on 2 Peter*, 49.
11. Flavel, *Whole Works*, 5:490.

The alertness you have been carefully cultivating over the years will help you spot this spiritual danger. When the body is failing, and sometimes even the mind falters, the Holy Spirit will make your faith stand firm!

INTENSIFYING TRIUMPHS

By faith, aided by happy meditative thoughts of God's *past* and *future* grace, you will not stumble but will run toward the *end* of your life with the most remarkable and powerful testimony. You can imitate Paul's rejoicing that "though our outer man is decaying, yet our inner man is being renewed day by day" (2 Cor 4:16). Like David ran toward his enemy Goliath (1 Sam 17:48), anticipating the faith victory he *fore*saw and *pre*dicted (vv. 27, 46–47), you will pick up the pace in your race of faith!

Your witness of increasing spiritual strength in seasons of decreasing physical weakness will show the authenticity of your faith to unbelieving friends and family. You will show them something in you, authentic and aggressive faith, that they lack. Just as many relive their wedding ceremony while watching another's wedding, watching your decline will prompt others to think about how they will or will not handle those ever-closer days. God plans for unbelievers to see your supernatural hope (1 Pet 3:15). They "will recognize by the way believers respond to difficulties that their hope is in God rather than in pleasant earthly circumstances."[12]

The triumph of your faith through the *final* testing of your faith will also inspire other believers, who are your fellow time travelers. Attitudes and actions will speak loudly, even without a voice. Jonathan Edwards (1703–58), cited several times as a model of spiritual maturity, died as he lived, confident in God's sovereign *past* grace and reassured about *future* grace. As you would expect, *after* a lifetime of practicing quiet contentment in Christ throughout his life, his death was the pinnacle of his peaceful faith. Reflecting on his last days, his attending physician and friend wrote: "Never did any mortal man more fully and clearly evidence the sincerity of all his professions, by one continued, universal, calm, cheerful resignation, and patient submission to the Divine will, through every stage of his disease, than he; not so much as one discontented expression, nor the least appearance of murmuring, through the whole."[13]

---

12. Schreiner, *1, 2 Peter, Jude*, 175.
13. Edwards, *Works*, 1:ccxx.

INTENSIFYING CHOICES

Wherever you are in your physical and spiritual seasons of life, you have vital decisions at hand. Many books and sermons focus on the call for younger generations to take up the cross and follow Christ faithfully, but what fantastic opportunities abound for older Christians! How can you improve the last seasons of your life? Making resolutions about how you intend to live and grow will help. Consider adopting four commitments. They would be helpful for any stage of life, but especially during the declining years. They are time travel commitments, anchoring to the *past* and reaching the *future*. Two resolutions look *ahead*, and two look *back* to your *past*.

The Bible often speaks counterculturally, pushing back against worldly assumptions. This is clear as you consider the forks in the road *ahead*. To resolve to follow Christ more intensely toward the end is to go against the flow. You can gain speed instead of losing it as you enter the latter stages of your life, but that is not what many of your peers will choose. Your life will ripen instead of rot. It should be a season of soul-ripening with an expanded "capacity for discerning choosing."[14] This is the triumph of the "inner self," possible only for believers, as it moves in the opposite direction of the "outer self" that is "wasting away" (2 Cor 4:16).

1. Resolved: To Choose Courageous Acceleration over Cautious Anxiety

Slowly weakening physical and mental abilities subtly signal the ongoing aging process, yet the two possible responses to such signals move in diametrically different directions! Most take the wrong path of caution and partial paralysis. The mottos of this road are well known: "Just play it safe," "Minimize your risks," and "Coast along"! These slogans might sound like good advice, but how misinformed they are! Such advice could be costly for your soul, too, for you must stay on the "narrow," "hard" way of following Jesus (Matt 7:14). Christians have no "time" for a last season of stopping kingdom work for "playing softball and collecting shells."[15]

Instead of seeing the end as a time to slow down, picture the signs of decline as the two-minute warning in football, the last lap of the race, or the last round of the boxing match. In light of all that God has given (*past*

---

14. Packer, *Finishing Our Course*, 19.
15. Piper, *Don't Waste Your Life*, 46.

appreciation recalled through meditation) and all that God will provide, what do you have to lose? Why not be courageous? Accelerate, do not decelerate, spiritually and relationally! Let the words of Jesus ring in your ears: "Whoever loves his life loses it, and whoever hates his life in this world will keep it for eternal life" (John 12:25).

Unlike unbelievers, who live in slavery to the fear of death (Heb 2:15), death should never terrorize you. Paul could even taunt the broken power of death, overturned by the resurrection of Jesus: "O death, where is your victory? O death, where is your sting?" (1 Cor 15:55). Since you have nothing from your *past* sin to fear, why feel timid when God calls you to risk even more, to give more, to pray more, to share the gospel more, and to worship him more boldly? You *now* have the spirit "not of fear but of power and love and self-control" (1 Tim 1:7). Your *future* stands secure, too! Peter urged Christians to remember their promised "inheritance that is imperishable, undefiled, and unfading, kept in heaven for you, who by God's power are being guarded through faith for a salvation ready to be revealed in the last time" (1 Pet 1:4–5). The Holy Spirit guards your inheritance, keeping it safe for you!

In addition to fears about the *future* slowing them down, unbelievers often have unresolved pain from their *past*. Unable to meditate biblically about their *past* suffering and harboring bitter, cynical fears that dissuade them from risking *again*, they play it safe, afraid of all the things that might harm them again. However, the believer clings to the hope that God has been working all things for good (Rom 8:28) and that all suffering in this life will someday seem like nothing (v. 18). As a result, they have learned that when God calls them to do more challenging things, even things they never succeeded at in younger years, they can attempt them with courage. Jesus will be with them always, especially as they seek to live out and spread the gospel (Matt 28:20). John Piper writes, "If death (I said, death—no pulse, cold, gone!)—if death is no longer a fear, we're free, really free. Free to take any risk under the sun for Christ and love. No more bondage to anxiety."[16]

When the inevitable seasons of sickness come, use them to quicken your pace spiritually instead of letting them slow you down. As badly as you may feel, you can pray, recite aloud verses hidden in your heart, and read and listen to deeper Christian books, even from a hospital bed. Upon recovery, if the Lord so wills that, you will discover that God used your days

---

16. Piper, *Joy to the World*, 40.

of physical convalescence as spiritual boot camp, *preparing* you to march *forward*. Thomas Chalmers (1780–1847) suffered from a liver disease that removed him from preaching for six months and pastoral ministry for an entire year. However, he emerged from that bed of sickness a spiritually improved man! He lived with a new sense of the "insignificance of time" and "human mortality," a new passion for deeper doctrines he *once* resisted, and an increased zeal for preaching God's word.[17]

More righteous risk-taking should drive you to serve God more zealously in the church, to give more to God's kingdom *now*, and to evangelize family and friends more energetically. Start taking "risks" *now*! Begin by seeking God more intensely through the spiritual disciplines. In *earlier* years, you might have thought it too "risky" to devote extended time to Bible reading, meditation, and prayer. You felt too busy, but *now* you see your mistaken thinking. Lemuel Haynes (1753–1833) noted that thinking of death improves spiritual perception: "When men are apprehensive that they are drawing near the eternal world, they commonly have very different views of many external duties that they despise in days of health."[18] Nothing is more important than fellowship with God *now* in the *present* that *prepares* you for *future* fellowship forever. Cultivate the desire to sense God's presence like the psalmist: "O God, you are my God; earnestly I seek you; my soul thirsts for you; my flesh faints for you, as in a dry and weary land where there is no water" (Ps 63:1).

Think of when you last tried to memorize a verse or a passage from the Bible. You might protest that you never could memorize, or perhaps you *once* could memorize in younger years but cannot any longer. Those thoughts are of the devil, who desperately wants to discourage memorization. Yet anyone can memorize, except those suffering from severe neurological issues. Maturing saints can be expert memorizers! Why? Because they have learned experientially what a child has not yet: the full value of having God's word with you anytime. While children show remarkable raw intellectual ability to memorize, they lack the seasoned appreciation of its lasting value. Those children will, in the *future*, learn the full value of the verses that seniors *already* cherish.

Be courageous enough to attempt to memorize or memorize again! Who cares if it takes you a month to memorize a verse? That would let you memorize any of the eighteen psalms with six verses or less in just

---

17. Hanna, *Life of Thomas Chalmers*, 28.
18. Anyabwile, *May We Meet*, 87.

half a year! For example, begin with Ps 1. Use this as the start of a journey of intensifying your *latter*-age quest to be the one who "meditates day and night" (Ps 1:2) and gains the promise of being a godly tree "that yields its fruit in its season, and its leaf does not wither" (v. 4). Do not let cynical "been there, done that" or "been there, couldn't do that" attitudes cut you off from the greatest spiritual satisfaction in your *later* years.

Try a powerful strategy for any age of a memorizer, but especially for older people. Redeem the cultural term of a "bucket list." While secular bucket lists linger long on everything people want to wring out of life, what if you put a passage of Scripture on your "bucket list"? Not only could you pursue something eternally worthwhile, but you will also have a humorous option for "failure." Perhaps you will not get finished! You could "kick the bucket" *before* you finish. How phenomenally fine! What better way to "fail" to finish than to awake in heaven, the destination for which you were practicing anyway? Then, gazing at God in the face of Christ, for whom you were memorizing, all is well. That is not a failure but a strong, accelerating finish to your spiritual life! You were joyfully in the process of studying for the final exam, but God graduated you early with honors!

2. Resolved: To Choose Heavenly-Mindedness over Earthly-Mindedness

All of us can drift! The allure of the world can draw our attention to this life, this world, this hope, this *present* age, and these pleasures. Unless you make a strenuous effort to avoid drifting (Heb 2:1), you will. How easy it is to become increasingly worldly as you age! Pain will accelerate the direction you are *already* heading in! You will accelerate your speed in either direction, depending on whether you have fixed your heart on heaven or earth. If you oscillate back and forth, trying to focus both on heaven and this world, trying to live for God while saddled with "the cares of the world and the deceitfulness of riches" (Matt 13:22), the pains of aging may well shove you off the path of growth altogether!

If you seek relief from pain by distracting yourself with worldly pleasures and pastimes, you will find neither lasting relief nor spiritual benefit. John Piper's observations from his time in a hospital should sober anyone. Disturbed by the prevalence of televisions in hospitals, he writes about the danger of drowning your pain in spiritually numbing entertainment: "It's the more subtle and pervasive dehumanizing banality of most television programming. This is the last thing a person needs who knows he is standing on the brink of eternity."[19] That dehumanizing danger applies to all forms of screen technology, such as cell phones, laptops, and tablets, that can distract in the most critical season for seeking God.

How easy it is to anesthetize the soul with many things enjoyed too much: reading, exercising, knitting, gaming, golfing, shopping, talking, listening to music, streaming movies! However, these are poor substitutes for turning your thoughts upward to God and *ahead* to eternity! The evil one is notoriously active in these seasons, seeking to keep you from thinking sobering spiritual thoughts.[20] Even more than *before*, you must heed Paul's plea to "set your minds on things that are above" (Col 3:2). Paul's instructions to seek the things above involve time travel from your *past* to your *future*. In your *past*, Christ gave you a new spiritual life (v. 1); in the *present*, your life flows from Christ, and in the *future*, your life will be revealed in Christ as his visible revelation (v. 4).

How can you set your mind on heavenly things instead of either being dragged down into the sorrows of this world or infatuated by its allures? Take the only path *forward* by employing meditation, that precious ability God has gifted to you. Commenting on this passage in Col 3:1–4, N. T. Wright concludes that "the command to aspire to the things of heaven is a command to *meditate* and *dwell* upon Christ's sort of life, and on the fact that he is *now* enthroned as the Lord of the world."[21] You can meditate on God himself, his beautiful creation, or his perfect providential control over your life. You can also contemplate your *future* continuation of this earthly life. *After* a brief period of living as a spirit in heaven until the glorious, triumphant return of Christ to this earth, eternity is here on a "new heavens and new earth" (Isa 65:17; 66:22; 2 Pet 3:13; Rev 21:1). That means that the pervasive cultural idea of needing a "bucket list" is tragically mistaken. If you are a child of God, then you do not need "to squeeze out of this life everything we can as though there is nothing more" because you have an unimaginably better physical eternity before you.[22]

A Christian woman I know discovered the freedom of meditating on memorized Scripture through painful days. When feeling alone and troubled during painful twenty-minute radiation treatments, she had just

---

19. Piper, *Lessons from a Hospital Bed*, 50–51.
20. Boice, *Psalms 1–41*, 339.
21. Wright, *Colossians and Philemon*, 136 (emphasis added).
22. Stevens, *Aging Matters*, 35.

enough time to recite aloud to herself chapters of Romans from memory. Her *earlier* investment in internalizing the meat of God's word sustained her better than the secular music soundtracks offered to her by radiation technicians. You may not have much memorized word-for-word *yet*, but you can recall Bible stories, Bible promises, Christian songs, Christian teachings, and even Bible songs from childhood from the vast storehouse of your mind.

Unless you experience a sudden illness, you can *pre*pare what you will use to nurture heavenly-mindedness in those times. Use technology in beneficial ways to *pre*plan and *pre*load the sermons and Christian music you might need for *upcoming* hospitalizations and prolonged recovery.[23] Redeem the same modern technology that most people will use to carry along worldly soundtracks by using it to carry along gospel-centered resources for your long hours of inactivity.

Strive to memorize Scriptures and songs that can lodge in your heart. You never need to recharge God's truth; you can take it anywhere. Even in *pre*-op and *post*-op, where personal technology is banned, the spiritual library of your brain is not! Excel at the spiritual disciplines you *once* thought you did not have time for! You likely have more free time to yourself as you get older. Be heavenly-minded enough to reinvest that time dividend into your spiritual life, reaping good rewards *now* and better ones in the world *to come*. Choose the best means for growth "when life moves at a slower pace: the practice of spiritual disciplines."[24]

3. Resolved: To Seek Significance in Christ, Not Commendations

Though many deny it, all people draw some degree of significance from the approval of others. But you can and should resist that mistake, seeking approval and significance from God alone. When you were born again (John 3:3), you were *already* freed from having to depend on others, from the life of slavery to the opinions of others. But people-pleasing is never quite a vanquished temptation. Even Peter fell into this trap (Gal 2:11–12) and had to be rebuked by Paul.

Living gracefully with God offers two opportunities for finding significance in Christ alone. First, reflecting more on your life should make you more humble and excited about giving all of the honor you receive to

---

23. Piper, *Lessons from a Hospital Bed*, 51.
24. Dunlop, *Wellness for the Glory of God*, 135.

Christ. It is God who has carried you safe this far, not yourself. So, receive compliments politely and enjoy them, but only a little! Hand them over to God in prayer without delay, acknowledging that Christ alone made all the things you did possible (John 15:4–5). Matthew Pool (1624–79) observed that praise each one receives tests them (Prov 27:21): "Either humbly and modestly with thankfulness to God, and a due sense of his own infirmities, which is the case and temper of a good man; or ambitiously and vain-gloriously, taking to himself the honor which he should give to God, as ungodly men generally do in that case."[25]

Second, when you think about yourself and your worth, move away from self-assessments that are dependent on your *past* achievements. Take joy in work well done, relationships marked by faithfulness, and your contributions to God's kingdom, but stop relying on the *past* for your sense of worth. Instead, lean more into your blessed identity in Christ. God defines your value solely in your relationship with Christ. That is shockingly countercultural, as the world always links achievements and values. Reflecting on how the culture casts people away at retirement age, R. Paul Stevens wrote,

> Society presses us into the mold of accomplishments—CVs, accolades for things made and done, the places to which we have travelled, the jobs held, even roles we have undertaken in the church and not-for-profit organizations. But gradually we get asked less and less, like an international speaker who recently wrote me that "the invitations have dried up." For people whose life was wrapped up in their daily work, who lived for their work, actual retirement is a kind of death. And it is not surprising that some, mostly men, sometimes die shortly *after* retirement. There is nothing left to live for. But, short of physical death, this transition can be life-giving if they shift to nurturing, discovering, and affirming who they are as a person, especially a person in Christ.[26]

Meditation is the key to internalizing your identity in Christ. As you read your Bible, pause to hear what God says about his children, his great love for them, his joy in them, and his *future* for them with him forever. A deepening view of your value in God avoids the sinful extremes of human-centered pessimism and optimism. Pessimistic atheist Bertrand Russell (1872–1970) said, "All the labors of the ages, all the devotion, all

---

25. Poole, *Annotations upon the Holy Bible*, 267.
26. Stevens, *Aging Matters*, 75 (emphasis added).

the inspirations, all the noonday brightness of human genius, are destined to extinction in the vast death of the solar system."[27] The optimistic, proud person says, "I have accomplished much, so I am worth much." Both are dead wrong!

But all Christians have entered God's kingdom as humbled spiritual beggars, mourning their inadequacies (Matt 5:3–4). Their forever *future* with God is bestowed on them by the overwhelming grace of God, not earned (Eph 2:8–9). As they grow, they learn to rejoice in that they are God's "beloved" (Rom 1:7), "chosen" *before* the foundation of the world (Eph 1:4; emphasis added), and "adopted" through the sacrifice of his Son (v. 5). Let your heart marvel with John: "See what kind of love the Father has given to us, that we should be called children of God; and so we are" (1 John 3:1). God calls you his "friend" (John 15:14–15), and Christ is your "brother" (Heb 2:11). What need do you have for the approval and applause of others?

4. Resolved: To Increase Appreciation While Avoiding Nostalgia

No one is more *prepared* to shower God with thanksgiving than those who have known him the longest. Those believers who have lived longer for God have been held tight by the grip of his grace and, in that grace, have resisted more temptations and attempted more spiritually ambitious endeavors. Throughout their lives, they have clung to more promises, had more prayers answered, and learned more about God from Scripture and experience than others: "The escalating joys stem from longer exposure to God's means of grace to his Spirit working through his word and to his inner work of renewal. Without Christ, we cannot know any of these higher joys, but in Christ, we can anticipate, experience, and enjoy them all."[28]

Furthermore, aging moves the mind naturally into the *past*, and God can use these trips down memory lane for his glory and your joy. Many tools exist for meditative time travel and can be used to remember and rejoice: old photo albums, scrapbooks, videos, and memos. Family members, especially fellow Christian time travelers, can help by asking aging saints specific questions to nudge *memories*.

Yet be careful! Satan loves to offer spiritual substitutes for God's precious gifts. There is a wide divide between appreciative journeys to the *past*

---

27. Russell, *Basic Writings*, 67.
28. Challies, *Aging Gracefully*, 17.

Transformative Time Travel

and the shipwreck of nostalgia. Dictionary definitions denote nostalgia as something neutral and harmless. But often, nostalgia is deadening, choosing not just to look lovingly at the *past* but to live there! Nostalgia, as "the human capacity for selective remembrance and forgetfulness," also permits the glorification of the *past* to the point where memory and imagination are blurred. Such reconstructions create a nostalgic experience or 'homesickness' for the *past*."[29] This temporal homesickness leads quickly to ingratitude for God's presence and power in the *present*.

Nostalgia can leech away the appreciation of God just as surely as anxiety hampers alertness. The alert person meditatively grasps the *future* dangers yet returns to live in the *present* and benefits in the *present* from this time travel. However, the anxious person mentally travels to the *future* and lives there, experiencing the possible pains and panics of *tomorrow today*. This panic makes the soul less equipped and enthused about living in the *present* because of warped mental time travel. In contrast, the healthy aging Christian visits the *past*, worships God for his goodness there, and returns to live in the *present*, full of joy and excitement about living *today* for that great God.[30] However, the nostalgic man visits the *past*, enjoys it too much, appreciates God there too little, and retires there. He returns little to the *present*, accelerating toward eternity while gazing at the rearview mirror![31]

Nostalgia, dangerous at any age, grows more hazardous with advancing years. First, living in the *past* empties your heart of the passion for living for God and others in the *present*. God wants his children to rise daily to seek him, praise him, and then serve him and others. The Bible's emphasis is on the importance of living and enjoying *today*. To leave your heart in the *past* is a subtle form of ingratitude for your *present* life. Sometimes, it is intentionally done to escape from mounting pain and perplexity in the *present*. Instead of humbly casting *today's* burdens on God (1 Pet 5:6–7), this is avoidance, seeking temporary "escape from the maladies of the moment."[32] Whatever those pains are, physical, emotional, or relational, you must bring them before God, lay them before him, and leave them there.

Second, the believer should be homesick for heaven, enjoying what God provides *now* but longing for his full presence and the *future* fulfillment of his promises. To regularly conclude, through nostalgic journeys,

---

29. Hill, *1 & 2 Chronicles*, 108 (emphasis added).
30. Karr, "Forgetting What Is Behind?"
31. Morse, "Most Dangerous Place."
32. Wilson, "Beauty and Burden," para. 3.

that the *past* outshines the *present* is nearsighted. The final *future* for believers will always be the best. Moreover, it must be reached by living in this *present* time with appreciation and alert anticipation. A clear focus on the *future* will give you the courage to try new things for God as you live for *tomorrow*. This *forward*-leaning hope also protects you from *backward*-leaning emotional entanglement.

So, look *back* and appreciate God for your *past*. Someday in heaven, you will be able to praise God even more for his goodness to you. You will see his good plans, sometimes accomplished with your cooperation but sometimes achieved despite your reluctance or unbelief. By "retrospect (meditation on the *past*) and prospect (anticipation for the *future*)" increase your appreciation for God as you age.[33] Practice praising him *now*, for that is your eternal purpose and joy! As you do that, you will be *pre*pared for your final resolution, making the most difference in this world as you *pre*pare for the next. C. S. Lewis (1898–1963) wrote, "If you read history, you will find that the Christians who did most for the *present* world were just those who thought most of the *next*."[34]

Goal: Aging out of Selfishness and into Service

These resolutions, taken together, depict the journey of the Christian life over time. As you master meditative time travel, more firmly anchored between *past* grace and *future* grace, you can let go of more of your stubborn tendency to put yourself first. You *once* renounced that self-absorption when God saved you, repenting of your self-centered ways, trusting Jesus for forgiveness, and committing to follow him fully and unselfishly. Keep going! These resolutions will remind you of what the road of discipleship looks like as you begin your *final* ascent up the mountain of the Lord. To seek less of you and more of Christ would be to imitate the humble ambition of John the Baptist, who would eventually lose everything for Jesus: "He must increase, but I must decrease" (John 3:30)! Moreover, this is a call to live as Jesus himself lived who" did not come to be served, but to serve" (Matt 20:28).

Tim Keller (1950–2023) believed that letting go of yourself brings freedom. He wrote, "True gospel humility means I stop connecting every experience, every conversation, with myself. In fact, I stop thinking about

---

33. Hill, *1 & 2 Chronicles*, 110.
34. Lewis, *Mere Christianity*, 134 (emphasis added).

myself. The freedom of self-forgetfulness."[35] Let your love of yourself decline, and your love for others and God increase! Then, the *final* season of your life (decline) and the *final* days (death) can be your best days, freed to serve God through prayer and worship. Having elevated God to the highest place (Matt 22:37–38), you will freely care for others (v. 39) by praying for them, encouraging them, exhorting them, and blessing them with other *final* touches of the grace of God.

J. I. Packer (1926–2020) expressed this thought by noting that senior saints have bodies and souls moving in different directions: "As seniors' powers of body, memory, and creativity grow less, their conscious focus on their hope of glory should grow sharper, and their meditations on it grow more joyful and sustained. As this happens, passion to continue being of use to God and his people in holiness, love, and what Scriptures conceives as neighborliness, should and will intensify, to the very end."[36]

Instead of being afraid (Ps 27:1–3), the psalmist longed to meditate more and more on God's beauty: "One thing have I asked of the Lord, that will I seek after: that I may dwell in the house of the Lord all the days of my life, to gaze upon the beauty of the Lord and to inquire in his temple" (v. 4). *Now*, in the *present*, you likely can still gather physically with God's people in church buildings. However, *later*, even if your health gives way, you can always pray, meditate, and likely either read or listen to Scripture. Thank God for modern technology like cell phones and tablets, which give you unprecedented end-of-life access to his word and people.

THE SEVEN FINALS OF YOUR FINALE

Having thought together reflectively about the aging process, we *now* look at our *final* days. You may be mistaken about when you will enter life's *last* and *final* phase. Isaac *prepared* to die (Gen 27:2) decades *before* he did (Gen 35:29)! But for most, a terminal diagnosis will be given or an injury suffered from which recovery seems unlikely.

In those *final* days on this earth, there are seven "*finals*" we will experience. "*Final*" is a broad word that has several dictionary definitions, of which we will use three interchangeably: "occurring at the *end*," "not to be altered," that is unchangeable, and "ultimate" result.[37] Live as a wise

---

35. Keller, *Freedom of Self-Forgetfulness*, 32.
36. Packer, *Finishing Our Course with Joy*, 96.
37. *Merriam-Webster Dictionary*, s.v. "final."

time traveler! *Pre*pare every day for whatever the Lord brings into your day, and those days will not come upon you suddenly and find you un*pre*pared. Throughout your Christian life, and especially in the decline, you will thrive in the *present*, aware of your *past* and *future*. Then, you will be ready for the days of your death, something only possible for believers in Christ. Your *last* days will entail your *final* testing, *final* dying, *final* testimony, *final* entrusting, *final* acceptance, *final* exchange, and *final* joy.

Final Testing

Do tests make you nervous? In school, could you master a subject but still disappoint yourself with your test results? Here is good news. The end of life is a different kind of test. It is a real test, the *final* exam of your soul, but you will pass it. That is guaranteed! How? God guarantees your success. How you pass the final testing depends on God's sovereignty and your spiritual sweat. You will pass the final test with flying colors, primarily because God will hold onto you. His Holy Spirit lives in you and will guarantee your success. You are a believer, one of his children, who by "God's power are being guarded through faith" (1 Pet 1:5). Hear the confidence of Paul about why Christians will finish well: "And I am sure of this, that he who began a good work in you will bring it to completion at the day of Jesus Christ" (Phil 1:6) Just as you have in the *past* learned to rely on God over and above your efforts, so you can lean on God until the *end*, praising him that "you are with me" (Ps 23:4).

Regarding your efforts to pass the *final* test, be confident because the Spirit has fully equipped you for what is *ahead*. You have learned to answer the question everyone should consider in *advance*: "What about what lies beyond death and the grave? Is it all worked out so you can face it with equanimity and never need give it another care? The answer of the believer is resoundingly and joyfully yes!"[38] In addition to knowing who you have believed (2 Tim 1:12), you can practice for the test by regularly thinking about the *end* of your life. Look *ahead now* and "picture yourself dying, conceive yourself breathing out your last breath, and see whether you can look at death without quaking."[39]

Further, your *final* days can be filled with the *final* prayers to God, summing up your spiritual journey here and *preparing* for your *next* life

---

38. Lloyd-Jones, *Authentic Christianity*, 299.
39. Spurgeon, "Last Enemy Destroyed," 648.

phase. Augustine (354–430) wanted to reflect on beloved psalms of confession, even when confined to his bed and death approaching. He asked for and received handwritten copies of David's "shortest penitential Psalms" (Pss 6, 31, 129, 142). More important than friends' visits, he "would look at these sheets as they hung upon the wall and read them." Not surprisingly, he passed his *final* test of faith confidently and entered eternity with his beloved Jesus, for whom he had so-long longed.[40]

Final Dying

No one enters the path to the kingdom of heaven without repentance. In fact, the first recorded words of both John the Baptist and Jesus are calls to repentance: "Repent, for the kingdom of heaven is at hand" (Matt 3:2; 4:17). That repentance involves dying. It is a spiritual death to one's will and old patterns of sin. That initial decision to die to self and be made alive in Christ must be renewed daily until God calls you home. Jesus "willed that the whole life of believers should be repentance," of daily death to self through sanctification.[41]

This daily sanctification requires two steps. Paul commanded Christians "to put off your old self, which belongs to your former manner of life and is corrupt through deceitful desires, and to be renewed in the spirit of your minds, and to put on the new self, created after the likeness of God in true righteousness and holiness" (Eph 4:22–24). Henry Bullinger (1504–75) described this process using the symbol of baptism: "Our old Adam must be drowned and extinguished, but our new Adam must be quickened day by day and rise up again. Therefore, mortification and vivification of Christians are excellently represented by baptism."[42]

Christians differ in their levels of understanding and embracing of this process! Additionally, even the spiritually ambitious do not rise every day from bed and have victory. What Christian has not had those "wretched" days of defeat (Rom 7:15, 19, 24)? But the journey begins anew each day with fresh supplies of grace. Practicing the pattern of death and life each day deepens your discipleship in the *present*. It *prepares* you for your *final* hour. Follow the Holy Spirit through disciplined decision-making in the *present* that kills sinful longings.

40. Possidius, *Life of Saint Augustine*, 57.
41. Luther, *Disputation*, 29.
42. Bullinger, "Sermon on the Purpose."

Final Testimony

You should live as light, which draws people's attention upward from yourself and to your Father (Matt 5:16). In your last days, others will see most clearly that you are a citizen of heaven, not of this earth, awaiting reunion with Jesus and the transformation of your body into his image (Phil 3:20–21). The way you have lived and the way you will die testifies loudly to two important groups. For the believers around you, your bold confidence in Christ, through *final* bouts of suffering, will prove the reality of what lies beyond the grave. If you have not reached the end of your life, remember that Christian deaths and Christian funerals, properly meditated upon, can encourage your faith. When asked if he had been to hear a sermon, Robert Leighton (1611–84) affirmed that he had: "I met a sermon—a sermon de facto, for I met a corpse, and rightly and profitably are the funeral rites performed when the living lay it to heart."[43]

For your unbelieving friends and family, your death proclaims your *final* living testimony to them. While not your *last* influence on them, as you will live on in their memories, this will be your *last* physical testimony to them. God plans that the gospel hope you have urged them to consider will be powerfully demonstrated one *last* time through your death. No one can deny the supernatural power that enables a saint to depart from this world at peace with God and their life. You will die "satisfied" by life (Gen 25:8 NASB). God surely gives dying grace only when you are actually dying; your enduring faith will give them confidence that God will also carry them peacefully through their deaths.

You can enhance the *final* testimony of your life by *preplanning* your *final* sets of words to be spoken. Your family and friends will not forget your *final* words spoken to them. What you need to communicate will likely vary depending on whom you will be speaking to. What encouragements and exhortations can you give beloved believers? What *final* invitation to follow you to heaven can you offer to dear unbelievers? Lady Margaret Steuart of Coltness (d. 1675) charged her eleven gathered children with serious words and commanded them to prove their faith by their disciplined devotion to God's words:

> I charge you before God and as you would wish meet with me again with happiness. Be diligent in reading the Scriptures and in prayer. Do not be satisfied with your morning and evening

---

43. Leighton, quoted in Spence-Jones, *Psalms*, 309.

prayers. I charge you in the sight and presence of the Lord not to judge your religion to be true and sincere, if it does not take you any further than morning and evening prayers. In all these things, I say to you, I will be a witness against you. Do not consider what I say *now* to be the same as instruction and reproof at any other time. The words I have spoken are the words of a dying mother. I pray to the Lord that you may never forget them.[44]

Her charge to her children displayed meditative time travel. In the *present*, she charged her children that in order to enjoy a great *future* and see her again in the *future*, they must demonstrate the spiritual disciplines in the *present* as evidence of their *past* faith commitment to Christ. You can also *pre*plan the words, hymns, songs, poems, and verses to be used at your funeral. As you think about verses that the Spirit has implanted into your life throughout your journey (Jas 1:23), which ones can someone read when you have the fullest attention of your family and friends? What hymns or songs of faith express your hope? How can the minister *re*tell the stories of your faith to encourage the saints and to invite sinners to be saved?

Final Entrusting

In this life, God has blessed you with family and friends. Your highest joys on earth have been your close relationships with friends and family, many stretching across decades of your life. How dear to you are your parents, children, siblings, dear friends, and fellow Christians! Just as God entrusts you with physical blessings, expecting you to enjoy them and handle them prudently, God gives you those close to you. These sweet relationships are stewardship relationships. Couples have mutual responsibility for each other. Likewise, God charges parents with raising their children in the knowledge and loving fear of the Lord. Adult children must look after their parents (1 Tim 4:4, 8, 16). While some saints may suffer loneliness at times in their lives, most believers have a whole web of wonderful, close relationships and responsibilities. They have at least church relationships. What will you do about those precious people when death approaches?

The prudent Christian will complete a process begun much *earlier*, entrusting these people to God for protection, provision, and spiritual well-being. Have you learned to hold onto these relationships lightly? Your

44. *Happy Faith and Assurance in Death*, 9 (emphasis added).

dearly beloved family members were "loaned" to you. Have you learned to hold onto them with a "loose hand"?[45] With all the strength, wisdom, and love you had to offer, you cared for them and will care for them. You will follow the model of Jesus, who, toward his disciples, "loved them to the *end*" (John 13:1). Yet even when healthy and active, you ultimately trusted God to take care of them, and you pointed them to God as their "Shepherd" (Ps 23).

God's love and care often flowed through you, but you either trusted God for their care or fell into the toxic time travel of anxiety. You surely tried to provide the best for them relationally, but you never lost sight of God's ultimate care. You encouraged them to appreciate God's provision and protection over, above, and through your love for them. What a blessing for children to have grown up knowing that their parents, although imperfect, were models pointing them to the infinite love of their heavenly Father! What a blessing for a wife of a devoted husband to know that though God blessed her through him, God was always her primary provider. Even if her husband dies *before* her, leaving her to care for her family, God will surely be with her to provide for them. He has always been the "father of the fatherless and protector of widows" (Ps 68:5).

Many of the burdens that you have been casting before God have been pleas for God to provide for you and yours (1 Pet 5:7). *Now*, at the end of your life, it is wise to point them to God as the one who has sustained them in the *past* and will sustain them in the *future*. Paul's departure from the beloved Ephesian elders was difficult, marked by grief, weeping, tears, hugging, and kissing (Acts 20:37). But Paul had peace from a sure knowledge that God would care for them. From that confidence flowed his benediction pronounced over them, his *final* words to his friends. He was clinging to God's promises and demonstrated faithfulness as he left his friends in heavenly hands: "And *now* I commend you to God and to the word of his grace, which is able to build you up and to give you the inheritance among all those who are sanctified" (v. 32; emphasis added). Paul knew that God could bring them home to heaven safely to enjoy their inheritance and to see him again. What a beautiful model of *final* entrustment!

Hopefully, through wise planning for the *future* and God's provision, you will leave your family in fine financial shape. However, even if they will face hard financial times, you can trust them to his care. Martin Luther's (1483–1546) last will and testament did just that: "I have nothing to leave

---

45. Spurgeon, "Last Enemy Destroyed," 647–48.

them, but I commit them unto thee. O Father of the fatherless, and judge of widows, . . . nourish, keep, and teach them."[46] Committing loved ones to God can be one of your most difficult emotional and spiritual steps!

John Flavel (1627–91) sympathized with those concerned about their family members' spiritual condition. He reminded his readers, "God can make your prayers and counsels effectual when you are dead."[47] That marvelous assurance should inspire you to pray more fervently for your family *now*, especially at the *end*. Even if they are not listening to your wisdom *now* and God does not seem to be heeding your prayers, know that you might be piling up a storehouse in heaven of *pre*mortem prayers to be answered *post*mortem!

Just as God has given you relationships to steward well, so he has given you financial resources. You regularly gave financially to support the Kingdom of God while alive; therefore, do not forget to plan to give generously to this greatest cause *after* your death. Through wise financial planning and your will, you can give a final blessing to Great Commission work by giving a substantial portion of your money to missions through your church or an agency.

As you meditate and pray, the Holy Spirit will show you how much to leave *behind* for your family and what you should give to God. The reward for being generous to God's causes will be a time-travel reward! Whatever you give to missions will contribute to more souls joining you in heaven someday in the *future*! How thrilling to plan to give some of your estate to support the ingathering of that great crowd "that no one could number, from every nation, from all tribes and peoples and languages, standing before the throne and before the Lamb, clothed in white robes, with palm branches in their hands, and crying out with a loud voice, 'Salvation belongs to our God who sits on the throne, and to the Lamb!'" (Rev 7:9–10). You will be funding *end*-times *forever* worship of the blessed God who bought you and brought you there by grace alone!

Final Acceptance

A sign of maturing in the Christian life is an increasingly earnest heart cry, echoing Jesus in Gethsemane, "Not as I will, but as you will" (Matt 26:39). God invites you to pray for what you desire and to pursue godly goals, all

---

46. Luther, quoted in Flavel, *Whole Works*, 5:494.
47. Flavel, *Whole Works*, 5:494.

with the understanding that he plans the best for his glory. Therefore, you will need to humble yourself to accept that from your earthbound perspective; his ways often remain "higher than" your ways (Isa 55:9). You may not understand and fully appreciate his will until you enter eternity. The heart of a child of God is to trust the Father and accept his will. As you have passed through the *previous* stages of life, God has proven that accepting his will is always wise. Blessings abound for those who have learned not to lean on their understanding (Prov 3:5)!

The *final* days of your life on earth will involve your *final* acceptance of several things over which you have no control. Meditative time travel here again will help your steps of submission. *Recall* God's perfect wisdom demonstrated in your *past* and use that as an encouragement to accept his will. You will need to accept the timing of your death, the deeds you might feel you are leaving undone, and his "just in the nick of time" dying grace. Not only does God know and plan all your days (Ps 139:16), including your last one, but you will die at the exact right time.

Like missionary John Paton (1824–1907), who "felt immortal until my work was done," nothing can cut your life short of the full number of the days God planned. Likewise, know *now* that you cannot and should not live a day longer than his plan.[48] God's tender control over your life can free you! You should work hard each day, not *pre*suming that you will have another day to serve God where he has placed you.[49] However, on the day you die, be assured that God's works for you are done. Just as there are actually no "*pre*mature" or "un*timely*" deaths of God's children, you will not leave *behind* any unfinished works that he intended you to finish. Your long to-do list was mistaken, not God's! So, when it is time to go, go without the guilt of what was never completed.[50]

Regarding the timing of your death, look to God's mercy. Trust that the timing of your departure spares you harder days *ahead*. For example, if believers have lingered in intense physical suffering toward the end, then in death, God has granted them the ultimate healing that comes from leaving broken bodies *behind* (Isa 53:4; Matt 8:17). God sometimes removes his saints from the scene *before* seasons of greater sorrow and pain. Think of Methuselah, who likely died on the eve of the flood.[51] As Paul anticipated,

---

48. Paton, *John Gibson Paton*, 133.
49. Anyabwile, *May We Meet*, 88.
50. Flavel, *Whole Works*, 5:494.
51. Flavel, *Whole Works*, 5:492.

you will experience the glory and grace of God's presence: "The sufferings of this *present* time are not worth comparing with the glory that is to be revealed to us" (Rom 8:18; emphasis added).

Anticipate that God will always provide enough strength to endure whatever lies *ahead*. He has never failed to guide you up to this point, and he will never leave you or forsake you (Heb 13:5). He will provide the dying grace you need when you are about to die. However, do not expect it *before* you need it for the *final* battle of faith, dying in peace. His grace never comes *pre*maturely! Instead, just as you accept each day as a gift of his grace, so too anticipate and accept his grace on your *final* day.

Having entrusted your family to God, relax in the thought that God will comfort and strengthen them through the season of your death, likely in ways you would never anticipate. Andrew Bonar's (1810–92) wife died suddenly in just one day. What neither of them could have known was how God had *pre*pared him *before*hand for it through his daily Bible reading and then used it in the *future* to refine him.

> Saturday, October 15th. O, what a wound! Last night most suddenly, *after* three hours' sinking, my dear, dear Isabella was taken from me. . . . She passed away so gently that, till I held her and touched her cheek, I could scarcely believe it was death. I have needed this affliction. It brings to my remembrance sins of many, many kinds: neglected prayer, neglected thanksgiving, self-indulgence, my life too much a life for myself and family. Lord, let me not love Thee less, but more, because of this stroke, and from this day may I work more for the ingathering of souls. I had been reading between dinner and tea my usual verse. Nah. i. 7 was that for the day. "The Lord is good," etc. Oh, little did I think how I would need it half an hour *after*! Lord, Lord, make this a time of the Spirit being poured out upon my family![52]

Final Exchange

The dying Christian will meet Jesus face-to-face (Matt 5:8)! While on earth, God calls us to meditate on himself and his promises, especially about heaven to come. He urges you to work daily toward heavenly-mindedness, especially amidst mounting suffering. Christians will differ in how much progress they make in this journey, but all will progress. Aspire to live so

---

52. Bonar, *Andrew A. Bonar*, 226–27 (emphasis added).

in touch with the things of God and leaning *forward* in your spiritual life that what was written of Richard Sibbes (1577–1635) could be said of you: "Of this blest man, let this just praise be given, heaven was in him, *before* he was in heaven."[53] When you die, you make your final exchange, swapping your life here on earth for a full and fantastic life in heaven with the blessed triune God, the angels, and the saints.

You will feel more comfortable about this exchange to the degree that you have *already* placed your mind and heart in heaven. All of earth's glimmers of God's glory and joy will pale compared to what is to come for you as you exchange your old life for the new one. That life you will experience will be so much better than anything or any relationship experienced on earth: "These are but shadows; but God is the substance. These are but scattered beams; but God is the sun. These are but streams, but God is the fountain. These are but drops; but God is the ocean."[54] Paid for by the precious life of your Redeemer, you are being brought home, but it will only happen *after* you exchange abodes. Indeed, Paul looked *ahead* to the death of the body and the coming resurrection of perfect bodies for that perfect eternity at the return of Christ. He reminded his readers that "flesh and blood cannot inherit the kingdom of God" (1 Cor 15:50). What a great final exchange awaits you! How this hope should daily dampen your pursuit of worldly things and pleasures soon to pass away!

Final Joy

All this life's joys point to heaven's higher and holier joys, chiefly the joy of living with God forever. This vision of God, seeing him face to face in the person of beloved Jesus, has inspired Christians across the centuries. Jesus promised this: "Blessed are the pure in heart, for they shall see God" (Matt 5:8). Hear and believe the blessed great news of the gospel. God justifies sinners such as us! Even if you still struggle with guilt, accept this eternal truth that God "justifies the ungodly" (Rom 4:5). Wayne Grudem writes, "When we realize that God is the perfection of all that we long for or desire, that he is the summation of everything beautiful or desirable, then we realize that the greatest joy of the life to come will be that we 'shall see his face' and experience the close interpersonal fellowship that this implies."[55]

---

53. Izaak Walton, in Sibbes, *Complete Works*, 1:20 (emphasis added).
54. Edwards, *Works*, 2:244.
55. Grudem, *Systematic Theology*, 224.

Final Encouragement

The "*final*" encouragement of the book is the most serious! You, the reader, have prayerfully journeyed to your *past* and *future* through this book's chapters. However, you must, absolutely must be certain, truly certain that you are a child of God, born again (John 3:3) and justified by faith alone in Christ (Rom 3:28). If you are not a believer *yet*, then none of the positive encouragements in any of the chapters apply to you—*yet*. Their advice will not help you! Like a student taking a true and false quiz in school, an unbeliever should mark "f" for "false" next to every encouragement and promise written to this point. There is no *future* hope or peace apart from Christ. Those who are not Christians *yet* should be anxious, have little reason to be appreciative, will not benefit from a disciplined life, and will have no true, lasting community around them. However, God can change that instantly, making the old you pass away, and God will make you a "new creation" (2 Cor 5:17).

If you are uncertain about your spiritual condition, read through the New Testament, especially reading slowly through the Gospels. Seek the help of an evangelical pastor or Christian you know. Right *now*, stop and meditate on the gospel hope, which Paul summarized in Romans so well. God will justify you by faith if you will "believe in him who raised from the dead Jesus our Lord, who was delivered up for our trespasses and raised for our justification" (Rom 4:24–25). Believing that extraordinary good news will drive you to repentance and confession: "If you confess with your mouth that Jesus is Lord and believe in your heart that God raised him from the dead, you will be saved. For with the heart, one believes and is justified, and with the mouth, one confesses and is saved" (Rom 10:9–10).

Again, have you *pre*pared for an eternal *future* with God? Make certain that you have been saved and can say joyfully with the saints of all the ages that "since we have been justified by faith, we have peace with God through our Lord Jesus Christ" (Rom 5:1). John Piper's gospel summary is encouraging regarding your possible *future*: "The best news in the world is that there is no conflict between your greatest possible happiness and God's perfect holiness. Being satisfied with all that God is for you in Jesus magnifies him as the greatest treasure and brings you more joy—eternal, infinite joy—than any other delight ever could."[56] If you are a believer, then know

---

56. Piper, *For Your Joy*, 39.

that God has an abundant life *ahead* for you (John 10:10). You are *already* blessed, and he will keep blessing you even more.

You can be a great disciple without thinking of your journey as transformative time travel. This book has not claimed otherwise. However, a healthy Christian, consciously or unconsciously, will learn to do what these chapters have pointed toward—staying alert, defeating anxiety, increasing appreciation, resisting amnesia, living a more disciplined life, living in a happy and holy community together with others, and being *prepared* to make your last season your best one. Picturing meditation as time travel is a helpful tool for seeing many aspects of the Christian life in one sweeping view. Test drive these recommended time-travel journeys to the *future*, to the *past*, and anchor the *present* between them both as we all await our eternal, indescribably joyful *future* together, worshiping our great God who lives beyond the finite bounds of time itself: "*Now* to the King eternal, immortal, invisible, the only God, be honor and glory forever and ever. Amen" (1 Tim 1:17; emphasis added)!

RECOMMENDED READING ABOUT DECLINE AND DEATH

Tim Challies, *Aging Gracefully* (Minneapolis: Cruciform Press, 2018).
J. I. Packer, *Finishing Our Course with Joy: Guidance from God for Engaging with Our Aging* (Wheaton, IL: Crossway, 2014).
John Piper, *Lessons from a Hospital Bed* (Wheaton, IL: Crossway, 2016).
R. P. Stevens, *Aging Matters: Finding Your Calling for the Rest of Your Life* (Grand Rapids: Eerdmans, 2016).

MEMORIZATION PASSAGES ABOUT DECLINE AND DEATH

1 Corinthians 15:54–55
When the perishable puts on the imperishable, and the mortal puts on immortality, then shall come to pass the saying that is written: "Death is swallowed up in victory." O death, where is your victory? O death, where is your sting?

2 Corinthians 4:16
Though our outer man is decaying, yet our inner man is being renewed day by day.

Transformative Time Travel

2 Timothy 4:6–8
The time of my departure has come. I have fought the good fight, I have finished the race, I have kept the faith. Henceforth there is laid up for me the crown of righteousness, which the Lord, the righteous judge, will award to me on that day, and not only to me but also to all who have loved his appearing.

Revelation 21:4
He will wipe away every tear from their eyes, and death shall be no more, neither shall there be mourning, nor crying, nor pain anymore, for the former things have passed away.

Revelation 22:4–5
They will see his face, and his name will be on their foreheads. And night will be no more. They will need no light of lamp or sun, for the Lord God will be their light, and they will reign forever and ever.

Conclusion

A common graduation gift given to students at the finish line of many different school levels is a beloved classic by Theodor Seuss Geisel, "Dr. Seuss" (1904-91)! The gift symbolizes the adventures that await graduates as they move *forward*. The book's title, *Oh, the Places You'll Go!* provides a whimsical description of the journey *ahead* of you (and *behind* you)![1] O believer, the place you *will go*—heaven! And the places you *have been*—by grace! How inseparable is the Christian faith from your *past* and your *future*! You live between them, and how you think of God's grace and your responsibilities toward the *past* and *future* will impact your *present*. Your *present* sets the stage for your *future*!

All healthy Christians "time travel" naturally as they read, meditate, sing, and pray, even if it is unrecognized! Is that not the power that moves your heart when you sing those stanzas of the beloved hymn?

> Amazing grace! How sweet the sound
> That saved a wretch like me.
> I *once* was lost, but *now* am found,
> Was blind but *now* I see.
>
> Through many dangers, toils, and snares,
> *I have already come*;
> 'Tis grace hath brought me safe *thus far*,
> and grace *will lead me home*.[2]

Periodically review the key memory verses recommended for you. And read further on the topics that either pricked your heart or encouraged

---

1. Seuss, *Oh, the Places You'll Go!*
2. Newton, "Amazing Grace" (emphasis added).

you the most. Let this book be an appetizer for reading great Christian books across the centuries! Blessed is the believer who lives in *present* grace, seeing the light of God's *past* and *future* grace. Hear the eternal words of the eternal Son of God afresh, Jesus's invitations to a great *future* and a worry-free *present*.

> Blessed are the poor in spirit, for theirs is the kingdom of heaven.
> Blessed are those who mourn, for they shall be comforted.
> Blessed are the meek, for they shall inherit the earth.
> Blessed are those who hunger and thirst for righteousness, for they shall be satisfied.
> Blessed are the merciful, for they shall receive mercy.
> Blessed are the pure in heart, for they shall see God.
> Blessed are the peacemakers, for they shall be called sons of God.
> Blessed are those who are persecuted for righteousness' sake, for theirs is the kingdom of heaven. . . .
> Therefore do not be anxious, saying, "What shall we eat?" or "What shall we drink?" or "What shall we wear?"
> For the Gentiles seek after all these things, and your heavenly Father knows that you need them all.
> But seek first the kingdom of God and his righteousness, and all these things will be added to you.
> Therefore, do not be anxious about tomorrow, for tomorrow will be anxious for itself. Sufficient for the day is its own trouble.
> (Matt 5:3–10; 6:31–34)

Bibliography

Adams, John Quincy. *Build Upon the Rock: Letters of John Quincy Adams to His Son on the Bible and Its Teachings*. Edited by Stephen Flick. Cleburne, TX: Christian Heritage, 2017.
Alcorn, Randy. "Can Cancer Be God's Servant? What I Saw in My Wife's Last Four Years." Eternal Perspective Ministries, Dec. 19, 2022. https://www.epm.org/blog/2022/Dec/19/cancer-servant.
———. *God's Promise of Happiness*. Carol Stream, IL: Tyndale House, 2015.
———. *The Purity Principle: God's Safeguards for Life's Dangerous Trails*. Sisters, OR: Multnomah, 2003.
Allcock, Linda. *Deeper Still: Finding Clear Minds and Full Hearts through Biblical Meditation*. Charlotte, NC: Good Book Company, 2020.
Allers, Roger, and Rob Minkoff, dirs. *The Lion King*. Burbank, CA: Walt Disney Animation Studios, 1994.
Allison, Gregg R., and Andreas J. Köstenberger. *The Holy Spirit*. Nashville: B&H Academic, 2020.
Amen, Daniel. *Stones of Remembrance: Healing Scriptures for Your Mind, Body, and Soul*. Carol Stream, IL: Tyndale Momentum, 2017.
Anyabwile, Thabiti M., ed. *May We Meet in the Heavenly World: The Piety of Lemuel Haynes*. Profiles in Reformed Spirituality. Grand Rapids: Reformation Heritage, 2009.
Archer, Clint. "Treasures of the Christian Life Pt 3: Thankfulness." *Cripplegate*, Dec. 9, 2019. https://thecripplegate.com/treasures-of-the-christian-life-pt-3-thankfulness/.
Ash, Christopher. *Married for God: Making Your Marriage the Best It Can Be*. Wheaton, IL: Crossway, 2016.
Baldwin, Joyce G. *1 and 2 Samuel: An Introduction and Commentary*. Downers Grove, IL: InterVarsity, 1988.
Ball, John. *A Treatise of Divine Meditation*. Charlotte, NC: Strait Gate Publications, 2009.
Barker, Glenn W. "2 John." In *The Expositor's Bible Commentary*, vol. 12: *Hebrews through Revelation*, edited by Frank E. Gaebelein, 360–67. Grand Rapids: Zondervan, 1981.
Barnett, John Samuel. *David's Spiritual Secret: A Life That Serves God*. Tulsa: Discover the Book Ministries, 2009.
Bates, William. *The Whole Works of the Rev. William Bates*. Edited by W. Farmer. Vol. 3. Harrisonburg, VA: Sprinkle Publications, 1990.

Bibliography

Bavinck, Herman. *Reformed Ethics: The Duties of the Christian Life.* Edited by John Bolt. Vol. 2. Grand Rapids: Baker Books, 2021.

Baxter, Richard. *The Practical Works of the Rev. Richard Baxter.* Edited by William Orme. Vol. 3. London: James Duncan, 1830.

———. *The Saints' Everlasting Rest.* Abridged by Benjamin Fawcett. ReadaClassic, 2012. https://openlibrary.org/subjects/person:benjamin_fawcett_(1715-1780).

Beeke, Joel R. *The Beauty and Glory of God's Word.* Grand Rapids: Reformation Heritage, 2016.

———. *Heirs with Christ: The Puritans on Adoption.* Grand Rapids: Reformation Heritage, 2008.

Beeke, Joel R., and James A. LaBelle. *Living in a Godly Marriage.* Grand Rapids: Reformation Heritage, 2010.

Bennett, Arthur. *The Valley of Vision: A Collection of Puritan Prayers and Devotions.* Carlisle, PA: Banner of Truth Trust, 1975.

Berkouwer, G. C. *Faith and Perseverance: Studies in Dogmatics.* Grand Rapids: Eerdmans, 1958.

Boice, James Montgomery. *Nehemiah: An Expositional Commentary.* Grand Rapids: Baker Books, 2005.

———. *Psalms 1–41: An Expositional Commentary.* Vol. 1. Grand Rapids: Baker Books, 2005.

———. *Romans: God and History.* Vol. 3. Grand Rapids: Baker Book House, 1991.

———. *The Sermon on the Mount: An Expositional Commentary.* Grand Rapids: Baker Books, 2002.

Bonar, Andrew A. *Andrew A. Bonar, D.D., Diary and Letters.* Edited by Marjory Bonar. Carlisle, PA: Banner of Truth Trust, 1960.

———. *Memoir and Remains of the Rev. Robert Murray McCheyne.* London: Oliphant, Anderson & Ferrier, 1894.

Bonhoeffer, Dietrich. *Life Together and Prayerbook of the Bible.* Translated by Ludwig Müller and Albrecht Schönherr. Dietrich Bonhoeffer Works 5. Minneapolis: Fortress, 2002.

Boston, Thomas. *The Whole Works of Thomas Boston.* Edited by Samuel M'Millan. Vol. 2. Aberdeen: George and Robert King, 1849.

Braga, Matthew. "Inside the First Audio Library of Alcohol-Addled Speech (Which Just Might Help Stop Drunk Driving)." *Fast Company,* Nov. 11, 2014. https://www.fastcompany.com/3038889/inside-the-first-audio-library-of-alcohol-addled-speech-which-just-m.

Brainerd, Richard. "Mr. Brainerd's Remains, Consisting of Letters and Other Papers." In *The Works of Jonathan Edwards,* 435–36. Vol. 2. Carlisle PA: Banner of Truth Trust, 1974.

Brakel, Wihlelmus à. *The Christian's Reasonable Service.* Translated by B. Elshout, edited by J. R. Beeke. 4 vols. Grand Rapids: Reformation Heritage, 1993.

Brant, Rebecca, and Jessi Strong. "The Catechism of Knowing God: An Interview with J. I. Packer." *Bible Study Magazine* 11.2 (Jan./Feb. 2019) 18–22.

Bridge, William. *The Sweetness of Divine Meditation.* Edited by Matthew McMahon. Crossville, TN: Puritan Publications, 2021.

Brooks, Thomas. *The Complete Works of Thomas Brooks.* Edited by Alexander Balloch Grosart. Vol. 1. London: James Nichol, 1866.

Bruce, Milne. *The Message of John: Here Is Your King!* Leicester, England: Inter-Varsity, 1993.

Bibliography

Bullinger, Henry. "Sermon on the Purpose of the Sacraments, 1551." In *Early Protestant Spirituality*, edited by Scott H. Hendrix and Bernard McGinn, translated by Scott H. Hendrix, 256–68. New York: Paulist, 2009.

Bush, Daniel, and Noel Due. *Live in Liberty: The Spiritual Message of Galatians*. Bellingham, WA: Lexham, 2015.

Butler, Trent C. *Hosea, Joel, Amos, Obadiah, Jonah, Micah*. Nashville: Holman Reference, 2005.

Calamy, Edmund, and C. Matthew McMahon. *The Art of Divine Meditation*. Edited by Therese McMahon. Crossville, TN: Puritan Publications, 2019.

Calvin, John. *Commentaries on the Epistles of Paul the Apostle to the Philippians, Colossians, and Thessalonians*. Translated by William Pringle. Bellingham, WA: Logos Bible Software, 2010.

———. *Commentary on a Harmony of the Evangelists Matthew, Mark, and Luke*. Translated by John Pringle. Bellingham, WA: Logos Bible Software, 2010.

———. *Commentary on the Book of Psalms*. Edited by James Anderson. Bellingham, WA: Logos Bible Software, 2010.

———. *Commentary on the Epistle of Paul the Apostle to the Hebrews*. Bellingham, WA: Logos Bible Software, 2010.

———. *Commentary on the First Book of Moses Called Genesis*. Translated by John King. Bellingham, WA: Logos Bible Software, 2010.

———. *Institutes of the Christian Religion*. 2nd ed. Edited by John T. McNeill, translated by Ford Lewis Battles. Vol. 1. The Library of Christian Classics. Louisville: Westminster John Knox, 2011.

Carson, D. A. *A Call to Spiritual Reformation: Priorities from Paul and His Prayers*. Grand Rapids: Baker Book House, 1992.

———. *For the Love of God: A Daily Companion for Discovering the Riches of God's Word*. 2 vols. Wheaton, IL: Crossway, 1998.

———. *Matthew: Chapters 13 through 28*. Grand Rapids: Zondervan, 1995.

———. *Praying with Paul: A Call to Spiritual Reformation*. 2nd ed. Grand Rapids: Baker Academic, 2015.

Castelot, André. *Napoleon*. Translated by Guy Daniels. New York: Harper and Row, 1968.

Challies, Tim. "Affluence and Discontentment." *Ligonier*, Nov. 25, 2015. https://www.ligonier.org/learn/articles/affluence-and-discontentment.

———. "Against Yous, Yous Only Have I Sinned." *Challies*, Feb. 7, 2017. https://www.challies.com/christian-living/against-yous-yous-only-have-i-sinned/.

———. *Aging Gracefully*. Minneapolis: Cruciform, 2018.

———. "It's Better to Suffer Wrong." *Challies*, June 28, 2022. https://www.challies.com/articles/its-better-to-suffer-wrong/.

———. "Not Worrying ≠ Not Caring." *Challies*, June 18, 2018. https://www.challies.com/articles/not-worrying-not-caring/.

Chambers, Oswald. "Approved unto God." In *The Complete Works of Oswald Chambers*, 1–23. Grand Rapids: Discovery House, 2000.

Chandler, Matt, et al. *Creature of the Word: The Jesus-Centered Church*. Nashville: B&H Books, 2012.

Chappell, Bryan. *Christ-Centered Preaching: Redeeming the Expository Sermon*. Ada, MI: Baker Academics, 2018.

———. *Grace at Work: Redeeming the Grind and the Glory of Your Work*. Wheaton, IL: Crossway, 2022.

Bibliography

Charnock, Stephen. *The Existence and Attributes of God*. Vol. 1. London: Robert Carter & Brothers, 1853.
Chester, Tim. *Stott on the Christian Life: Between Two Worlds*. Wheaton, IL: Crossway, 2020.
Chesterton, G. K. *St. Francis of Assisi*. New York: Clydesdale Press, 2020.
Clowney, Edmund. *Christian Meditation*. Vancouver: Regent College Press, 1979.
Cole, R. Alan. *Exodus: An Introduction and Commentary*. Downers Grove, IL: InterVarsity, 1973.
Crosby, Fanny. *Fanny Crosby's Life-Story by Herself*. New York: Every Where, 1903.
Dallimore, Arnold A. *George Whitefield: God's Anointed Servant in the Great Revival of the Eighteenth Century*. Wheaton, IL: Crossway, 1990.
"Data Scientists Chart the Tragic Rise of Selfie Deaths." *MIT Technology Review*, Nov. 15, 2016. https://www.technologyreview.com/2016/11/15/156018/data-scientists-chart-the-tragic-rise-of-selfie-deaths/.
Davis, Andrew. *An Approach to Extended Memorization of Scripture*. Greenville, SC: Ambassador International, 2014.
Demarest, Bruce A. *The Cross and Salvation: The Doctrine of Salvation*. Wheaton, IL: Crossway, 1997.
Diamond, Dan. "Just 8% of People Achieve Their New Year's Resolutions. Here's How They Do It." *Forbes*, Jan. 1, 2013. https://www.forbes.com/sites/dandiamond/2013/01/01/just-8-of-people-achieve-their-new-years-resolutions-heres-how-they-did-it/?sh=7cbc8410596b.
Dickens, Charles. *A Tale of Two Cities*. New York: Reader's Digest Association, 1984.
Dickson, David. *A Brief Explication of the Psalms*. Vol. 1. Glasgow: John Dow, 1824.
Duguid, Barbara R., and Wayne Duguid Houk. *Prone to Wander: Prayers of Confession and Celebration*. Edited by Iain M. Duguid. Phillipsburg, NJ: P&R, 2014.
Dunlop, John. *Wellness for the Glory of God: Living Well after 40 with Joy and Contentment in All of Life*. Wheaton, IL: Crossway, 2014.
Earls, Aaron. "Americans Most Thankful for and to Family This Thanksgiving." Lifeway Research, Nov. 17, 2020. https://research.lifeway.com/2020/11/17/americans-most-thankful-for-and-to-family-this-thanksgiving/.
Edwards, Jonathan. *Ethical Writings*. Edited by Paul Ramsey and John E. Smith. Vol. 8. New Haven: Yale University Press, 1989.
———. *The Works of Jonathan Edwards*. Edited by Edward Hickman. 41 vols. Carlisle, PA: Banner of Truth Trust, 1834.
Elliff, Jim. "The Nod and the Pause: Where the War Begins." Christian Communicators Worldwide, Jan. 28, 2022. https://www.ccwtoday.org/2022/01/the-nod-and-the-pause-where-the-war-begins/.
Erickson, Millard. *Christian Theology*. 2nd ed. Grand Rapids: Baker, 1998.
Fee, Gordon D. *Philippians*. Vol. 11. Westmont, IL: IVP Academic, 1999.
Ferguson, Sinclair. *Grow in Grace*. Carlisle, PA: Banner of Truth Trust, 1989.
———. *In Christ Alone: Living the Gospel-Centered Life*. Sanford, FL: Reformation Trust, 2007.
Flavel, John. *On Keeping the Heart*. Monee, IL: Lulu Publishers, 2022.
———. *The Whole Works of the Reverend John Flavel*. 6 vols. London: W. Baynes and Son, 1820.
France, R. T. *The Gospel of Matthew*. Grand Rapids: Eerdmans, 2007.
Franklin, Benjamin. *The Autobiography and Other Writings*. Edited by L. Jesse Isaacson. New York: Signet Classics, 1961.

Bibliography

Gill, John. *An Exposition of the Old Testament*. Vol. 2. London: Mathews and Leigh, 1810.

Goldman, Russell. "A Solution for Drunk Dials and Accidental Emails." ABC News, Mar. 20, 2009. https://abcnews.go.com/Technology/AheadoftheCurve/story?id=7134834&page=1.

Goodwin, Thomas. *The Vanity of Thoughts*. Pensacola: Chapel Library, 1999.

Green, Gene L. *The Letters to the Thessalonians*. Grand Rapids: Eerdmans, 2002.

Grudem, Wayne. *Systematic Theology: An Introduction to Biblical Doctrine*. 2nd ed. Grand Rapids: Zondervan Academic, 2020.

Gundersen, David. "Why You Need Sermons That Don't Directly Apply to You." The Gospel Coalition, Jan. 9, 2020. https://www.thegospelcoalition.org/article/sermons-apply-you/.

Hall, Joseph. *The Art of Divine Meditation*. Lafayette, IN: Sovereign Grace, 1964.

Halloran, Kevin P. *When Prayer Is a Struggle: A Practical Guide for Overcoming Obstacles in Prayer*. Phillipsburg, NJ: P&R, 2021.

Halsey, Ashley, III. "Flying and That Oxygen Mask: Here's the Correct Way to Use It." *Washington Post*, Apr. 18, 2018. https://www.washingtonpost.com/news/dr-gridlock/wp/2018/04/18/flying-and-that-oxygen-mask-heres-the-correct-way-to-use-it/.

Hannah, William. *Life of Thomas Chalmers*. Miami: HardPress, 2017.

Happy Faith and Assurance in Death. Bathgate, Scotland: Reformation Scotland Trust, 2015. PDF.

Haq, Sana Noor. "This Is the Day You're Most Likely to Let Your New Year Fitness Goals Slip." *Runner's World*, last updated Jan. 8, 2020. https://www.runnersworld.com/uk/training/a776013/today-is-the-day-youre-most-likely-to-let-your-new-year-fitness-goals-slip/.

Heidelberg Catechism. Cleveland: Central Publishing, 1907.

Hibbs, Pierce Taylor. *Struck Down but Not Destroyed: Living Faithfully with Anxiety*. Middletown, DE: Truth Ablaze, 2020.

Hill, Andrew E. *1 and 2 Chronicles*. Grand Rapids: Zondervan, 2003.

Hodge, Charles. *Systematic Theology*. Oak Harbor, WA: Logos Research Systems, 1997.

House, Brad. *Community*. Wheaton, IL: Crossway, 2011.

Hubbard, Scott. "Set Your Mind on Things Above: How to Live Heavenly Minded." *Desiring God*, Mar. 1, 2021. https://www.desiringgod.org/articles/set-your-mind-on-things-above.

———. "Will You Praise Him While You Wait?" *Desiring God*, Mar. 20, 2021. https://www.desiringgod.org/articles/will-you-praise-him-while-you-wait.

Hughes, R. Kent. *Disciplines of a Godly Man*. 2nd ed. Wheaton, IL: Crossway, 2019.

———. *Luke: That You May Know the Truth*. Wheaton, IL: Crossway, 1998.

Hulyer, Jake. "Inside the Booming Business of Background Music." *Guardian*, Nov. 6, 2018. https://www.theguardian.com/news/2018/nov/06/inside-the-booming-business-of-background-music.

Jamieson, Robert, et al. *Commentary Critical and Explanatory on the Whole Bible*. Oak Harbor, WA: Logos Research Systems, 1997.

Jefferson, Thomas. "Thomas Jefferson to John Adams, 8 April 1816," Founders Online, National Archives. https://founders.archives.gov/documents/Jefferson/03-09-02-0446.

Johnson, Dennis E. *Philippians*. Edited by Richard D. Phillips. Phillipsburg, NJ: P&R, 2013.

Bibliography

Karr, Andrew. "Forgetting What Is Behind?" *Gentle Reformation*, Jan. 4, 2020. https://gentlereformation.com/2020/01/04/forgetting-what-is-behind/.

Keller, Timothy. *Counterfeit Gods*. New York: Penguin, 2009.

———. *The Freedom of Self-Forgetfulness: The Path to Christian Joy*. Leyland, UK: Norhaven, 2012.

Kidner, Derek. *Psalms 73–150: An Introduction and Commentary*. Downers Grove, IL: InterVarsity, 1975.

Kistemaker, Simon J., and William Hendriksen. *Exposition of the Second Epistle to the Corinthians*. Grand Rapids: Baker Book House, 1953.

Lawson, Steven J. *Foundations of Grace (1400 BC–AD 100)*. Vol. 1 of *A Long Line of Godly Men*. Lake Mary, FL: Reformation Trust, 2006.

Leeman, Jonathan. *Church Membership: How the World Knows Who Represents Jesus*. Wheaton, IL: Crossway, 2012.

Lewis, C. S. *The Joyful Christian*. New York: Macmillan, 1977.

———. *Mere Christianity*. C. S. Lewis Signature Classics. New York: HarperOne, 2015.

———. Preface to *On the Incarnation*, by Athanasius, 9–15. Yonkers, NY: St. Vladimir's Seminary Press, 2011.

———. *Screwtape Letters*. New York: HarperCollins, 2001.

Lindgren, Caleb. "Someday You Will Read or Hear That Billy Graham Didn't Really Say That." *Christianity Today*, Feb. 21, 2018. https://www.christianitytoday.com/ct/2018/february-web-only/billy-graham-viral-quote-on-death-not-his-d-l-moody.html.

Lloyd-Jones, D. Martyn. *Authentic Christianity*. Vol. 1. Wheaton, IL: Crossway Books, 2000.

———. *The Christian Soldier: An Exposition of Ephesians 6:10–20*. Ada, MI: Baker Books, 1998.

———. *The Christian Warfare: An Exposition of Ephesians 6:10–13*. Carlisle, PA: Banner of Truth Trust, 1976.

———. *Expository Sermons on 2 Peter*. Carlisle, PA: Banner of Truth Trust, 1983.

———. *God's Sovereign Purpose*. Carlisle, PA: Banner of Truth Trust, 1991.

———. *God's Ultimate Purpose: An Exposition of Ephesians 1*. Carlisle, PA: Banner of Truth Trust, 1978.

———. *Healing and the Scriptures*. Nashville: Thomas Nelson, 1988.

———. *Preaching and Preachers*. London: Hodder & Stoughton, 1971.

———. *Spiritual Depression: Its Causes and Cures*. Grand Rapids: Zondervan, 2016.

———. *Studies in the Sermon on the Mount*. 2nd ed. Grand Rapids: Eerdmans, 1971.

"Lonely Patients with Heart Failure Least Likely to Follow Treatment Recommendations." European Society of Cardiology, May 26, 2019. https://www.escardio.org/The-ESC/Press-Office/Press-releases/Lonely-patients-with-heart-failure-least-likely-to-follow-treatment-recommendations.

Longman, Tremper, III. *How to Read the Psalms*. Downers Grove, IL: InterVarsity, 1988.

Luther, Martin. *The Christian in Society*. Vol. 44 of *Luther's Works*, edited by James Atkinson. Philadelphia: Fortress, 1966.

———. "A Disputation of Doctor Martin Luther on the Power and Efficacy of Indulgences." In *Works of Martin Luther with Introductions and Notes*, 29–38. Vol. 1. Philadelphia: A. J. Holman Company, 1915.

———. *First Lectures on the Psalms I: Psalms 1–75*. Vol. 10 of *Luther's Works*, edited by Hilton C. Oswald. St. Louis: Concordia, 1974.

MacArthur, John, Jr. *Different by Design*. Wheaton, IL: Victor Books, 1996.

Bibliography

———. *Matthew*. MacArthur New Testament Commentary 1. Chicago: Moody, 1985.
Manton, Thomas. *The Complete Works of Thomas Manton*. 22 vols. London: James Nisbet & Co., 1870–75.
Markwald, Rudolf K., and Marilyn Morris Markwald. *Katharina von Bora: A Reformation Life*. St. Louis: Concordia, 2002.
Marsden, George. *Jonathan Edwards: A Life*. New Haven: Yale University Press, 2004.
Marshall, Glenna. *Everyday Faithfulness: The Beauty of Ordinary Perseverance in a Demanding World*. Wheaton, IL: Crossway, 2020.
Mathis, David. *Habits of Grace: Enjoying Jesus through the Spiritual Disciplines*. Wheaton, IL: Crossway, 2012.
———. "Time Alone for God: The Ageless Habits of Jesus Christ." *Desiring God*, Aug. 6, 2020. https://www.desiringgod.org/articles/time-alone-for-god.
M'Cheyne, Robert Murray. *The Works of the Late Rev. Robert Murray McCheyne*. 2 vols. New York: Robert Carter, 1848.
Merriam-Webster Dictionary. 11th ed. Springfield MA: Merriam-Webster, 2019.
Miller, J. R. *Workday Religion*. Scotts Valley, CA: CreateSpace Independent, 2014.
Mohler, Mary K. *Growing in Gratitude: Rediscovering the Joy of a Thankful Heart*. Charlotte, NC: Good Book Company, 2018.
Mohler, R. Albert, Jr. *The Prayer That Turns the World Upside Down: The Lord's Prayer as a Manifesto for Revolution*. Nashville: Thomas Nelson, 2018.
Moreland, J. P. *Finding Quiet: My Story of Overcoming Anxiety and the Practices That Brought Peace*. Grand Rapids: Zondervan, 2019.
Moreland, J. P., and Klaus Issler. *The Lost Virtue of Happiness: Discovering the Disciplines of the Good Life*. Colorado Springs: NavPress, 2006.
Morgan, Robert. *Worry Less, Live More: God's Prescription for a Better Life*. New York: HarperCollins, 2017.
Morris, Leon. *The Gospel according to Matthew*. Grand Rapids: Eerdmans, 1992.
Morse, Greg. "The Most Dangerous Place to Live: The Subtle Perils of the Past." *Desiring God*, July 17, 2018. https://www.desiringgod.org/articles/the-most-dangerous-place-to-live.
Mosse, Kate. "Eleven Days: When Agatha Christie Went Missing." *BBC*, Sept. 14, 2015. https://www.bbc.com/culture/article/20150914-eleven-days-when-agatha-christie-went-missing.
Mounce, Robert H. *Matthew*. Grand Rapids: Baker Books, 2011.
Müller, George. *Autobiography of George Müller: A Million and a Half in Answer to Prayer*. London: J. Nisbet and Co., 1914.
———. *Counsel to Christians*. 3rd ed. San Pedro, Belize: Eternally Blessed, 2013.
———. *A Narrative of Some of the Lord's Dealings with George Müller*. Vol. 1. London: J. Nisbet & Co., 1860.
Nettles, Tom. *Ready for Reformation? Bringing Authentic Reform to Southern Baptist Churches*. Nashville: Broadman & Holman, 2005.
Newcomb, Harvey. *The Young Lady's Guide to the Harmonious Development of Christian Character*. Vestavia Hills, AL: Solid Ground Christian Books, 2003.
Newton, John. "Amazing Grace, How Sweet the Sound." In *Baptist Hymnal*, 104. Nashville: Lifeway, 2008.
———. *The Works of John Newton*. Vol. 1. London: Hamilton, Adams & Co, 1824.

Bibliography

"NHTSA Safety Advisory: Reducing Crashes Caused by Pedal Error." *Automotive World*, May 29, 2015. https://www.automotiveworld.com/news-releases/nhtsa-safety-advisory-reducing-crashes-caused-pedal-error/.

O'Donnell, Douglas Sean. *Matthew: All Authority in Heaven and on Earth*. Wheaton, IL: Crossway, 2013.

Orr, Charles E. *Helps to Holy Living*. Guthrie, OK: Faith, 2016.

Owen, John. *The Works of John Owen*. Edited by William H. Goold. Vol. 4. Edinburgh: T&T Clark, 1862.

Packer, J. I. *Concise Theology: A Guide to Historic Christian Beliefs*. Wheaton, IL: Tyndale House, 1993.

———. *Finishing Our Course with Joy: Guidance from God for Engaging with Our Aging*. Wheaton, IL: Crossway, 2014.

———. *Knowing God*. Downers Grove, IL: InterVarsity, 1973.

Pao, David W. *Thanksgiving: An Investigation of a Pauline Theme*. New Studies in Biblical Theology 13. Westmont, IL: InterVarsity, 2002.

Pascal, Blaise. *Pensées*. Oxfordshire, UK: Marston Gate, 2013.

Paterson. "Heaven Came Down." In *Baptist Hymnal*, 573. Nashville: Lifeway, 2008.

Paton, John Gibson. *John Gibson Paton, Missionary to the New Hebrides: An Autobiography*. Stafford, UK: Pantianos Classic, 1890.

Perkins, William. *The Works of William Perkins*. Edited by J. Stephen Yuille, et al. Grand Rapids: Reformation Heritage, 2014.

Pink, A. W. *The Arthur Pink Anthology*. Bellingham, WA: Logos Bible Software, 2005.

———. *The Nature of God*. Chicago: Moody, 1999.

Piper, John. *Desiring God*. 3rd ed. Sisters, OR: Multnomah, 2003.

———. *Don't Waste Your Life*. Wheaton, IL: Crossway, 2003.

———. *For Your Joy*. Minneapolis: Desiring God, 2005.

———. *Future Grace*. Sisters, OR: Multnomah, 1995.

———. "Guard Yourself with Gratitude." In *Sermons from John Piper (1980–1989)*. Minneapolis: Desiring God, 2007. Accessed using Logos Bible Software.

———. "If My Words Abide in You." In *Sermons from John Piper (2000–2014)*. Minneapolis: Desiring God, 2014. Accessed using Logos Bible Software.

———. "Is an Audio Bible Sufficient for Devotions?" *Desiring God*, Jan. 15, 2021. https://www.desiringgod.org/interviews/is-an-audio-bible-sufficient-for-devotions.

———. *Joy to the World: Daily Readings for Advent*. Minneapolis: Desiring God, 2013.

———. *Lessons from a Hospital Bed*. Wheaton, IL: Crossway, 2016.

———. *Life as a Vapor: 31 Meditations for Your Faith*. Sisters, OR: Multnomah, 2004.

———. *Seeing and Savoring Jesus Christ*. Wheaton, IL: Crossway, 2004.

———. *Taste and See: Savoring the Supremacy of God in All of Life*. Sisters, OR: Multnomah, 2005.

———. *This Momentary Marriage: A Parable of Permanence*. Wheaton, IL: Crossway, 2009.

———. "Thy Word I Have Treasured in My Heart." In *Sermons from John Piper 1990–1999*. Minneapolis: Desiring God, 2007. Accessed using Logos Bible Software.

———. *When I Don't Desire God: How to Fight for Joy*. Wheaton, IL: Crossway, 2004.

Piper, John (@JohnPiper). "One of the great uses of Twitter and Facebook will be to prove at the Last Day that prayerlessness was not from lack of time." Twitter, Oct. 20, 2009. https://twitter.com/johnpiper/status/5027319857?lang=en.

Bibliography

Plumer, William S. *Studies in the Book of Psalms: Being a Critical and Expository Commentary, with Doctrinal and Practical Remarks on the Entire Psalter.* Philadelphia: J. B. Lippincott, 1872.

Plummer, Robert, and Matt Haste. *Held in Honor: Wisdom for Your Marriage from Voices of the Past.* Ross-shire, UK: Christian Focus Publications, 2015.

Poole, Matthew. *Annotations upon the Holy Bible.* Vol. 2. New York: Robert Carter and Brothers, 1853.

Possidius of Calama. *The Life of Saint Augustine: A Translation of the Sancti Augustini Vita.* Translated by Possidius, Bishop of Calama. Merchantville, NJ: Evolution, 2008.

Powlison, David. "Sane Faith in the Insanity of Life, Part 1." Christian Counseling & Educational Foundation, Apr. 14, 2016. https://www.ccef.org/sane-faith-insanity-life/.

Prince, David. "A Different Kind of Profanity." Reformation 21, Dec. 11, 2018. https://www.reformation21.org/blogs/a-different-kind-of-profanity.php.

Ranew, Nathanael. *Solitude Improved by Divine Meditation.* Grand Rapids: Soli Deo Gloria Ministries, 2019.

Raymond, Erik. *Chasing Contentment: Trusting God in a Discontented Age.* Wheaton, IL: Crossway, 2017.

Raynor, Jordan. *Redeeming Your Time.* Colorado Springs: WaterBrook, 2021.

Reju, Deepak. "Christian Amnesia." Ligonier, Sep. 21, 2019. https://www.ligonier.org/learn/devotionals/christian-amnesia.

Reyner, Edward. *Precepts for Christian Practice: Or, the Rule of the New Creature; Containing Duties to Be Daily Observed by Every Believer.* Cambridge, MA: Samuel Green, 1668.

Ross, Allen P. "Genesis." In *The Bible Knowledge Commentary: An Exposition of the Scriptures.* Edited by J. F. Walvoord and R. B. Zuck, 15–105. Wheaton, IL: Victor Books, 1985.

Russell, Bertrand. *The Basic Writings of Bertrand Russell.* Forge Valley, MA: Murray Printing, 1961.

Ryken, Philip. *Exodus: Saved for God's Glory.* Wheaton, IL: Crossway, 2005.

Ryle, John Charles. "Are You Looking?" In *109 Sermons and Tracts.* West Linn, OR: Monergism, 2015. https://www.monergism.com/109-sermons-and-tracts-ebook.

———. *Fighting for Holiness.* Wheaton, IL: Crossway, 2022.

———. *Holiness: Its Nature, Hindrances, Difficulties and Roots.* Moscow, ID: Charles Noland, 2001.

Sanders, Linley, and Kathy Frankovic. "Thanksgiving 2021: What Are Americans Thankful For?" YouGov, Nov. 24, 2021. https://today.yougov.com/society/articles/39612-thanksgiving-what-are-americans-thankful-for.

Santayana, George. *The Life of Reason.* New York: Open Road Media, 2015.

Sauls, Scott. *A Gentle Answer: Our "Secret Weapon" in an Age of Us against Them.* Nashville: Thomas Nelson, 2020.

Schreiner, Thomas R. *1, 2 Peter, Jude.* The New American Commentary Series 37. Nashville: Broadman & Holman, 2003.

———. *Hebrews.* Bellingham, WA: Lexham, 2021.

———. *Magnifying God in Christ.* Ada, MI: Baker Academic, 2010. Kindle ed.

———. *Paul, Apostle of God's Glory in Christ: A Pauline Theology.* Westmont, IL: IVP Academic, 2006.

———. *Run to Win the Prize: Perseverance in the New Testament.* Nottingham, UK: Apollos, 2009.

Bibliography

Schwertley, Brian. *The Sermon on the Mount: A Reformed Exposition.* Iowa, WI: Covenanted, 2010.

Seneca, Lucius. *Letters from a Stoic.* London: Penguin, 1975.

Seuss, Dr. *Oh, the Places You'll Go!* New York: Random House Books for Young Readers, 1990.

"Shenandoah—James Stewart: Charlie Anderson." IMDb. https://www.imdb.com/title/tt0059711/characters/nm0000071.

Sibbes, Richard. *The Complete Works of Richard Sibbes.* Edited by Alexander Balloch. 7 vols. Carlisle, PA: Banner of Truth Trust, 1982.

Smith, James K. A. *How to Inhabit Time: Understanding the Past, Facing the Future, Living Faithfully Now.* Grand Rapids: Baker, 2022.

Spence-Jones, H. D. M. *Psalms.* Vol. 1. London: Funk & Wagnalls, 1909.

Sproul, R. C. *How Can I Be Sure I Am Saved?* Orlando: Reformation Trust, 2010.

Spurgeon, Charles H. *Barbed Arrows from the Quiver of C. H. Spurgeon.* London: Passmore and Alabaster, 1896.

———. "Christ's Estimate of His People." In *The New Park Street Pulpit Sermons* 5:457–64. London: Passmore & Alabaster, 1859.

———. *Farm Sermons.* New York: Passmore and Alabaster, 1882.

———. "The Incomparable Bridegroom and His Bride." In *The Metropolitan Tabernacle Pulpit Sermons* 42:277–85. London: Passmore & Alabaster, 1896.

———. "The Last Enemy Destroyed." In *The Metropolitan Tabernacle Pulpit Sermons* 12:637–48. London: Passmore & Alabaster, 1866.

———. *Lectures to my Students.* Vol. 1. London: Passmore and Alabaster, 1875.

———. *Morning and Evening: Daily Readings.* London: Passmore & Alabaster, 1875.

———. "My Times Are in Thy Hand." In *The Metropolitan Tabernacle Pulpit Sermons* 37:285–86. London: Passmore & Alabaster, 1891.

———. "Paul—His Cloak and His Books." In *The Metropolitan Tabernacle Pulpit Sermons* 9:661–72. London: Passmore & Alabaster, 1863.

———. "Prayer, the Cure for Care." In *The Metropolitan Tabernacle Pulpit Sermons* 40:109–17 London: Passmore & Alabaster, 1894.

———. *Psalms 1–26.* Vol. 1 of *The Treasury of David.* Peabody, MA: Hendrickson, 2021.

———. *Psalms 56–87.* Vol. 2. of *The Treasury of David.* Peabody, MA: Hendrickson, 2021.

———. "Return unto Thy Rest." In *The Metropolitan Tabernacle Pulpit Sermons* 47:601–10. London: Passmore & Alabaster, 1901.

———. "Why Lay Aside?" In *The Sword and Trowel 1876*, 397–400. London: Passmore & Alabaster, 1876.

Standridge, Jordan. "The Day King David Became an Atheist." *Cripplegate*, Jan. 5, 2021. https://thecripplegate.com/the-day-king-david-became-an-atheist/

Stanley, Charles F. *10 Principles for Studying Your Bible.* Nashville: Thomas Nelson, 2008.

Stein, Robert H. *Luke.* The New American Commentary Series 24. Nashville: Broadman & Holman, 1992.

Stevens, R. P. *Aging Matters: Finding Your Calling for the Rest of Your Life.* Grand Rapids: Eerdmans, 2016.

"Stop, Drop, and Roll." U.S. Fire Administration. https://www.usfa.fema.gov/gallery/pictographs/pictograph49.html.

Stott, John. *The Bible: Book for Today.* Leicester, England: Inter-Varsity, 1982.

———. *The Message of Galatians: Only One Way.* Downer's Grove, IL: InterVarsity, 1986.

Strauch, Alexander. *Biblical Eldership.* 3rd ed. Colorado Springs: Lewis and Roth, 2003.

Bibliography

Stuart, Douglas K. *Exodus*. The New American Commentary 2. Nashville: Broadman & Holman, 2006.

Swinnock, George. *The Works of George Swinnock, M.A.* Vol. 3. Edinburgh: James Nichol, 1868.

Tautges, Paul. *Anxiety: Knowing God's Peace*. Phillipsburg, NJ: P&R, 2019.

Taylor, Howard. *To Die Is Gain: The Triumph of John and Betty Stam*. Denton, TX: Westminster Resources, 2004.

Taylor, Howard, and Geraldine Taylor. *Hudson Taylor's Spiritual Secret*. Louisville: GLH, 2018.

Thomas, Geoff. "The Authority of Scripture." In *The Beauty and Glory of God's Word*, edited by Joel R. Beeke, 17–28. Grand Rapids: Reformation Heritage Books, 2016.

Thomas, W. H. Griffith. *Life Abiding and Abounding: Bible Studies in Prayer and Meditation*. Chicago: The Bible Institute Colportage Association, 1910.

Thorn, Joe. *Note to Self: The Discipline of Preaching to Yourself*. Wheaton, IL: Crossway, 2011.

Tocqueville, Alexis de. *Democracy in America*. Translated by Harvey C. Mansfield and Delba Winthrop. Chicago: University of Chicago Press, 2000.

Tolstoy, Leo. *My Confession*. London: Fount, 1995.

Tripp, Paul David. *Awe: Why It Matters for Everything We Think, Say, and Do*. Wheaton, IL: Crossway, 2015

———. *Dangerous Calling: Confronting the Unique Challenges of Pastoral Ministry*. Wheaton, IL: Crossway, 2012.

———. *Journey to the Cross: A 40-Day Lenten Devotional*. Wheaton, IL: Crossway, 2021.

Um, Stephen T. *1 Corinthians: The Word of the Cross*. Edited by R. Kent Hughes. Wheaton, IL: Crossway, 2015.

Ussher, James. *A Body of Divinity: Or, the Sum and Substance of Christian Religion*. 8th ed. London: A. and J. Churchill, 1702.

Ware, Bruce A. *God's Lesser Glory: The Diminished God of Open Theism*. Wheaton, IL: Crossway, 2000.

———. *The Man Christ Jesus: Theological Reflections on the Humanity of Christ*. Wheaton, IL: Crossway, 2012.

Watson, Thomas. *A Christian on the Mount, or a Treatise Concerning Meditation*. Monee, IL: Lulu Publishers, 2022.

Webb, Jill Iroz. "The Function of Gratitude in Marriage: Building Ties That Bind." *Family Perspectives* 2.1 (2020) art. 2. https://scholarsarchive.byu.edu/familyperspectives/vol2/iss1/2.

Weidmann, Josh. *The End of Anxiety: The Biblical Prescription for Overcoming Fear, Worry, and Panic*. Washington, DC: Salem Books, 2020.

Welch, Edward T. *Running Scared: Fear, Worry, and the God of Rest*. Greensboro, NC: New Growth, 2007.

Wenham, Gordon J. *Genesis 16–50*. Dallas: Word, 1994.

Wesley, John. *The Works of John Wesley*. 3rd ed. 29 vols. London: Wesleyan Methodist Book Room, 1872.

Wesley, John, and George Eayrs. *Letters of John Wesley: A Selection of Important and New Letters with Introductions and Biographical Notes*. London: Hodder and Stoughton, 1915.

Whitney, Donald. "Pursuing a Passion for God through Spiritual Disciplines: Learning from Jonathan Edwards." In *A God-Entranced Vision of All Things: The Legacy of*

BIBLIOGRAPHY

Jonathan Edwards, edited by John Piper and Justin Taylor, 109–28. Wheaton, IL: Crossway, 2004.

———. *Simplify Your Spiritual Life: Spiritual Disciplines for the Overwhelmed*. Colorado Springs: NavPress, 2003.

———. *Spiritual Disciplines for the Christian Life*. Colorado Springs: NavPress, 1991.

Wilson, Jared C. "The Beauty and Burden of Nostalgia." For the Church, Nov. 25, 2019. https://ftc.co/resource-library/blog-entries/the-beauty-and-burden-of-nostalgia.

Winslow, Octavius. *The Precious Things of God*. Louisville: GLH, 2015. Kindle.

Witmer, Timothy Z. *Mindscape: What to Think About Instead of Worrying*. Greensboro, NC: New Growth, 2014.

Witsius, Herman. *The Economy of the Covenants between God and Man: Comprehending a Complete Body of Divinity*. Translated by William Crookshank. Vol. 2. Edinburgh: CrossReach Publications, 2017.

Wood, A. Skevington. "Ephesians." In *The Expositor's Bible Commentary: Ephesians through Philemon*, edited by Frank E. Gaebelein 11:3–92. Grand Rapids: Zondervan, 1981.

Workman, A. W. "I Look Forward to Drinking Chai with You in the New Jerusalem." *Entrusted to the Dirt*, Oct. 23, 2020. https://entrustedtothedirt.com/2020/10/23/i-look-forward-to-drinking-chai-with-you-in-the-new-jerusalem/.

Wright, N. T. *Colossians and Philemon: An Introduction and Commentary*. Downers Grove, IL: InterVarsity, 1986.

Zylstra, Sarah Eekhoff and Megan Hill. "Build Spiritual Habits in Just a Few Minutes." The Gospel Coaltion, Dec. 31, 2021. https://www.thegospelcoalition.org/article/spiritual-habits-few-minutes.

Author Index

Adams, John, 33
Adams, John Quincy, 126
Alcorn, Randy, 7, 86–87, 88
Alcorn, Nanci, 86
Allcock, Linda, 11, 14, 48, 68, 104, 110, 132
Allison, Gregg, 60
Amen, Daniel, 2
Anyabwile, Thabiti, 148, 163
Archer, Clint, 53
Ash, Christopher, 121, 138
Augustine, 158

Baker, Glenn, 134
Baldwin, Joyce, 25
Ball, John, 98
Barnett, John, 37
Bates, William, 36
Bavinck, Herman, 17
Baxter, Richard, 13, 37, 42, 97, 100, 103
Beeke, Joel, 15, 58, 121
Bennett, Arthur, 71
Berkouwer, G.C., 20
Boice, James Montgomery, 48, 63, 80–81, 127, 150
Bonaparte, Napoleon, 6
Bonar, Andrew, 14, 164
Bonhoeffer, Dietrick, 131, 138
Boston, Thomas, 138
Brainerd, David, 99
à Brakel, William, 5, 134
Bridge, William, 11, 24, 98, 99

Brooks, Thomas, 47, 87, 99
Bruce, Milne, 60
Butler, Trent, 81
Bullinger, Henry, 158
Bush, Daniel, 37

Calamy, Edmund, 4, 15, 37, 66, 103, 106
Calvin, John, 35, 71, 109, 143
Carson, D.A., 124, 125
Castelot, André, 6
Challies, Tim, 33, 64, 130, 153, 167
Chalmers, Thomas, 148
Chambers, Oswald, 96
Chandler, Matt, 77
Chappell, Bryan, 86, 137
Charnock, Stephen, 78
Chester, Tim, 26, 136
Chesterton, G.K., 54
Clowney, Edmund, 112
Cole, R. Alan, 89
Crosby, Franny, 84–85

Dallimore, Arnold, 67
Davis, Andrew, 112
Demarest, Bruce, 109
Diamond, Dan, 174
Dickens, Charles, 140, 142
Dickson, David, 41
Dunlop, John, 47, 151

Edwards, Jonathan, 45, 107, 127–128, 145, 165

Author Index

Erickson, Millard, 39–40

Fee, Gordon, 48
Ferguson, Sinclair, 21, 43
Flavel, John, 26, 29, 43, 90, 136, 144, 162–63
France, R. T., 22, 125
Franklin, Benjamin, 4

Geisel, Theodor (Dr. Seuss), 169
Gill, John, 79
Goodwin, Thomas, 99
Green, Gene, 131
Grudem, Wayne, 2, 61, 76, 165
Gumpert, Gary, 82
Gundersen, David, 135

Hall, Joseph, 15, 100, 110
Halloran, Kevin, 49
Hannah, William, 148
Haste, Matt, 121, 138
Havner, Vance, 30
Haynes, Lemuel, 148, 163
Hibbs, Pierce, 50, 51
Hill, Andrew, 64, 69, 154–55
Hill, Megan, 69
Hodge, Charles, 76
House, Brad, 131
Howard, Taylor, 13, 96, 141
Hubbard, Scott, 59, 67
Hughes, R. Kent, 78, 113

Jamieson, Robert, 46
Jefferson, Thomas, 33
Johnson, Dennis, 87

Karr, Andrew, 154
Keller, Timothy, 36, 155–56
Kidner, Derek, 56
Kistemaker, Simon, 134
Köstenberger, Andreas, 60

Leeman, Jonathan, 138
Lewis, C. S., 2, 28, 31, 51, 99, 155
Lindgren, Caleb, 143

Lloyd-Jones, D. Martyn, 12, 19, 27, 30–21, 49, 51, 93, 95, 104, 131, 134, 137, 144, 157, 176
Longman, Tremper III, 54, 56, 176
Luther, Martin, 45, 121, 158, 162, 176

MacArthur, John Jr., 35, 136
Manton, Thomas, 17, 59, 78, 136
Markwald, Marilyn, 121
Markwald, Rudolf, 121
Marsden, George, 40
Mathis, David, 96, 113
M'Cheyne, Robert Murray, 14
Miller, J.R., 40
Mohler, Mary, 72
Mohler, R. Albert, Jr., 105
Moreland, J. P., 46, 87
Morgan, Robert, 11, 42, 47
Morris, Leon, 44, 87
Morse, Greg, 154
Miller, J.R., 40
Mounce, Robert, 35
Müller, George, 9, 35, 100–101

Nettles, Tom, 138
Newcomb, Harvey, 12
Newton, John, 56, 131, 169

O'Donnell, Douglas, 91
Orr, Charles, 39
Owen, John, 49

Packer, J. I., 42, 61, 103, 104, 108–109, 113, 146, 156, 167
Pao, David, 54, 72
Pascal, Blaise, 68–69
Paton, John, 163
Perkins, William, 67, 97
Pink, A.W., 41
Piper, John, 8, 16, 18, 29, 31, 38, 47, 66, 68, 87, 96, 98, 111, 117, 126, 138, 143, 146, 147, 150, 151, 166, 167
Plumer, William, 78, 122
Plummer, Robert, 121
Poole, Matthew, 267
Possidius of Calama, 158
Prince, David, 87

Author Index

Ranew, Nathanael, 110
Raymond, Erik, 92
Raynor, Jordan, 81
Reju, Deepak, 74
Reyner, Edward, 99
Ross, Allen, 90
Russell, Bertrand, 152–53
Ryle, J.C., 1, 4, 95
Ryken, Philip, 78

Santayana, George, 74
Sauls, Scott, 132
Saxton, David, 113
Schreiner, Thomas, 6, 22, 29, 36, 76, 95, 137, 145
Schwertley, Brian, 35
Seneca, Lucius, 4
Sibbes, Richard, 6, 165
Smith, James, 91
Spence, H.D.M., 159
Spurgeon, Charles, 10, 37, 50, 62, 82, 104, 127, 129, 135, 137, 140, 142, 157, 161
Stam, Betty, 13
Standridge, Jordan, 79
Stanley, Charles, 46
Stein, Robert, 59
Stevens, R. Paul, 150, 152, 167
Stott, John, 12, 26, 123, 136
Stuart, Douglas, 67

Swinnock, George, 110

Tautges, Paul, 50
Taylor, Howard, 13
Taylor, Hudson, 96
Thomas, W. H. Griffith, 25
Thorn, Joe, 21, 29
de Tocqueville, Alexis, 142–43
Tolstoy, Leo, 39
Tripp, Paul, 13, 44, 90, 92

Um, Stephen, 88
Ussher, James, 64

Ware, Bruce, 24, 86, 96
Watson, Thomas, 82, 101
Weidmann, Josh, 47
Welch, Edward, 30, 51
Wenham, Gordon, 114, 124
Wesley, John, 142
Whitefield, George, 67
Whitney, Donald, 45, 66, 94, 98, 113
Wilson, Jared, 154
Winslow, Octavius, 42
Witsius, Herman, 106
Workman, A.W., 42
Wright, N. T., 150

Zylstra, Sarah, 69